The Two Faces of Economics

Anthony Dalston Dawson

LONGMAN
LONDON AND NEW YORK

Addison Wesley Longman Limited
Edinburgh Gate
Harlow, Essex CM20 2JE, England
and Associated Companies throughout the world.

Published in the United States of America
by Addison Wesley Longman Limited, New York

© Addison Wesley Longman Limited 1996

First published 1996

ISBN 0 582 27451-6 PPR

British Library Cataloguing-in-Publication Data
A catalogue record for this book is
available from the British Library

Library of Congress Cataloging-in-Publication Data
Dawson, Anthony Dalston, 1927-
  The two faces of economics / Anthony Dalston Dawson.
    p. cm.
  Includes bibliographical references and index.
  ISBN 0-582-27451-6 (pbk.)
  1. Economics. 2. Economic policy. I. Title
HB171.D32 1996
  330--dc20   96-4824
                                                           CIP

Set by 7 in 10/12 sabon
Produced through Longman Malaysia, LSP

The Two

The London School of Economics and Political Science (1895–1995) celebrates its centenary as this book is published. It is dedicated to the memory of my Professors at the LSE between 1944 and 1946:

Friedrich von Hayek and Harold J. Laski

Ubi saeva indignatio ulteris
cor lacerare nequit.

He lies where fierce
indignation can no
longer rend his heart.

From the *Epitaph* written for himself by Jonathan Swift (1668–1745), Dean of St Patrick's Cathedral, Dublin. Quoted in a sermon of Henry Richard Dawson (1792–1840), Dean of St Patrick's Cathedral and great-great-grandfather of Anthony Dalston Dawson.

Contents

List of Boxes   x
Abbreviations   xii
Introduction and Summary   xiii

Part I Our Inheritance   1

The prehistory and history of making a living   3
The economics of subsistence   4
Community and cultivation   5
Regional differences and location of cities   7
Trade in people and things   7
Robbery and invasion, government and taxation   8
Population growth   12

Part II Unemployment   15

Unemployment: a new focus for economics   17
Frictional unemployment: signs of freedom and vitality 24
Seasonal unemployment: rest? recovery? second job? or? 25
Cyclical unemployment: booms, busts; euphoria, misery   26
Economic collapse: disaster and hyperinflation   28
Until Keynes, economists said unemployment was voluntary! 30
Achieving full employment: the abstract answer   31
Cyclical and non-cyclical industries   32
The importance of consumers and their confidence   34
Investors, their confidence and expectations   37
The acceleration of downs and ups   37
Why cycles are endemic to capitalism   39
How recessions start   40
Errors of judgement   41
Under-consumption and over-investment   45
The way recessions bottom out and recovery begins   47
Reducing the impact of cycles on workers   52
Keynes' proposals wrongly applied for six decades   52
Recession opens the 1990s: how will they close?   59
The business cycle outside the USA   60

Part III Structures in the Population, Economy and Society   65

Reducing long-term unemployment: population transcendent   67
Structural unemployment: the pain of adjustment   69
The interaction of economic and social structures   69
Labour unions and employment   73
Economic migrants   75
Age and sex structure and skills   78
Exogenous factors in structural change   81
Endogenous factors in structural change   88
International displacement of workers and jobs   91
Japan as a problem for the USA   95
The rise and fall of industries and countries   98
Baumol's disease   110
The mixed blessings of machines   112
Chronic unemployment: too many workers, fit or not   114
Part-time employment   119
Contractors and consultants   120
Under-employment and low productivity in poor countries   121
Employment policy and human resources planning   123

Part IV 'The Poor Ye Have Always'   131

Justice in a policy of income and wealth   133
Wages   135
Salaries   136
Paid holidays, enforced idleness, workaholism   136
The meaning of real wages   138
Working and living conditions   140
Wages and employment   144
Profit-sharing   148
Recent socio-economic history   150
Wages and productivity   154
Minimum wages   155
Labour unions: the pros and cons   160
Labour law and relations   166
The notion of maximum salaries   172
Fixed incomes and profits: parity of esteem   182
Why is inequality of incomes increasing?   185

Part V The Paradox of Prosperity and Disillusion   189

Malaise and optimism growing fainter   191
Changes in the economic system   193

The illusion of the low American cost of living   199
Services after the sea-change   199
The good bits   200
Swings and roundabouts   202
The two messages of this book   204
Seven big bills   207

Part VI Reform and Policy   213

Good government grown fat and senile   215
Lessons from recent history   216
Reforms needed in public life   219
Cost efficiency in the public sector   221
Money-takers spend carefully, as earners do   224
Do not print money to seize wealth   224
Equal terms of public and private employment   225
Downsizing government and bolstering community action   226
Immunising governments from bribery   227
Downsizing dissimulation and hypocrisy   228
Total expenditure and borrowing   228
Reform of the taxation system   230
Objects of expenditure   230
Radical change in taxation   232
   A. Upper revenue limit: one dollar in four   232
   B. Simplification of the tax code   233
   C. No income taxation   233
   D. Estates over $10 million: 50 per cent to charity and
     community   235
   E. Value-added tax (20 per cent) on non-vital goods and
     services   236
   F. All land nationalised; low-rent long leases 238
   G. No exemptions from the new taxation system   239
   H. Centralisation and standardisation of social relief 239
   J. Property tax unchanged; education systematised 239
   K. Power shift and endowment to community action 239
Flood protection from a torrent of criticism   240
Adequacy of revenues   241
Regressivity   244
Impact on employment   244
Balance of power, public and private   247
Realism, and the truth for its own sake   247

Notes   249
Index   258

List of Boxes

1.1   Asia: Economic progress 1980–1993   11

2.1   Underestimation of unemployment   20
2.2   Keynes on politicians   23
2.3   Consumer confidence   35
2.4   Book box: Birth of the Foundling Mouse   42
2.5   Job-creating in the USA   47
2.6   Average mid-recession inflation rate: 1992   48
2.7   Pace of American economic recovery 1993–1994   49
2.8   American worker productivity falls in advanced recovery   51
2.9   Recession hits Hispanics in the USA   52
2.10   The big chill on social relief   58
2.11   Unemployment in rich capitalist countries, 1993–1994   59
2.12   Unemployment and economic growth during the recession   61
2.13   GDP in selected OECD countries, % change   62
2.14   The European recession   63

3.1   The USA and the UK: Structure of GDP and labour force 1992   70
3.2   Union membership in OECD countries, 1980–1990   71
3.3   Hosting economic immigrants   76
3.4   International migrants   77
3.5   Defence industries after the cold war   82
3.6   Production in the biosphere   83
3.7   Book box: Regulation and deregulation   84
3.8   America's airlines   85
3.9   Book box: Transforming threatened businesses   86
3.10   Employment structure in G-7 countries, 1920–1990   89
3.11   Job-creating in the USA   92
3.12   Multinationals' Foreign assets 1992   93
3.13   USA trade with Japan   97
3.14   The European Union   98
3.15   Employment in manufacturing 1962–1993   99
3.16   Getting away from New York City   100
3.17   Unemployment 1993–1994 in Western countries   114
3.18   EU unemployment   116
3.19   Economic and social indicators for poor countries   122
3.20   Economic growth in the Third World   123
3.21   Career-planning   125

3.22	Supply and demand for PhDs: 'Eggheads unite . . .'	126
3.23	JOBMAP	128
3.24	Subsidising wages	128
4.1	UK and USA: Distribution of income	134
4.2	Global income distribution 1960–1989	134
4.3	Poverty-level wage-earners and other poverty	135
4.4	Workaholism in the USA	137
4.5	The UK and the USA: The quality of working life	141
4.6	Book box: The homeless	143
4.7	Ground lost by blue-collar workers	145
4.8	USA: average weekly earnings by occupation	147
4.9	United Kingdom: range of employee earnings	147
4.10	Glass half full or half empty?	149
4.11	Recent thought on minimum wages	161
4.12	British labour unions	166
4.13	Worker ownership of companies	168
4.14	Dunlop Commission on American labour	170
4.15	Latest views on labour unions: who needs them?	171
4.16	The cost of talent in the USA	174
4.17	USA: Executive salaries	176
4.18	High pay in the UK	179
4.19	'The new inequality'	187
5.1	The pot calls the kettle black	201
5.2	The veil of money	203
5.3	Baumol's disease and health care	211
6.1	China's economic history	217
6.2	A male Thatcher sighted in Philadelphia	219
6.3	Big, and big losers	222
6.4	Arrogant capital	226
6.5	Book box: *Reinventing the Left*	234
6.6	Investment-led recovery	245

Abbreviations

BG	*Boston Globe* newspaper
EB	*Encyclopedia Britannica*
EBY(19 . . .)	*Encyclopedia Britannica Yearbook* (for year)
EU	European Union
FAO	UN Food and Agriculture Organisation
GDP	Gross Domestic Product
GNP	Gross National Product
OECD	Organisation of Economic Cooperation and Development
IBRD	International Bank for Reconstruction and Development, or World Bank
ILO	United Nations International Labour Organisation
IMF	International Monetary Fund
MIT	Massachusetts Institute of Technology
TENL	*The Economist* London (New York edition)
UN	United Nations
UNCTAD	United Nations Conference on Trade and Development
UNDP	United Nations Development Programme
UNHCR	United Nations High Commissioner for Refugees
UNICEF	United Nations International Children's' Endowment Fund
WFP	UN World Food Program
WHO	UN World Health Organisation

Introduction and summary

Epictetus remarked, about jugs with two handles, that they can be carried more easily with one handle than with the other. This book is not too heavy to carry and it contains economics with an easy handle.

It is written for students and working people, and for unselfish politicians and others who care deeply about everyone's careers and their economic security. It explains how the economy of the world works and can be made to serve the needs of the poor and the rich in a more balanced way. It could also be of direct interest to businessmen. They may not like some of the message, but will find themselves in familiar territory when reading it. It is the stuff of which their working days are made and a part of their sweet dreams of profit and their nightmares.

Unlike most introductions to economics, this book does not speak about economic theory directly. It focuses, through the spectacles of an economic theorist, on the behaviour of the visible economy. The hidden or underground economy is large enough in several countries to throw their official economic statistics out of whack; mainly making them under-estimates. It is sometimes called 'the gray economy' because it is populated by tax evaders, smugglers, insurance swindlers, confidence tricksters, fences, illegal immigrants, plagiarists, pimps, prostitutes, protection racketeers and welfare cheats – somewhat less criminal than the black market and the billion-dollar business operations of mafias and drug traders. These last considerably warp the official statistics. The total unseen economy is probably as large as the massive world tourist trade. I lived in Italy for twelve years, which prospered more in its gray than in its white economy, until the recent purge. Through a lifetime I visited such ups and downs of the world as Cali and Rio Hacha in Colombia's drug world; factories employing child slaves in caves of the Asian sub-continent; the basement emporia in Seoul, South Korea, selling on a shopping mall scale the goods 'leaked' from the PX (army store system) of the US Army. I contended, as a banker in Central Africa, with diamond smuggling and the ubiquitous corruption. This gave me a nodding acquaintance with less visible parts of economic life. Not all economists are prudish. There are those who, when analysing models of the economic behaviour of governments, assume that they will encounter characteristics shared with criminal organisations. That relationship is getting ominously close in Russia today.

The two faces of economics are not white and black respectively, nor are they capitalism versus something else. All shades of the world economy, in all countries, wear two masks alternately, which make and break social classes: the smiling face of wealth and welfare and the frightening face of poverty and insecurity, profit and loss, boom and slump, growth and shrinkage, hope and despair, more-for-them and less-for-us. But inflation and deflation both reflect the scowling face; price stability is the smiling face, though it may seem a cold comfort to house owners and debtors.

The national economies of the world are now nearly all capitalist, or more so than before. The global economy is the only economy not ruled by a government; the world market no longer has large, nearly closed economic enclaves of Marxian or other religious/fanatical experimentation with governance and planning. North Korea, governed by 'communism's' first hereditary monarchy, is the last remnant of the Left's lunatic fringe. The thought of true communism infects capitalists with paranoia, but remains only a thought. The true 'socialist' and 'democratic' countries did not, and do not, use those words in their official names. Economists looking at countries simply distinguish between market-driven and (central) command economies.

The USA still has the largest capitalist economy, and is further down the *laissez-faire* road toward the withering away of the State than any other country. There is widespread interest in the look of the American capitalist road and its travellers, insofar as private enterprise and a market-driven economy is being adopted, eagerly or gingerly, by a large majority of countries.

Canada tends to be ignored in the USA. Even the American weather forecasts stop at the border, though Canadian weather calls for careful attention and sympathy. Poor debt-ridden, overtaxed Canada, a humane society still admired by the wider world, is a major but slipping economic power that, more British than American since 1776, has moved further away from the American toward the European model, favouring social justice over economic advancement when they conflict. Canada's short-term prospects are poor but it could eventually have a glowing future, if we are to experience global warming that falls short of human extinction. God gave Canada a huge and fruitful territory rather blighted, for the present, by excessively cold air.

The future holds many surprises for us, and we should prepare for outcomes as sudden, surprising and unforeseen as the collapse of the Berlin Wall and the disintegration of the USSR. Canada might, perhaps in desperation, take a U-turn just as suddenly as did New Zealand some years ago; though federal states are less capable of major yet peaceful reforms. New Zealand, the antipodean, early-to-bed paradise of social security and welfare, felt the need, quite soon in the current global renaissance of market-driven solutions, to pull up its socks.

This book concentrates on North America, where I have lived in Boston and Montreal for the last fifteen years. It compares America, I hope impartially, with my old home: a Kingdom still United, where I touch base annually. Little England, that congested and monoxided but still kindly and patient isle, is recalled from our distant Brit childhood as the heart of a mighty empire that was blown away when the Pax Britannica and Britain's material wealth were extinguished by two world wars. Yet England remained quietly proud of the Commonwealth, almost a fraternity of peoples it has endowed with institutions and traditions that nurture prosperity and fairness. Can the Commonwealth's remnant amity and partly worthwhile nostalgia survive the dessication of the Royal glue?

Work-a-day Britain has recently moved away from the feather-bedded European type of economy towards a leaner and meaner American model. Figuratively speaking, we witness the westward-bound British vessel steaming past the eastward-bound Canadian vessel. They both reinsure and refuel financially in mid-ocean at a capitalist haven: British (ahem) Bermuda, the world's only oceanic island to have eliminated poverty (better than Hawaii). Bermuda, Hong Kong and Singapore are the richest islets there are, and their workers do enjoy that rarity, trickle-down prosperity. Amid busy seas, they grew affluent while still British colonies, and are now astonishingly rich. Space is not necessary for wealth creation; but communications (and a propitious culture) are.

In Africa, one of the globe's largest land masses, the former British territories have done better, in business and in government, than many other former colonies. A sad exception is bankrupt, war-torn, Sudan. Sudan's Mahdi (a name meaning the Prophet returned), killed General Gordon of Khartoum in the last century; he was the frightening fore-runner of today's extremist amd militant Islam. Political disturbances and threats can bedevil the most healthy and flourishing economy. Beirut, destroyed in a year or two, will probably not rebuild its economy up to the level of productivity it had before 1975 until about 2010. Another ex-British colony in Africa, Tanzania, did poorly economically despite a morally excellent leader and cultivable land to spare. Its agriculture was said to have had a new crop disease: Socialism.

The political and economic changes in country after country may just be swings in the pendulum of our contemporary political life; or, in a brainstorming session, we could imagine outcomes as startling as the end of the USSR. Obviously, the USA will not re-enter an Anglo-Saxon empire, as once imagined by George Bernard Shaw ("The Applecart"), but might in the next century receive Britain into the North American Free Trade Agreement if the European Union further ossifies. Were Quebec eventually to be cut in two, would the eastern, more francophile half, its trade with the other Canadian provinces bitterly clipped by the latter, enter the European Economic Union or, in desperation, would it be welcomed by France, proud guardian of the purest spoken French?

An increasingly heterogeneous and fractured America could conceivably stumble into a second civil war. A moment for that could be in fifteen years, when the American economy will undergo a sharp demographic jolt. It would be a guerrilla war with no battle lines drawn: several massive splinter groups firing the 220 million guns now owned and held in a majority of private homes and in the informal barracks of the local militias. Oddly, the USA, paranoid after both world wars about almost non-existent communists in its midst, now fails to perceive its 'constitutional' and terroristic militias as a form of treason capable of doing real harm to the country they proclaim to love. Sucked into the mayhem of this second civil war would be the extremely-right wing, now more militant than religious, which might have to face a class-conscious burst of rage from the four Americans in five being ripped off by each fifth American since the 1970s. In the slowed growth of American productivity since those years, the fours, the 80 percent of Americans, have grown poorer, while the plutocratic fifth has cornered the assets of the world's wealthiest nation. As a way out, America may find and empower its own Tito, to put an iron-clad clamp on any home-grown balkanisation. The justification for such a ruthless salvage could be damage control. There would be other intervenors in the fray, ranging from the outsider and criminal classes in the inner cities to the hungry mobs breaking across the southern border as soon as the nation's attention is forced inward. Within the spectrum of violence would be the sharp tensions between racial, religious, sexual and other particular groups ignited by conflagration. There are many shoplifters awaiting any uproar that facilitates looting.

'It can't happen here!' Well, guns are fired in anger every night at least as frequently as a man batters a woman or a child. Children in more peaceful families, only semi-literate, are left free to remain focused on the TV violence and training in crime.

I have mentioned these extremities because they interact with, and are potentially triggered by, the economic and social forces at work, and considered in this book. The risks represent a strong reason for a wide understanding of those forces and their mitigation.

A majority of Americans (the outside world's 'rich uncles') still own only part of a house and part of a car, and have part of a hope for an adequately financed retirement or sick bed. That flickering hope of tranquillity at life's end is dashed by a sensitive and festering sore destined for future eruption. Americans are now exploited and harassed by their bosses more than ever during the past three or four generations. Their insecurity disturbs their sleep and calm; they do need proper holidays, repose, retirement. The American Dream is, for most, either a mirage or nothing more today than an old-time movie recalled nostalgically. In fact, that Dream as Dream-come-true lay behind the warm appeal of the movies remembered by parents and grandparents. In contrast, today's movies have the cold appeal of a nightmare, and seem more likely to become true.

The character of the economic and social situation is similar worldwide. The scale of deprivation and suffering differs: but everywhere the rich grow richer and the poor grow poorer. ('The Two Faces in the Third World' awaits close attention in a separate book.)

The job of the world economy, with the help of economics, is to be at least a survival kit for all our human brothers and sisters. Economists were notorious for their pessimism, induced by Reverend Malthus' doom and gloom. Now numerous non-green economists, and *The Economist* itself, have become optimistic about the limits to the extent and durability of overpopulation and poverty. By force of habit, and needing shorthand forms of expression, economists think and speak more and more in aggregates, medians and secular or other major trends; they muse and mumble in detached and generalised paradigms. They rejoice in the thought of technological progress, which (arithmetically speaking) raises productivity per human head and reduces the numbers of human bodies required.

Speaking frankly, we have too many brothers and sisters. Millions more are born every week, representing an unprecedented explosion. This burst of people far exceeds the availability of natural resources, capital and technology required for the space, shelter, equipment, power and materials we need to have a productive job and earn an adequate living for a family.

The market-driven economic system prevailing in the present world has the effect, perhaps unintentionally, of increasing the gap between the wealth of the few rich and the poverty and insecurity of the many poor. We can hope that technology will continue to enable the satisfaction of total demand for goods and services, including purchasing power – **the capacity to pay for them**. Beyond that hope, however, I will wager that technology and economics alone cannot and will not satisfy the most basic needs of **the many more people whose purchasing power is bound to remain pitifully weak**. Moreover, the increased purchasing power of those doing better will eventually drive up the price of food and make it more unattainable for the poor.

Causes of the inequality of wealth and income are examined at length later. A major factor engendering the situation is the lack of productive and remunerative employment for everyone who wants and needs it.

The unemployed suffer privation and a sense of rejection. The employed suffer from the fall-off in their pay, advantages and conditions of work as the surplus of labour reduces the amount employers need to offer in order to obtain and retain their workforce. The workers also suffer part of the burden of supporting the unemployed (who include their friends and relatives), whereas there is less help for the unemployed from those who make profits under the status quo. The profit-makers dominate and maintain the setup. They thus bear some of the responsibility for unemployment. Some, not all.

Population growth shares a large and increasing part of the blame for chronic unemployment and economic inequality. The capitalist system – rather than its blinkered, robotic inmates and individual practitioners – is to blame for the business cycle of boom and bust. Adam Smith's "invisible hand" in the economic system alternately caresses and slaps us.

There is a need for government to stabilise the economy, notably through counterbalancing action with money supply and public investment during boom and slump and through a revised taxation system that encourages the additional saving and investment required to pay for new jobs and housing. Government cannot do this well until it is adequately democratic, honest or efficient.

Advances in technology make possible labour savings which release workers from agriculture to work in industry. Industry, in turn, becomes highly capitalised and can manage with less labour. Then the service sector expands – as is now happening.

Despite computerisation, many of the services suffer from low productivity. The application of appropriate technology has been a lengthier process than with agriculture and industry. Professor William Baumol has drawn this low productivity in services to our attention. The growing preponderance of services in the economy has lowered the average productivity growth across the economy and helps to explain the slower rate of economic growth in the USA during the last two decades.

Another problem most advanced in the USA is the increasing expense of certain services and most top jobs in all services due to poor administration and restrictions on supplies of high-level manpower. One restriction is the drag imposed on the economy by too sluggish and uneven an improvement and expansion in education and training. Another cost-increasing factor is the emergence of a star system, no longer confined to Hollywood. In essence, these are employment markets where personnel near the top get a huge share of the earnings (econojargon: a huge 'rent'). The star system encourages the public's search for the best, only the best, talent, and strikingly illustrates the old adage that the best is the enemy of the good. Professors Frank and Cook assert that markets for high-level human resources have become "an increasingly important feature of modern economic life. These winner-take-all markets have permeated law, journalism, consulting, medicine, investment banking, corporate management, publishing, design, fashion, and even the hallowed halls of academe."[1a]

The population explosion, outreaching the capacity for technology to stretch the supply of natural resources, together with the bottlenecks in education and training and supplies of other forms of capital, add to other tendencies that lead to increased inequality of wealth and incomes.

The book closes with my recommendations for the reform of government and of policies to address these problems. In no instance do these recommendations coincide with those of existing political parties. Each politician is expected to like some of the recommendations and hate others. There is, notably, a plea for a shift from direct to indirect taxation in order to encourage employers to hire more people and all classes to increase their savings; for an increase in investment in economic development; for progress toward less economic inequality by heavy taxation of large estates; and for balancing public and private power by changing from freehold to thousand-year leaseholds of all land, with the government as the landlord with limited rights of eviction based on proper land use.[1b]

Towards the end of the book (pages 204–27) readers will reach the two main messages, succinctly stated. The second of the two messages concerns the service sector, so large in modern economies and some developing economies. Though that major and growing sector is labour-intensive and of low productivity, an innovative economist, Andre Gorz, has warned us that due to technological progress 'the amount of labour required by the economy will have diminished in the next ten years by about 22 per cent; in the next fifteen years it will have diminished by about a third.' Gorz therefore proposes that the half of the population eventually unemployed or under-employed should be absorbed by shortening normal working hours in 'waged employment,' without reducing wages at all, and spreading the short-time jobs much more widely. Moreover, he urges self-help and activities of social value, including protection of the ecology for the spiritual betterment of leisure and family life during everbody's ample spare time. All work and workers, whether creating wealth commercially or socially, would by means of a social policy receive a similar share of purchasing power from the amount of wealth produced. An impossible dream?[2]

Meanwhile, the policy recommendations offered here, if they can overcome the opposition of special interests and be applied appropriately, will stimulate the economy, and strengthen employment and social life substantially.

Acknowledgements

I thank warmly, for their continual assistance, encouragement and editorial acumen, Geoffrey Black and Stuart Wall of the Guidance Partnership agency and Chris Harrison, Jane Toettcher and other over-worked but always friendly and willing staff members of Addison Wesley Longman, including their consultant Valerie Mendes, Director of WordWise. I am most grateful for encouragement, sound advice, sobering comments and information received from Professors Will Baumol (Princeton and New York), Reuven Brenner (McGill), Robert Cox (York, Toronto), John Dunlop (Harvard), J. Kenneth Galbraith (Harvard), Peter Gill (M.I.T.), Clark Kerr (UC, Berkeley), Simon Maxwell (Sussex), and Sir Hans Singer (Sussex). Thanks also are proffered to the authors cited in the Notes. My loneliness as a long distance writer has been immensely reduced by my wife Sony, my children Jenny, Robert, Stella, Raffi, Sevan, and grandchildren Joe, Sophie, Lucia and William so far, and the rest of our loving and patient circle of family and friends. The publisher, a sound economist, accepted this book on the assurance that each of them would buy a copy.

None of these innocent souls thanked here share any blame for errors that managed to remain unslayed; while they should be credited for their mercy toward me. Knowing myself to be incurably error-prone, I resolved when reaching the age of discretion to concentrate on errors of commission and avoid errors of omission. I take full responsibility for the mistakes and for all the ideas and facts expressed, except those specifically credited to anyone else. In particular I am heavily indebted to the *Boston Globe* and *The Economist*, both as necessary to me as a bowl of raisin bran, to start each day well primed. I assure all concerned that coincidences between my views and those of public figures are not complete, contemporaneous, or causally related, and should not give rise to the false assumption that I and they are bedfellows in politics, religion, commerce or collusion.

Finally, my thanks in advance to readers for their support and fidelity, which will help to repay my debt to my publisher, my agent and their staff. In a noisy, busy world, to listen to someone is to offer them a great compliment.

Chestnut Hill
Massachusetts
March 1996.

PART I

OUR INHERITANCE

The prehistory and history of making a living

About 3,200,000 years ago in north-eastern Africa (Hadar, Ethiopia), a woman who was three and a half feet high lived a primitive existence. She mated, reproduced and died a natural death on the edge of a lake, leaving a skeleton preserved until today in the modern dryness and heat of the world's largest rift valley. It contains the Red Sea, northward. Don Johansson of Chicago, who found her bones and pieced them together, called her Lucy (not Eve, since no Adam lay dead beside her). In Aramis, not far away, some tell-tale teeth, knee-joints and other bones of the same age were found. These belonged to the common ancestor we share with that woman and with the whole gorilla and chimpanzee family.

Lucy and her companions were not big or strong enough to engage in direct battles with the larger and fiercer animals that certainly lived around them. They proved superior in their use of the bones of other animals as knives to cut up the dead meat they ate and that also served as tools. They and their descendants lived by scavenging near water-holes where many animals gathered, battled, left carcasses and hid the meat for their next dinner up trees (which Lucy easily climbed). Their knees let them stand upright. *Homo erectus* moved across the continents. In France, Neanderthal men and women lived a separate existence for 200,000 years before dying out. They were replaced by more 'modern' man: the knowing *homo sapiens* with a larger skull giving room to a substantial brain.

Since then, people have learned how to reach a standard of living which is acceptable for a majority and to attain a higher standard to delight the affluent minority. In the last ten millennia we have developed and indulged our tastes for conventional necessities such as clothing, artificial heating, cooling and other comforts not required by the animal kingdom. In warm and watered places, the sparsely populated world was like a garden as wild as that of Eden. The Bible does not describe the Garden of Eden in detail; it mentions one tree offering poison fruit and resident snakes. On a visit to Lebanon before their civil war, I saw a luscious mountain valley high above its fine view of the blue, sun-bathed Mediterranean sea. That place, called Ehden, would have made Adam and Eve happy, with its babbling streams, fruitful trees and spring-like weather most of the year. Life on this beautiful planet can be blissful. It can also be turned into a living hell in a few days by its human but destructive inhabitants.

The economics of subsistence

Before history – before writing itself – began, our ancestors lived by wandering about in an uncrowded world, hunting for meat, catching fish and picking anything edible from the trees and meadows. People today could live like that. In fact, a few still do, but only if they are lucky to be in the few remaining empty areas we still have. For example, the Intuit and Cree Indians in the north of Canada's Quebec Province number only about 7,500 hunters and fishers occupying well-watered and vegetated land as spacious as the whole of Northern Europe and not much colder in winter.[3]

For the five billion other people crowded on our planet, that is an impossible dream. The southern border of Quebec, where the northern border of the USA dips southward to the 45 degree parallel, is halfway between the equator and the North Pole. (Perhaps you thought cold Quebec was not far from the North Pole? It is as far from there as it is from Ecuador.) The empty north is indeed vast: too cold for many people, but it may attract millions if we find cheap sources of energy or if our planetary climate grows warmer in future. Almost costless energy – which abounds in the universe – could, when harnessed, serve to warm cold regions and desalinate seawater to irrigate and cultivate the world's deserts.

There is still some space to spare in other parts of the New World which are not as cold as much of central and eastern Canada. The New World has two of our globe's five habitable continents but less than a seventh of the world's population. The USA, with its large area affording room galore for its farmed acres and piles of property, houses only one-twentieth of the entire human race. Australia is even more sparsely populated than North America; much of it is desert. Most of the Old World, with the other two habitable continents, is congested with people, half of them hungry, three-quarters unhealthy. More than half of them are women, many of them downtrodden and treated as chattels. Whereas one person in twenty is an American, one person in five in the whole world is Chinese – but in their case females are distinctly less than half.

One anthropologist-cum-economist, W. E. Armstrong of Southampton University, had a fantasy about the advantages of a world peopled mainly by women with very few men. Less aggression and sufficient fertility, for example, might be anticipated; only a few men are needed to happily fertilise all the women.

Africa is vast. It remains spacious even when you deduct the area of the Sahara and other deserts. Although Africa has grave geographic problems, such as the tsetse fly which limits otherwise prosperous meat production, the poor use of natural resources there is a human failure. Civil servants and other African city-dwellers force food prices down so far for their own benefit that not enough food is produced. Land that should also grow staple foods for Africans is producing crops for export like cotton and tobacco. Michael Lipton, in his book about why poor people stay poor, blames worldwide rural poverty on the systematic tendency of cities to exploit the countryside.[4]

South Africans (of all colours), Australians and New Zealanders enjoy enough fertile space for themselves and most of them eat enough or too much.

World population has grown rapidly since prosperity and advances in technology increased output per head. Medical technology has also enabled more babies to survive and adults to live longer. This has happened mainly since 1800. How did we get to that point of breakthrough, after the centuries of a high death-rate when lives were nasty, brutish and short?

Lucy and her friends could stand up straight on their knee bones: novel in animal history and permitting erect stature. Those bones proved she was no monkey though a cousin of the chimpanzees. In due course, humans won the throne of the animal kingdom thanks to the first thumbs and opposing fingers holding things well. They further improved their lot by making work tools and hunting weapons. Our official name, *homo sapiens*, meant we were good at thinking. The skulls of Lucy and her *homo erectus* family were low-browed and monkey-like, enough for only a small brain. Brain growth and skull change occurred after the human ability to stand erect. We ended up having proportionately more skull space for our brain than the mental attic where dinosaurs stored their puny intellects.

Dinosaurs weren't such fools, though: not as self-destructive as we are. It will be surprising if humans succeed in surviving longer than the hundred-and-fifty million years the dinosaur family continued to crash about the globe. Before we are wiped out by a large meteor hitting Earth, as happened to them, our weapons, combined with our filthy, wasteful habits, risk destroying this planet as a habitat for most living things.

Community and cultivation

In the earliest days, the affinity between the sexes led to family life. This gave rise to the emergence of human interdependence and communal life. When cultivation first appeared, it was initially undertaken by child-bearing women who preferred to settle down. They found a wandering life harder to bear than their nomadic, hunting-and-killing husbands.

History's worst wars have been the most recent, yet in just a few years the numbers killed were easily replaced by the subsequent baby booms. That may not be so simple in future. A few centuries ago the population of Easter Island in the South Pacific suddenly dropped from eighteen thousand to about one thousand. Today it is even smaller. It became so hopelessly overcrowded that the islanders killed each other in squabbles over available food. There were no boats large enough to carry them all away.

Boatloads of Vietnamese were sent back from Hong Kong and – far more brutally – raped, robbed, killed and rejected from Thailand and

Malaysia. Boatloads of Haitians were turned back by the USA which, with unconscious irony, tried to find a home for them in Central American and Caribbean countries already crowded with poor people. France and Italy are threatened within by many other outsiders – North Africans – spearheaded by the fanatical militants of Islam.

Let us return to that happier image, the garden of Eden. Some of the hunters, nomads and migrants eventually discovered and were tempted to dally in attractive places with plentiful fresh water and rich soils. There they started gardening and cultivating crops and fruit. Many of those who, after the ice ages, poured out of Mongolia and eastern Siberia across the chain of the Aleutian islands easily found verdant, warmer and welcoming places as they moved southward through North and South America. Such settlers, anywhere, have to move on, when the soil has given of its best and yields only shrinking crops and harvests. If the settlers particularly liked their former home, they might return to find that the rested soils had recovered their nutrients.

Man discovered how to make fire. He used it to clear vast areas of forest for cultivation and enclosure. Slash-and-burn practices have their pros and cons; more cons, as the population increases. Luxuriant tropical forests, when cleared, leave soils less rich than perhaps expected and disappointing within a short period of cultivation. Recently a Mr Ludwig invested a billion dollars trying to clear a Brazilian forest for pulp and paper production. He failed. The hinterland of the new capital, Brasilia, centrally located in a forest clearing, could not sustain the market-gardening and truck-farming whose produce the city required.

Ancient people learned to improve their farming through techniques such as crop rotation and irrigation and by exploiting the value of silt deposited by rivers in flood basins and deltas. That made possible one of the world's greatest and most ancient civilisations: Egypt, the land of the Pharaohs. Siltation helped much of China and giant river valleys like those of Indochina, Thailand and Bengal to grow rice. Once, they all had great dynasties, wealth and civilisation. Now they all suffer from chronic over-population despite typhoons and 'the killing fields'.

Bengal and other river basins suffered from a deficiency of stones and rocks with which to build homes, fortifications and bridges. In many other countries and land-clearings across the world – particularly on the fringes of the great glaciers of the ice ages – there were so many stones and rocks they had first to be 'harvested', so as not to break early wooden ploughs. The stones were used for buildings and for walls and enclosures to retain farm animals.

Egypt makes bricks from its earth but now, with one million more people to feed every nine months, and with Cairo growing so large its homeless even have to sleep on and between tombstones, it can ill-afford to have vast areas of fertile soil submerged under urban sprawl or consumed in bricks.

Regional differences and location of cities

Some regions and countries had certain advantages and favourable climates; others had different ones. When not far away from each other, there began a swapping of the different products each region was able make, so trade began to grow. Not far away was, in those days, a few miles, especially if the traders were in landlocked or mountainous areas where transport for trade had to be on foot or in carts drawn by pack animals. It could be a few hundred miles if two complementary trading regions were situated up and downstream on a river where cargo boats could ply unimpeded by rapids, falls or cataracts. Such boats would sail down with the current and, when against it, be pulled upstream by animals on a towpath. With the improvement of boat-building, not far away became a few thousand miles as trade developed between regions with ports and ocean-sailing ships taking advantage of prevailing winds. Wood for ship-building, not too far away, was necessary. It was abundant in Scandinavia to make the Viking boats; in England and New England to build ships for their merchant fleets and navies; in Portugal, Spain and Italy for their explorers' ships.

Today, the world's greatest cities are still by the sea. Even Chicago, Toronto, Montreal and Quebec City would be far smaller were it not for their location on the Great Lakes and the St Lawrence Seaway.

Later, large towns sprang up at rail and road junctions, at strategic military posts and near rich agricultural regions. Mining and mineral-processing industries also became centres of population. When exhausted, such places became ghost towns. Shifts of centres of production and population occurred with changes in comparative advantages in terms of the cost and productivity of labour and other inputs.[5]

Trade in people and things

The first economic contacts between countries and communities were to barter goods or to buy and sell them in exchange for silver and, later, gold coins and other precious substances which were in limited supply and impossible to counterfeit. Some items brought in by travellers, such as mirrors, salt and spices, were regarded as acceptable forms of payment to locals wherever such commodities were scarce.

One of the commodities that travellers in Africa and elsewhere came to buy – or just seize – were slaves, most of whom were badly treated. Some economic historians suspect that slavery, efficiently organised, could be a profitable, though repugnant system of production. The abolition of slavery on moral and humanitarian grounds was one of the first examples of mankind trying to give economics a human face. Aristotle did not propose to set them free. Thomas Jefferson harboured thoughts of emancipation ahead of his time.

In Shakespeare's *The Merchant of Venice*, and in many other stories, people were often characterised as waiting for their 'ship to come in'. They prospered when it did and were ruined when it did not. On 'Widows' walks' along the roof-tops, the wives of the men on the whaling ships waited anxiously. For these people modern communications, providing news of where what you want to buy is cheapest and where what you want to sell gets the best price, together with news of the safety and whereabouts of their loved ones, would have been an enormous benefit.

The economic theory of international and interregional trade confirms what common sense leads us to expect. Trade between different places makes everyone more prosperous than they would be without it. It enables each area to specialise in making those goods and services each makes most efficiently. Each can then export their better goods and services, earning the money to buy other goods and services which are made better and more efficiently – and thus more cheaply – in other countries. They can also import goods and services, such as tropical fruits, which they cannot produce at all.

It is easy to imagine how a country would suffer if it had no trade with any other and had only those goods and services it was able to make, whether good, bad or indifferent, and had to do without things it could not make at all. This autarky, as it is called, would cause the greatest suffering in the smallest countries. Hong Kong, an economic miracle, would have been unable to develop without trade. Countries such as Albania which have experimented with autarky have paid a heavy price.

At the other extreme, countries as large as the USA, Russia and China can be almost self-sufficient and could survive even if the rest of the world were cut off or destroyed. By trading with the world, though, they can get richer and enjoy a wider range of better-produced goods and services than would have been possible without travel and trade. Finally, trade induces the cosmopolitan, a colourful trait for all but bigots and fanatics.

The next stage, now predominant, was the exchange of ideas and information and entitlements to money, by telecommunications.

Robbery and invasion, government and taxation

A large majority of human beings see no alternative to hard work. They endure the sacrifices and practise the thrift required for investment to increase productivity and economic security. Whatever they have, they earned the hard way.

Almost every page of history since it was first written focuses on some individuals, organised groups, clans and tribes, feudal lords and those over whom they hold sway, monarchs and emperors, all of whom gained their wealth mainly by seizing it from the hard-working people who had created it. (There are parallels of large-scale robbery and parasitism in the animal kingdom, though animals on the whole behave better.) In fact history is mostly about these dominant predators and their activities; others seem hardly to exist or to matter. As Napoleon explained after his Russian fiasco, a million men lost do not matter; only one man mattered – Napoleon.

This kind of example having been set by 'our betters' since time immemorial, it is natural that recourse to armed violence and robbery, since the accumulation of wealth began, has been an obvious, strong temptation for many different kinds of artful dodgers, bullies and bystanders consumed with jealousy.

What are the varieties of these predators?

- the able-bodied but lazy;
- those with more brawn than brain who have, or expect to have, difficulty in doing and keeping a regular job;
- those born or brought up with better instincts but driven to a life of robbery or quiet fraud by a desperate need for money. They may be driven to extremes to feed their families when no employment or relief can be found, or impelled by drug addiction, or hunted by creditors, criminals or terrorists that hound them for money. There are children and youths brought up by criminals at home, on the streets, in prison or in the army, who are trained only to beg, steal or kill; and desperate orphans in poor countries, unadopted by anyone kind and able enough to set them on the right path;
- people well-endowed with intelligence and capacity, even the capacity to make a fine career, yet set apart by their impatience and greed. They find life nasty, brutish and short and prefer to acquire wealth and power by force rather than merit. They might carve out an empire while fairly young, like Alexander the Great, Napoleon and Hitler in their heyday, using treachery, regicide, force of arms or glib propaganda and violent revolution. Others might settle more modestly for a criminal fortune as large as that of Al Capone, using his cunning and ruthlessness.

These are ancient categories, still with us and still preying on us.

In addition to these shamed classes, we have the unashamed and exalted ones of the Establishment, notably the military and the police. The current procedure for those in authority to obtain wealth and power by force is through taxation and the confiscation of assets in the name of penalisation or political correction.

A terrible element at one end of the spectrum of benefits and dangers brought to us by technological advance are weapons in the hands of both official and criminal enforcers. These weapons enable them to dominate far greater numbers of comparatively humble, unarmed people. Even when governments and the forces of law and order are democratic and do not seek to shift much wealth toward themselves under legal arrangements, there remains the illegal shift of wealth through the fraudulent, corrupt practices of dishonest officials. Corruption occurs in rich and poor countries alike, both democratic and dictatorial. When corruption is not driven by necessity among poor officials it is occasioned by greed among well-paid officials. It can be worse in democracies than in dictatorships because in the latter they can terrorise their administrations to reserve the spoils of the corrupt system for the top people alone.[6]

The share of national income and wealth carved out by national rulers for their own ends and requirements is just as much a part of economic history and is just as powerful in determining the growth and distribution of our material blessings as is the whole process of normal and honest trade.

History, like transport, has been speeded up considerably since 1800. In previous centuries, we had the spectacle of great empires rising and falling far less frequently. The Egyptian dynasties lasted for several millennia. The Chinese hegemony was comparatively durable – is perhaps still durable. The Chinese 'emperors' are not yet dead and gone. They are comrades instead of majesties and less ceremonially dressed. The 'communist' leaders have become major capitalists of the rawest kind. Their children are financiers and major stockholders in Hong Kong and have usurped the State's money for their personal investments even before 1997.

The Roman and the Turkish empires were shorter-lived, but they survived successfully for seven or eight centuries. All these empires were built on military superiority. We know from Yale's Professor Kennedy (whose book's widespread publication may even have helped to end the cold war) that the collapse of great empires is largely due to the economic strain of maintaining them.[7]

The ancient empires were also costly to maintain, but the degree of democracy so far achieved in recent times, together with the enormous cost of world wars and modern weaponry, made it hard for empires to survive. The British empire, strong for more than a century, crumpled after the First World War and dissolved after the Second World War. Hitler announced in 1939 that his empire would last a thousand years, but it collapsed in 1942 no more than three years after reaching its widest extent. The Führer's men suffered and perished, like Napoleon's men, on the Russian front.

The USA has seen a decline in the *comparative* power and wealth it had in the late 1940s. It is said to be the only great power since the collapse of the USSR, though its power is somewhat dulled by deficits in its government financing and in its balance of trade; once the world's largest creditor, it has become the world's largest debtor.

China is a major power, ostentatiously unnoticed although it has nearly a quarter of the world's population and the world's fastest-growing national income. It will soon include Hong Kong, a single city with a larger income than half the member countries of the United Nations. China has streamlined and improved its army of less than four million soldiers and made its nuclear missiles more accurate and longer-ranging. Its scruples do not exclude the assistance of unpleasant allies and vassals, such as the

Khmer Rouge and the North Koreans. Over-population is the writing on the wall for the longevity of the Chinese empire. Nevertheless, if China comes to regard its soldiers as expendable and not superannuated, its army with its 'cannon fodder' of a billion might still conquer much of the world to obtain the extra cultivable land it needs. Or, to be optimistic, it might go out and buy more, as the USA once did.

When we think of the economic progress since 1948 of Japan, Hong Kong, Singapore, South Korea, Taiwan and now China (Box 1.1), we see the other half of Professor Kennedy's equation.

Box 1.1: Asia: Economic progress 1980–1993

From 1980 to 1993 gross domestic product (GDP) and GDP per person increased each year as follows:

GDP: 8–10% China
     6–8%   South Korea, Taiwan, Singapore, Thailand
     4.6%   Hong Kong, Malaysia, Indonesia
     2–4%   India
     0–2%   Philippines

GDP per person: 6–8% China, South Korea, Taiwan, Singapore
                 4–6% Thailand, Hong Kong, Malaysia, Indonesia
                 2–4% India
   (decrease) – 2–0% Philippines

(Source: Economist Intelligence Unit)

In its *World Economic Outlook* (Washington DC, 1994 – six-monthly editions) the International Monetary Fund forecasts that developing countries will grow (in terms of GDP) by an average 5.5% in 1994 and by almost 6% in 1995. This would be more than twice as fast as the rate of growth expected in the rich industrial world. Asia's GDP will have increased by no less than 44% over the period 1990–95, compared with 16% and 11% respectively in Latin America and Africa. In contrast total output in Eastern Europe dropped by 32% in 1991–93 and will continue down in 1994. China's growth will slow down from 13% in 1992–93 to 10% in 1994, but remain the fastest growing economy. Thailand comes second, whose growth will speed up to 8.2% Venezuela will fall by 2.5% and Russia by almost 10% after an average decline of 14% in 1991–93.

Empires often fall under the burden of financing their maintenance while, on the other hand, real power accrues to those who are winning the competition in world trade. Empires were formerly built by military bullies.

Now they are built by economic bullies. Different and successive phases in the history of commerce during recent centuries are highlighted first by one and then by another country with a major and efficient economy, which exploits great competitive advantages in world trade and then, being a confident winner, presses hard for freedom of trade. The less strong trading partners are usually dominated and exploited in this process. Then, in a matter of a decade or so nowadays, other countries build up their industry and competitive edge and win growing shares of a world market formerly hogged by a single pioneering industrial nation such as Britain, the USA or Japan.

A question of major policy interest now is the extent to which the old and fading economic bullies can afford to maintain free trade or can keep their working people willing to maintain it when, despite differences in productivity and capital employed per worker, they face competition from countries with huge forces of low-wage labour. We return to this complex question in the sections on reducing unemployment and on trade policy.

Population growth

In recent times, there has been one transcendental factor in economic life which was neither known nor imagined by historians before American independence: the explosive population growth. Despite the killing of millions in the Second World War, the impact on world population of those tragic losses was insignificant. The baby boom in some countries in the years from 1947 to 1960 included extra births delayed by the wartime separation of couples and by uncertainty about their future. Most powerful of all was the secular rate of expansion of the population of the whole world, stepped up by gains in health and longevity. World population has more than quadrupled since 1800. This was a sudden and unique acceleration of population growth which had been extremely slow in all previous human history.

Unlike the developed countries, the marked population growth in many countries of the Third World, however, has occurred *prior* to much economic growth. This spurt reflects the spread of modern medicine and health care from their rulers. Colonialism arguably brought a mixed benefit. Since the start of the human race any increase in its numbers was almost imperceptibly slow and vulnerable to disastrous setbacks.[8] In the fourteenth century the Black Death killed a third of Europe's population.[9] World population only reached one billion people in 1800, after more than three million years.

The industrial revolution and advances in science followed, notably in medicine and public health, which by 1920 increased the world population to 2 billion. That was 1 billion extra people achieved in 120 years – at an average of 8.33 million more people each year. Then, in the thirty years from 1920 to 1950, despite factors such as the Great Depression under capitalism, the massacres under communism, the Third World famines and the Second World War, world population grew another half billion to reach a total of 2.5 billion in 1950, averaging 16.66 million more people each year. In the twenty years from 1950 to 1970, it grew by another 1.2 billion to a total of 3.7 billion in 1970. The growth rate in the nineteenth century was doubled by the middle of the twentieth century and in only another twenty years, to 1970, it had more than tripled, averaging 50 million more people each year.

In the twenty-four years from 1970 to 1994, the rate of growth slowed but with so many mothers then living many babies were born. People increased at an average rate of 83 million a year, some 2 billion in twenty-four years, raising the total to 5.7 billion in 1994: more than six times the number of people who had been living on earth throughout history before 1800.

We must expect substantial growth in the future – and catastrophic growth is possible. Population growth has slowed to a rate of 1.6 per cent annually but because there are now so many people alive, even that rate adds 90 million more people a year, which is a higher annual number than the growth we have experienced in the recent past. The forthcoming increase in the number of women of child-bearing age means the 'momentum of population' can carry the annual growth rate above 100 million more people a year by 2050. In another fifty-six years, 1994–2050, world population could exceed 11 billion.

It took more than 3 million years to produce 1 billion people by 1800, 120 years to double it by 1920, 75 years to double it again by 1995. In each decade in the future, expect an extra billion: one more Mexico each year and one more China every ten years.

Most ominous of all the consequences of high population growth is that, despite technological progress, it will certainly exceed the world's maximum capacity to produce food. Moreover, the high rate of urbanisation means that cities spread over land formerly growing food, so that food output may well contract in the most crowded countries. Yet increasing prosperity in some areas and in the numbers of people overall combine to push up the demand for food. By 1993 Japan was importing 77 per cent of its grain, South Korea 64 per cent and Taiwan 67 per cent.

The escalating demand for food in China alone could soon convert the world grain market from a buyer's to a seller's market. Allowing only for the projected population increase, China's demand for grain would increase to 479 million tons in 2030 whereas its falling production by then would call for imports of 216 million tons – more than the world's entire 1993 grain exports of 200 million tons.[10]

This prospective sellers' market for food, together with relatively gentle population pressure on food resources in America, should help protect the USA from the dire threats of famine, economic difficulty and political unrest facing the rest of the world. This may help to explain why the American man in the street is oblivious to this world issue. He may be astonished when its consequences, good and bad, arrive on his doorstep. Wealthy Americans have the least reason to worry. How about everyone else? The United Nations General Assembly declared that 1996 should be International Year for the Eradication of Poverty. It has indicated that the proportion of poor people has dropped from 32 per cent of world population in 1985 to 25 per cent in 1995. But about 50 babies every minute are born into poverty. Of the 5.7 billion people on earth, 1.5 billion are desperately poor – a figure which increases by 25 million a year (*Secretariat News*, December 1995, p. 5). The UN will become bankrupt during 1996 if the USA and other Member States continue to be in arrears in paying member-ship fees and peace-keeping UN forces.

Economics, the science that grapples with problems of scarcity, has two faces. Like the smiling and scowling masks in the world of theatre, in the real world there are booms yet there are busts. The rich become richer while the poor are exploited or, like Jesus, 'despised and rejected'. Government is mediocre at best or downright bad. The American Dream yields to cold-hearted awakenings. There are the educated and the uneducated; insiders and outsiders; kind people who care for the sick or hypochondriac while those who are sickest or poorest wither away untended. One child is born with a silver spoon in its mouth; another sucks at the withered breast of a drug addict or a famine-stricken mother. Good fathers are an endangered species. Others are jobless or disappear and are often cruel, whether they are there or not.

PART II

UNEMPLOYMENT

Unemployment: a new focus for economics

Economics exists to increase wealth and income wherever there are scarcities. In nineteenth-century America there was natural abundance and rapid exploitation of it. In that era of relative prosperity, seen by many as forming the basis for the American Dream – a frankly materialistic fantasy – there were few American economists or Americans interested in economics.[1] Today, despite decades of concern with social problems, economists are still mainly interested in output, productivity, the economy and the employed. The employed are called by statisticians 'the economically active population'. Economists are typically less interested in the unemployed, the economically inactive, than they are in the scarce resources used in production. It is exceptional for workers to be scarce, other than in the tiny area of highly educated and trained manpower.

The general public, on the other hand, are deeply concerned about unemployment. Joblessness undermines the security and prosperity of almost everybody. Many people are now urgently interested in finding effective ways of reducing the unemployment that is now also impacting on classes higher up the social scale than 'the workers'.

In defence of their focus, most economists would probably retort that increasing the number of jobs depends on expanding the economy. When economists get on with their task of expanding and enriching the economy, the creation of jobs will be a by-product of the process of economic development and growth. This argument is only half true. Fewer jobs are now being created than the number of people being born and eventually seeking them. Output can now be increased more efficiently by advances in knowledge and technology than by taking on more 'hands'.

Why not focus on reducing unemployment rather than on the traditional preoccupation with expanding output? While in theory the increase of output and productivity provides more wealth to be shared by workers, whenever or wherever workers are not at all scarce there will be little resistance to the many strong influences leading to greater inequality of incomes and of wealth. Increased output invariably gravitates into the hands of the wealthy and powerful; indeed, wealth and power do overlap.

Expanding employment without expanding output is pointless and can even be grievously harmful. We must continue to use economic analysis to promote increases in quantity and quality of output but – this is the crunch – do it in ways that seek to avoid throwing a lot of people out of work, some perhaps for life. We now focus directly on the search for more employment and more income for more people.

Short-term unemployment is about joblessness, which is often called 'a lay-off'. That can be painful, but workers eventually expect to return to work. Long-term unemployment is about a more tragic 'blight': workers fear they may be out of work for years and perhaps may never have another job. School-leavers may not even get their first job. At worst, long-term unemployment can cause more suffering than being crippled in an accident.

The two problems – short- and long-term – are different, but not entirely so. Policies and fortunate trends can extract workers from the ranks of the long-term unemployed group into a job and then 'only' expose them to the usual risks of short-term lay-offs in future. More probably and all too frequently, the least fortunate workers who are laid-off short-term are not taken back and fear they will not get another job for years, if ever. At the top of a recovery from a business slump, for example, national production can return close to capacity yet leave more workers unemployed than was the case before the slump.

The business cycle goes up and down but there is a strong possibility in the capitalist system of the cycle *not* returning to full economic capacity and associated employment activity. It gets stuck in what Keynesian economists call 'an under-employment equilibrium'.[2] That is one of the defining characteristics of a Great Depression, as happened in the 1930s and was destined not to end in peacetime, despite semi-recoveries. It could happen again toward the end of this present century. It is mentioned here as an illustration of how short-term unemployment can slide into long-term unemployment. The business cycle generates short-term employment; an incomplete recovery from it leaves a significant residue of long-term unemployment.

Technological unemployment can be either short- or long-term. A new technological development may be taking over the activities performed by a specific occupation rather gradually, so that it will displace some workers who are still able to find another job in the same occupation. For example, Sabre computerised programmes are widely used by American travel agents for locating empty seats at acceptable fares and booking and ticketing them, but Worldspan programmes performing the same function are catching on fast. If the boss switches to Worldspan, his employees can either take time out to learn Worldspan or they can resign and seek work in another agency, remaining with Sabre. You may think the boss has a duty to keep you on while he retrains you, but in the USA, 'adaptability' is considered to be the workers' responsibility.

Then there are the bigger, sometimes quicker, changes in technology. In the transport industry, which has been revolutionised by such progress, there is almost no demand for those who can look after a horse-and-cart; similarly there is almost no demand for stokers for steam engines and a shrinking demand for locomotive drivers. What is currently needed in large numbers are truck-, van- and bus-drivers.

We now look closely at what causes short-term unemployment, so as to know how to reduce it. First, we have to define the idea of unemployment, though the fact itself may seem simple and clear.

Labour left fallow

The worst economic problem in our world is 'fallow labour'. Labour left fallow includes unemployment but it means you have no paid work, no earned income. You are 'between jobs', as they say bravely. Till the next paid job comes along, you get payment from an unemployment insurance or social security system. It comes first as an insurance benefit until your share in the fund is exhausted. Then it might be followed up by a social relief payment. In the USA, $20 billion a year in free food is distributed to the poor and jobless under a food-stamp scheme. This exceeds the value of the food which the USA gives annually to the unemployed and needy in other countries.

In less-developed countries no insurance or relief is usually available. People not earning money from a job have to manage somehow: possibly helped by limited support from relatives, friends and even unfriendly money-lenders. They are usually too poor to have much in savings. The wife might sell some jewellery handed down to her, but she usually clings on to that until the end. Exceptionally, there are a few local church and other charities and a little foreign assistance such as food aid, which might help temporarily. The down-and-out in less-developed countries find it hard to keep going by begging; they live where there is little wealth to be shared. The most destitute of those without earned income, without even a plot of land on which to grow food, finally face starvation.

Anyway – anywhere – people without income are desperate. They take up any job or activity, often on a part-time or freelance basis like selling apples on a street corner, for very little money, eating anything on hand to survive. That happened even on Wall Street in the 1930s. Today the unemployed in countries that pay more adequate unemployment benefits may not bother to work for very little money and may refuse any job paying much less than they earned before.

The word 'unemployment' has two meanings: no job, is one; the other is the money 'they' may pay you when you have no job. Jobless workers in the USA say optimistically that they 'are between jobs' but meanwhile they 'have only "unemployment" to live on'. Unemployed people want work, but they may not look for it if they lose hope; usually only those regarded as actively looking for work are counted by statisticians (Box 2.1).

Outside the monetary economy, safety nets and rich countries, there are too many examples of 'labour left fallow', humans of working age (more than nine years) who are left to starve if they cannot work. Thus, whereas 'unemployment' is a statistical and administrative category in developed

Box 2.1: Underestimation of unemployment

Improved measurement has suggested effective rates of unemployment *above* the official rates (expressed as percentages of the labour force) at the end of 1993, as follows:

	France	Britain	Japan	USA
Official rate	12	10	2.9	6.4
Effective rate	13.7	12	9.6	9.3

(Source: Tappan Datta, The Amex Bank Review, New York, quoted by TENL)

In the USA, many women 'keeping house' were also looking for a job and therefore had to be counted as unemployed. The US figures for the effective rate still exclude 'discouraged workers' (who would like a job but have given up looking), and the underemployed (workers who would like a full-time job but have to work part-time during a downturn). Japan has even more discouraged workers, particularly women. Japanese official figures are based on a pretty narrow definition of employment. Europe has fewer discouraged workers.

countries, in the less developed countries there is no unemployment in either of the two senses: no job and no compensation paid for failing to find a job. Instead, in poor countries, there is what the economists call 'under-employment and low productivity'. Whether or not workers in these less-developed countries have any employment – typically characterised by long working hours – their earnings and their total income are painfully low.

Many people but not everyone likes to have work to do; for some, work gives status and a defined role. An even more universal concern is having enough (money, etc.) to live on. Poor pay and poverty are caused first by workers being in over-supply, making it easy for employers and landowners to beat down their earnings. Second, with so few tools and poor health, their output is of little monetary value. They will not be paid a wage above the value of the goods they produce.

This personal input can be measured by observing how much production is lost if one worker is laid-off or absent for a while. Production may not in fact drop at all with one less worker. It may even rise. The employer may have hired too many hands from the flood of desperate, cheap applicants for an urgent job. On his crowded worksite, people get in each other's way and waste the supervisor's time. A smaller working force would in this case be more efficient.

We come to the crux of the matter. Many people enjoy leisure and will only work because they have to earn their keep. They may complain about how little they earn. It may be little because of their low productivity. Only when, worldwide, the value of output is increased per person 'employed', can every person have a better income. And even then they will get it if – and only if – they are given a share in the increased output.

'Low productivity of a worker' is not a statement about laziness or personal weakness. It is a statistical ratio and it is usually a low ratio when capital – machinery and power – for labour to work with is insufficient, so that still more effort is demanded from the worker. Driving through the streets of Calcutta in a heavy rainstorm, we passed a pitiful spectacle exemplifying a demand upon a worker beyond his strength. A thin-bodied, elderly man, whose wet, ragged clothes outlined his ribs underneath, struggled between the shafts of a cart where a horse should have been, to pull a load that a horse should have pulled. At the intersection, the nearest drain was blocked and the cart and man were hardly moving: he was stuck in the middle of a corner pool with water up to his waist. Vehicle drivers screamed at him and honked their horns. The torrential rain beat down on his head and back. Our bus was no luxury vehicle but our driver had a comfortable seat under a roof because other people's capital had been invested in the bus. And 'of course' he was paid more. Why 'of course'? His skill was not so remarkable or scarce.

Where 'highly productive workers' are at work, you can be sure that a significant supply of power is being used. Men loading, unloading and driving huge trucks and trailers up to 60 feet long used to be among the strongest of American workers. When power brakes and power-steering were introduced, forklift trucks loaded and unloaded bulk and weight and giant cranes dropped three-ton containers on to flat-top trailers. The drivers of power machinery may have become wizards at manoeuvring but they are less likely to be the tough guys of old. Indeed, some of them are now being replaced by women.

In contrast, workers all over the mainly poor world slave away until their back is ready to break and the sun has parched their skin. They have to do this in order to accomplish a small fraction of what another worker can achieve with machinery – and sometimes they must even compete with the latter. Without modern tools and machines, the work done by muscle and fingernails alone looks pathetically small. I have seen workers on their knees cutting a lawn outside the boss's office with ordinary domestic scissors. I have seen women in Bangladesh breaking clods of mud in parched, fissured road beds with sticks and their shrivelled, bony fingers. They were said to be in a food-aided project for 'prostitutes being rehabilitated'. They were certainly no welfare cheats. In a culture where female dress and decorum are mandatory and the cruel tropical sun burned their flesh, their bodies were pitifully ill-covered with the remains of their rags.

In a rich country we often see the opposite extreme: a lazy, inept, over-equipped worker who delivers by truck a stack of bricks on to the roadside for a new garden wall. A crane on the back of his truck seeks to pick up a modest load of bricks and pyramid them on to the ground a foot away; it seems like taking a hammer to kill a gnat! The crane is big and unwieldy, intended to handle heavier loads. In casual hands the 'load' is swung round, smashing one block of bricks against another and dropping a lot of other bricks in the road. It would in fact have been quicker, easier, safer and less damaging to use the traditional method of hand-carrying the bricks in the customary six-packs held in a hand-tool grip and stack them neatly. Adequate capital equipment may be a necessary, but not sufficient, condition for high productivity!

In a nutshell, high productivity is the efficient and combined use of brain and brawn, fuel and the right tools for the job. It depends on a combination of capital, intelligence, skill and diligence.

Fallow labour is the sum total of millions of unemployed who sit around waiting for the sun to set after it has risen. It arguably includes the idle time of those who are under-employed and under-equipped. It may even encompass the low productivity of billions of workers who, in a formal sense, are called 'fully' employed merely because they are kept available in case something may turn up that is something they can do.

The number of workers is far greater than the number of wage-earners. In fact, worldwide, wage-earners are in a minority. The majority of workers are employed on the land as cheap-day labour, share-croppers, tenant farmers, small-holders and truck-farmers. There are actually more self-employed people than employees worldwide. The totality of workers and entrepreneurs is called 'the economically active population' by statisticians. Statisticians, if they were interested, might call fallow labour 'the economically inactive population'.

Fallow labour is a more concise name and less of a tongue-twister. It may be compared to land 'left fallow', a phrase that accurately connotes a fertile resource left aside for the time being or not fully used and that may well be surplus to requirements. Unfortunately, though, there is also a painful difference. Land left fallow benefits from crop rotation. It renews its strength and fertility during its 'rest' from intensive cultivation. Labour left fallow and idle can only do one thing: deteriorate in both body and mind.

With sufficient land, capital and good management – 'sufficient' in relation to the number of people – unemployment can be easily overcome. Without those factors, it cannot.

No single politician can deliver a miracle

For decades, politicians have foolishly and arrogantly claimed they have the knowledge and power to solve employment problems and will do it in short order (Box 2.2).

> **Box 2.2: Keynes on politicians**
>
> 'Practical men, who believe themselves to be quite exempt from any intellectual influences, are usually the slaves of some defunct economist. Madmen in authority, who hear voices in the air, are distilling their frenzy from some academic scribbler of a few years back.'[3]

No one, not even the President of the United States, the so-called 'most powerful man in the world', who nevertheless has to contend with the Supreme Court, Congress and the Federal Reserve System, can, by himself alone, eradicate chronic unemployment. Take this typical statement for example:

> *Despite all his troubles, Clinton is presiding over a fairly impressive economic comeback. After generating just 2.4 million jobs in the four years George Bush was president, the nation has created 3.8 million in 18 months under Clinton.*

Note 'the nation' did the creating; Bush was unlucky and Clinton was lucky. Even though we are speaking of less than a quarter of the total influences on employment over this time period, one might say Clinton's impact was more positive than Bush's.

President Hoover went to the opposite extreme. He stood firm in his belief that he could do nothing, as President, to alleviate the Great Depression. He believed that the capitalist system, combined with the good hardworking character of the right kind of American worker and citizen, would ultimately bring about a recovery. He was rather unfairly pilloried by those who called it 'Hoover's Depression', since it was a depression he did not start and could not stop. He may, however, have suffered from excessive modesty, insufficient imagination and a surprising unreadiness to show the same mercy to American down-and-out families that he had shown to foreign families in postwar Europe to whom he carried relief in the 1920s.

President Roosevelt and his well-chosen advisers demonstrated brilliantly and courageously what sort of things could be done during depression to raise the effective demand of the population for goods and services and to work on improving the economic infrastructure. Even so, it took production for war to bring about full recovery.

Stalin did not really achieve genuine full employment, even after killing millions of 'kulaks' (small farmers), which left their land free to be seized and worked by others. His so-called Leninist–Stalinist system claimed to have eradicated unemployment. Actually he dropped a number of Lenin's better economic ideas and had little right to call himself Leninist. And there were major questions Stalin did not answer. How much work could rural

Russia do in a Russian winter? What was the occupation of millions of Soviet soldiers on a year-round basis? How could anyone get another job, since they could not leave one job and move to another address without Stalin's permission to travel and to change residence? How could anyone be free to change jobs – as required in an efficient economy in a free society – if, as the USSR regularly reported to the UN International Labour Organisation (ILO), the level of unemployment was permanently 'zero'?

Optimistic unemployment reports by the USSR began to look all the more incredible when, in the 1950s, the ILO adopted a convention (a kind of international treaty) on the promotion of full employment. The convention stated that the 'full employment' to be achieved by the signatory countries (including the USSR) was, precisely, 'full, productive and freely chosen employment'.

Even before that exacting but humanly just standard was introduced, there were already other ILO conventions forbidding forced labour and slavery. The first conventions were adopted in the 1930s, though the problems still abound today. We might have no unemployment worldwide if all employment was forced and the wages, in money or just food, were minimal. The total work achieved would probably be less and inferior. World income would certainly be lower and arguably civilisation would collapse.

Before considering the most serious unemployment, we look first at two universal kinds of unemployment that are partly necessary and not too serious. They are frictional unemployment and seasonal unemployment.

Frictional unemployment: signs of freedom and vitality

People voluntarily resign from a job:

- to take a better job elsewhere;
- to move to an area where they prefer to be and where they might expect to find another job if they wish;
- to get married and have children, perhaps planning to return to employment when their children go to school;
- to retire or to live restfully on doctor's orders;
- to do further study and training to advance their career.

In most of these cases the job they leave remains to be done and usually it is soon filled by someone else. These are the most desirable examples of *frictional employment*, where people are voluntarily between jobs or voluntarily leaving the active labour force and returning later if they wish.

To deny individuals this freedom would be harmful to them and harmful to society. Workers may change jobs to escape sexual harassment or to follow a spouse or friend who has changed job or address. Both sexes may quit following the appointment of a hated boss and seek another job.

Others feel obliged to move because of an increase in local taxation, a deterioration in the quality of schools attended by their children or other adverse factors.

Workers may have to move to other areas because of various changes, for example, in markets; in technology; in diminished conditions of security (even war itself); the depletion of natural resources (as happened recently in the fishing industry); or because ill-health in the family requires a change of climate. Alternatively, workers may move for more positive reasons: more fish to be found elsewhere, a gold rush, an oil strike, a part in a Hollywood film, a job abroad with a tax-free salary or a better job opened up after completing evening courses.

The worst instances of frictional unemployment often occur under 'casual employment' systems. Dock-workers and other manual labour used to be employed by the day before 'decasualisation', which in turn was followed by the rapid spread of container-cargo technology. Consultants, actors and actresses, private detectives and others are often employed by the day or under contract for short periods (such as the making of a film or the run of a play). Some of them are well paid (to compensate for the off-time and for the absence of fringe benefits) and in a few cases are almost fully employed.

Some unemployment at first sight caused by frictional factors, may prove *not* to be short and temporary, but unfortunately to last far longer. In this case, it then enters the serious, large category of *structural* unemployment. The massive problems of international trade and of economic and social structural adjustment may involve this type of unemployment and are discussed later.

Seasonal unemployment: rest? recovery? second job? or?

Temporary work stoppages, or reductions of workload due to climatic and other changes that come with the natural annual cycle of the seasons, cause substantial but temporary seasonal unemployment for part of each year. It is more meaningful to talk about whether 'unemployment is now worse than it was' if, instead of comparing it with last month, we compare it with the same month the previous year.

Only a fortunate few can escape the seasonal factor, such as professional sports stars who move from the northern to the southern hemisphere for their championships, and orchestras, ballet and opera groups that also go on tour. Others just take a second job in their off-season, or take a holiday. Many teachers who are paid ten months of the year do the latter. To a major extent, the seasonal unemployment problem is reduced by man's mastery over nature which has come with technological and economic progress. We have heating and air-conditioning in buildings and transport, wherever it can be afforded. Construction work can continue in foul

ˈunder plastic sheets. Some crops, fruits and flowers are grown
er.

However, far worse than frictional and seasonal unemployment, we now
examine the deepening horrors of completely involuntary unemployment.
This occurs more massively and more durably, often far exceeding the
alleviating income support provided temporarily in a few countries.

Cyclical unemployment: booms, busts; euphoria, misery

The best-known aspect of the unemployment of millions is the 'cyclical'
one. There is a business cycle of booms and busts. It is not as regular in its
duration or magnitude (a decade) as was once supposed. But it is regular in
being like a wave – with crests and troughs – and with few if any eccentric
plateaux or double summits. Like ocean waves, the cycles vary in size.

Some unemployment may even remain at the top of the boom; but there
is so much unemployment at the bottom of the bust (recession or
depression) as to expose totally the complacency and arrogance of
ideologists advocating entirely free market systems. Beyond the painful
social suffering, there is the economic fact of lost output – the gross
wastage of unused production capacity. The whole world economy is upset
by the business cycle, which hits hardest in the industrialised, capitalist
countries.

This is what happened to the world's gross domestic product from the
top of the last boom until 1994, when recovery from the recession was
nearly complete. The figures show the percentage rise in world income and
output (GDP) from one year to the next:

1987–1988: nearly 5 per cent rise in world GDP
1988–1989: around 3.5 per cent rise in world GDP
1989–1990: around 2 per cent rise in world GDP
1990–1991: around 0.5 per cent rise in world GDP
1991–1992: nearly 2 per cent rise in world GDP
1992–1993: slightly more than 2 per cent rise in world GDP
1993–1994: nearly 3 per cent rise in world GDP

The point is that the world economy can grow as fast as five per cent per
annum, as it did in 1987–1988. Yet in five years it 'lost' some 14 percentage points of possible growth (at a compound rate), with no prospect
of a return to 5 per cent growth in sight in 1994. Of course an economy
can grow too fast – it can become 'overheated' and liable to inflation – but
inflation (though certainly harmful) is arguably less serious than unemployment. An economy growing below capacity is rusting away its skills and
dilapidating its idle plant: a downcast, wounded economy.

It was announced that 'recovery was nearly complete' in 1994. That was true in the USA and the UK; and the European Union as a whole stated at its meeting early in September 1994 'the union is definitely in a growth pattern again' and that the group's economy would expand by 2 per cent in 1994, a rate below the world average.

The recession had thrown nearly 18 million people out of work in the European Union, with unemployment at a rate of almost 11 per cent in 1994. Finance ministers of the Union considered this jobless rate too high. Moreover, it was said 'We are now coming out of the recession with the highest level of public debt . . . in Europe since the Second World War. Deficits must be brought down as the recovery takes root.' The danger here is that a policy of paying-off debt means less investment and/or consumption by debtors.

The OECD reported that from 1990 to 1994 unemployment (by standardised definition) rose from 9 to 12 per cent in France, from less than 7 per cent to nearly 11 per cent in Italy and from 4 per cent (in 1991) to nearly 7 per cent in Germany. In Britain it rose to a level over 10 per cent by 1993 before dropping toward 9 per cent in 1994. In the USA it rose from just over 5 per cent to over 7 per cent in 1992 but dropped under 6 per cent in 1994.

Recessions and depressions

Cyclical unemployment is caused by the ups and downs in the economy, the alternating good times and bad. The busts, politely called recessions, occur when the rate of growth in the national income recedes toward nil. Their start is marked by two or three successive quarters involving a falling-off in the economic growth rate. If economic growth drops to a standstill, the economy may actually start to shrink so that the national income and many personal incomes fall in the current year below what they were in the previous year. We then have a situation in which, should the shrinkage be prolonged for many months, even years, we have what is called a major depression.

Politicians often seek to avoid that frightening word, which recalls the Great Depression of the 1930s. But it would certainly be dishonest not to use it if there is both a failure to recover and the total output is dropping. Almost no new jobs are created while so many are sought, causing grave unemployment. People have fewer babies in a depression, but that cannot change the fact that many young people already born are finishing or dropping out of school or university and are finding it hard to get their first job. One person in four was out of work in North America in the 1930s and it is staggering to find the same thing happening in Spain in 1994 despite the supposed benefits of European Union! Ireland is almost as badly blighted by unemployment.

Economic collapse: disaster and hyperinflation

There is something worse than a depression that really goes beyond the business cycle: an economic breakdown or collapse. In such a situation comparatively few people can keep their normal employment and many are driven to acts of desperation. It occurs in a country reduced to ruins by a massive war, such as Germany in 1945, Lebanon in the 1980s and probably southern Yugoslavia by 1996.

Since the world abandoned the gold standard and used paper money, a number of countries have been wrecked by hyperinflation as well as depression. Hyperinflation wrecks the economy and society and is a far more deadly kind of manmade sabotage than mere terrorism. The value of money, like the value of anything else, falls when it enormously increases in supply. Many people feel they can never have too much money; that can only be true as long as each dollar will buy as much as before. That can only happen when the increased supply of money in a country is matched by an increase in the supply of all the things people want to buy.

Hyperinflation occurs when so much money is printed that in less than a year or two it loses all its value: it will buy nothing. Light the fire with it. Paper the walls. Use it as toilet paper. Lenin once said that gold would be used to make lavatory bowls in a communist society. He forgot that it is limited in supply so that it can always be used valuably to buy anything, anywhere. Buying things is money's 'exchange value'; lighting the fire is an example of its limited usefulness or 'utility value'. However, gold has and keeps more of both kinds of value.

The printer of too much money and he who gives the orders to the printer are the saboteurs. That happened in Germany in the 1920s, ruining millions of families; Nazism rose from the wrecked society. The memory and history of it still terrifies Germany today so that it has the most independent central bank in the world, which stubbornly fights the smallest signs of rises in the rate of inflation. The German Bundesbank kept interest rates unrelentingly high during the recent recession, when West Germany paid out of its current income most of the bills of bankrupt East Germany after the Berlin Wall and the prison it enclosed crumbled away.

In the 1940s, war drove Italy, France, Greece and Japan close to the edge of hyperinflation: France is the only one of the four which later converted to a new currency. Italy, Greece and Japan continue to pay people salaries denominated in millions of wispy currency units that had been worth thousands more in the 1930s. Other governments, notably in South America, have in more recent years allowed hyperinflation to make a mockery of established currency units. Civil war caused it in Lebanon although that country had an independent central bank; the latter's large gold holdings had to be used up, covering the cost of government when tax collection fell extremely low. Something similar to Germany's disaster in the 1920s was well under way in the Russia of 1994: hyperinflation leading to civil war and civil war soon involving neighbours and spreading internationally seemed well on the cards. (That fate has not yet been ruled out but it is rivalled by the risk of Russia being overtaken by large criminal organisations, with economic and political effects quite novel in world economic history.)

When hyperinflation gets beyond a certain point it is impossible to stop it. A new and credible currency has to be introduced and that may be impossible without massive foreign support. Today, that support would usually have to be from the International Monetary Fund (IMF). The IMF is the world's central bank, which has a kind of world currency called SDRs (special drawing rights). Only the central banks of Member Countries[4] can keep an account in that money.

Spendthrift and bankrupt countries hate the IMF. Its job is to be a tough creditor who refuses to put the world's money, earned and saved by hard and thrifty workers, to undue risk in irresponsible countries. Unfortunate countries are not bad credit risks if their misfortunes do not also include a weak 'character'.

Gold is the only form of money always credible: no one could print it or fake it. However, other 'currencies' have emerged in periods of hyperinflation. In Germany in the mid-1940s, for example, packets of cigarettes became effective means of payment: one could print the packets but not the contents, so their supply was limited and they were valued in terms of use and even more in terms of exchange.

Dollar bills are very often the preferred form of payment in countries such as Russia or Lebanon, especially in times of high inflation. US dollars, long the form of payment in Liberia, Panama and the tourist enclaves of the Caribbean islands, demonstrate that a single world currency need not cause grave problems if it is as reliable as gold (the former world currency).

When a government is generously printing and pumping money into the economy, but not to such an extent as to cause hyperinflation, it will not entirely override the business cycle. During a boom, it will dangerously encourage speculation, notably the over-pricing and over-building of offices and also houses (still needed in principle by modest families but often priced beyond their reach).

Increasing the money supply by printing money was once a popular gimmick for creating employment and prosperity but eventually and fairly soon it makes things worse. Printing money does not increase the supply of 'real' money because it loses value as prices rise. More 'nominal' money is trying to buy relatively few more goods, so prices rise.

There will still be recessions under inflationary conditions. Recession is particularly nasty if the cost of living keeps rising: we have a situation called 'stagflation', i.e. inflation in a stagnant economy. In a stagnant economy there is not much physical addition to the real assets of the economy – buildings, factories, ports, roads, bridges, etc., merely over-pricing of these assets. During recessions there is unemployment of both people and of the existing production capacity: factories lie idle, roads are less crowded, ships are mothballed. The incomes of the proletariat (the property-less) fall, while the owners of property, including the assets just mentioned, can live riotously well on the capital gains they enjoy from the inflationary money issue being thrown at the fixed stock of assets in the market place.

Providing a lot more credit is, in its adverse effects, rather like printing money. It increases the current demand for goods but reduces future demand: people buy less while they pay off their debts.

Until Keynes, economists said unemployment was voluntary!

Let's think a little more about inflation. It leads to speculative 'investment in' (or 'over-paying for') the fixed supply of existing buildings and old stocks and shares that just rise in price. This may be distinguished from real investment in new buildings and in purchasing new shares issued by companies expanding their capacity. It will then be easier to understand a major point made by the economist J. M. Keynes. He explained why the so-called 'classical' economists were wrong when they quoted, with approval, J. B. Say, a French economist, to prove that all unemployment is voluntary.

More than a century ago Say contended that there cannot be any unemployment except that of voluntary unemployment – those choosing not to work – because all the goods and services produced create a national income in the form of the value of what was produced. In other words, Say contended that total supply is equal in value to the money or means received in payment for producing that supply. Thus, there must be enough money available to buy all that has been produced.[5]

Keynes pointed out that this will not be true if some of those receiving money choose not to spend all of it. They might well prefer to save some of their earnings. For example, many people remember occasions when they and their friends have experienced 'rainy days' when it was painful to run short of money. They might therefore save for their old age if they can, especially if they expect to live to a ripe old age.

Keynes also pointed out that, under capitalism, the total level of production in the predominant private sector will be no more than the amount of things it proves profitable to produce. If profits were found to be greater with some continuing level of unemployment, which is quite possible because full employment tends to bring rising wages and inflation, then some unemployment will continue indefinitely. A country then has what Keynes called an 'under-employment equilibrium', which will not be relieved unless and until some external influence improves the profitability situation.

When we have deflation – falling prices – people are afraid to invest in more production capacity as even existing capacity is now rendered unprofitable at lower prices. In these ways a business cycle can come to a stagnant pause as killingly as an arrested heartbeat. The economic recovery is rendered incomplete because growing output stops at some profitable level, which happens to be an 'under-employment equilibrium'. That is what happened in the Great Depression. Output and employment never returned to their high level in the 1920s; the 'recovery' from the 1937–1938 downturn only returned half-heartedly to an under-employment equilibrium. It took war in the USA from 1941 onward to force the economy back to full employment and output towards capacity production.

Such an under-employment equilibrium and even a serious depression could occur again before the end of the century because of the current lean, mean tendency of the capitalist system. We had cut-throat competition, cost-cutting and lay-offs right through the last American recovery from 1993 to 1995, even in companies that were already quite profitable. This diminishes discretionary income for the masses and with it their free-spending power. It sets a country's economy on a collision course, with a swelling national debt and prospects of still further indebtedness. These soaring debts are caused by:

- the governmental, health-care and legal services sectors acquiring larger shares of the national income each year;
- burdensome population growth; and
- a shortage of capital associated with the super-rich absorbing a large and growing slice of the national income and wealth in ways that prevent that income and wealth being fully recycled into the national economy through real investment and their own consumption. The 'super-rich' are headed by 136 American billionaires, each with total assets exceeding $1,000,000,000. One of them, Bill Gates, owns $12,900,000,000; another, Warren Buffett, owns $10,700,000,000. During the 'golden age' of the late nineteenth century, the Vanderbilt family had more money than the US Treasury.

In Keynes' own language, there may exist a strong 'liquidity preference' (hoarding of money and easily cashed-in speculative investments) and a 'diminishing marginal propensity to consume'. These factors imply that money previously earned in the economy is not being fully returned as aggregate effective demand for goods and services.[6]

Achieving full employment: the abstract answer

Although most of the readers of this book are non-economists, many may have the kind of mind that enjoys the abstract and can fully conceive the meaning and implications of the following brief statement. It does include some economic jargon which has leaked into the general media. Others may wish to move fast forward to the next section.

Full employment can be approached and maintained in a country if . . . well! there are two big IFs:

First, IF the total effective demand by consumers, business-people and governments for goods and services remains as high as, and grows with, the capacity to supply them. 'Effective demand' is what buyers want and have the money to pay for (the ability to pay). Total or aggregate effective demand is what *all* buyers in a country want and can afford.

Second, IF the number of workers required for full capacity production in shops, offices, factories, farms and other workplaces equals the number of workers looking for jobs, and the workers looking for jobs are qualified for the jobs to be done, THEN a country will be well on the way to having and keeping full employment.

So far we have only discussed points about the business cycle that many people know. What many do not know and others argue about is why it happens at all. Why does it start? Why and when does a recovery eventually arrive? Why do the costs and benefits affect some people more than others?

Cyclical and non-cyclical industries

We can get an idea of how business cycles operate by looking at the differences between cyclical and non-cyclical industries. Some industries are much more strongly affected than others by booms and busts. In any of the kinds of economic downturns just mentioned we see certain industries more badly affected than others and they are often the ones laying-off the most workers. When the recovery comes, employment goes up again but the unemployment does not disappear. In fact it tends to remain higher than it was during the previous boom.

If we compare two major recessions in the USA – in 1975 and 1992 – we find that unemployment became worst in construction (18.0 per cent and 16.7 per cent of those workers unemployed, respectively), in manufacturing (10.9 per cent and 7.8 per cent unemployed) and in wholesale and retail trade (8.7 per cent and 8.4 per cent unemployed). Unemployment in agriculture was also severe, but it did not recover in better times either: it remained above 10 per cent most years from 1975 to 1992.

The non-cyclical businesses largely produce and sell necessities, not luxuries. They provide items we have to buy every day. Some items such as milk, eggs, fresh fruit, meat and fish are perishable and must be used soon, or stored protectively. However, deep freezers are popular and allow some purchases to be more intermittent: you can buy food for storage when prices are low, shop less frequently and always have supplies on hand for unexpected occasions. But frozen food loses quality, taste and all its value if there is a power failure. Medicines and other items, in contrast, have a limited shelf-life for hygiene, health and other reasons and must be replaced.

There are clear seasonal patterns in the purchases of some items: logs, gloves, antifreeze in winter; swimsuits, sunglasses, strawberries-and-cream in summer. However, most outlets providing multiple choices, such as supermarkets, department stores, shopping malls, hardware stores, pharmacies, general stores, service stations, medical centres, clinics, doctors, dentists and hospitals, are open every day for business and sell thousands of items daily, irrespective of the time of year.

There is the remarkable fact in the USA (perhaps elsewhere too) that more than half of the total retail sales in a year occur in less than a quarter of it, between Thanksgiving Day and New Year's Day. However, in a recession, holiday sales for retailers can drop frighteningly and spring up suddenly in a recovery once consumer confidence is re-established.

Suppose you or your partner or both of you are out of work and spending as little as possible. Or it may be that you are economising in order to have a security reserve of cash because you are frightened by the lay-offs of friends, neighbours and colleagues in the office and people in the news. You are frightened that such lay-offs may hit you next. Even so, you have to go on buying certain necessities, so far as possible.

Since people cannot help dying when their time has come, we assume funeral parlours and burial services would be needed and used at all times. Amazingly, a friend who runs such a business told me that morticians feel the pinch during slumps. This reminds us that for almost every item of expenditure there can be a choice about whether or not to purchase and in the quantity or quality of item to be bought.

There are a few things that many people cannot do without. Companies making and selling alcohol seldom go out of business. Despite all the adverse publicity and official discouragement, sales of products for smokers hold their own, though possibly on a declining long-term curve. Gambling has its addicts and in bad times attracts the desperate. Today in the USA it is passing through an unparalleled boom at many places between Atlantic City and Las Vegas. The 'world's oldest profession' earned its title by maintaining a steady business that has never collapsed.

The cyclical industries often involve the production of less necessary or less frequently needed items: luxuries, special treats and other postponable items. They are mainly bought with what is sometimes called people's 'discretionary income': income spent on things we choose to take or leave, or to save and invest.

The cyclical industries often produce durable goods. These kinds of goods consumers can decide to make last longer, for example, by getting them repaired. They tend to wait for better times to buy such costly items. The most obvious and common examples are cars, recreational vehicles, boats, planes, a new house or an addition to the current one, a new central-heating system, an air-conditioning system, a swimming pool or tennis court, furniture, musical and other entertainment equipment, computors, refrigerators and deep-freezers, washing machines, driers, dish-washers, disposals, air and water purifiers and humidifiers, white goods, garden furniture and equipment.

Houses are the biggest single purchases in many people's lives. The stock of existing houses is so large and the purchase of any new or old house is so postponable that in a recession new house construction can virtually come to a standstill. Old houses, often cheaper than new ones, are preferred by buyers in recessions. Plenty are offered for sale and buyers often insist on finding a house not in need of repair. Many house purchases are delayed – but house repairs and extensions may well increase. Similarly, new-car sales drop but used-car sales may rise and car repairs certainly increase. The onset of a recession is usually heralded by a longer delay for a car-repair appointment.

The importance of consumers and their confidence

Until now we have referred mainly to the consumer goods and services provided by non-cyclical and cyclical industries. They are important: consumers buy two-thirds of everything sold and when they splurge or save money *en masse*, the entire economy is galvanised or gutted, respectively, by the impact.

Consumer confidence always has to be watched carefully. This was first realised long ago by the economist George Katona, who over several decades prior to his death in 1981 set up a research centre which blended economics and psychology at Ann Arbor, Michigan.[7] National indexes of consumer confidence are watched like a barometer and are equally reliable. The media have a considerable impact on consumer confidence, both by providing facts and by giving opinions and analyses concerning the current and prospective behaviour of the economy.

Note that consumer confidence was not shaken by the stock-market crash of 1987 (Box 2.3). The stock market is a jittery indicator, but hints at a capacity for some foresight.[8] Workers looking at headlines about the stock market must often feel that their interests are contrary to those of shareholders. When the economy is expanding, jobs are easier to find and wages are harder to cut, while the stock market is gloomy because of the fear of inflation. When there is recession and interest rates are pushed low to stimulate recovery, long before recovery comes and there are still millions of unemployed the stock market is bullish. This is because shares can become high-priced in relation to the dividends they are paying and can easily compete with low-interest bonds and bank accounts. If there is any loose anchor at all in the stock market, it is expectations regarding company profits (or losses).

Box 2.3: Consumer confidence

'Americans are worried that the turbulent economy has become a hurricane, one that can wipe out their jobs with no warning, leaving them without the income and the benefits they once took for granted.' That was written in the *Boston Globe* on 21 November 1993, in an article 'Can Clinton quiet their anxiety? And at what cost?' By mid-1994 people felt somewhat better after some economic recovery but the next thing to worry about was inflation – the rich and the stock market feared it, while the poor feared that attempts to quell inflation would lead to overkill of the recovery.

The employers' group The Conference Board maintains an index of consumer confidence – peoples' view of current and future economic conditions. It has summarised it in a graph pinpointing how the annual average of the index of consumer confidence has varied since the recession of the early 1980s. Taking the mid-boom year of 1985 as the baseline equal to 100, the graph roller-coastered up and down as follows:

1981 – 75	1989 – 118
1982 – 59.3	1990 – 90
1983 – 80	1991 – 66
1984 – 102	1992 – 61
1985 – 100	1993 – 59.4
1986 – 94	1994 – 102[*]
1987 – 101	1995 – 100[*]
1988 – 116	1996 – 87[*]

[*]With economic recovery, consumer confidence rose throughout 1994 from a low point of 58.6 in mid-1993 to 102 at the end of 1994. That level was reached again twice in 1995, but plunged to 87 in January 1996. In the latter month the economy was partially stalled by severe weather and discouraged by the poor Xmas shopping season. Though some commentators were saying recovery came well before 1993, consumers had in 1993 less confidence than in 1982, the bottom of the preceding recession said to have been worse. The stock market was far more cheerful than consumers in early 1996; consumers were again cash-short and falling heavier into debt. Economists had up to that point assessed the 1982 downturn as being more severe than the more recent one.

Consumer decisions about when to buy durable goods, most of which they purchase with credit cards and instalment (and, nowadays, leasing) schemes, involve a number of trade-offs because incomes are limited:

- There is the trade-off between now and the future in the amounts of their total purchases.
- There is the trade-off between buying some goods or other goods.
- There is the trade-off between proportions of their income consumers spend or save.
- Similarly, there is the trade-off between the proportions of expenditure paid for now (in cash) and the proportion paid for in future (on credit).

The amount of credit-card borrowing power available in rich countries increases the discretionary income (present plus future income). This enables card-holders to make large changes in total effective demand for goods and services at a point in time. Even during a boom period, there may be signs in the economy that cause concern and diminish consumer confidence. I was not alone during the 1980s boom in noticing three worrying trends:

1. Structural and other problems were already occurring in the 1980s, as reflected in the massive corporate mergers and buyouts, regrouping of holdings and re-engineering of management. The completion and solution of these trends and problems took time and proved turbulent. In particular, they involved a heavy increase in the indebtedness of the corporations involved.
2. Above all, there was the huge increase in consumer debt which would have to be reduced before consumers could plunge into the market to take advantage of the bargain prices and perpetual 'sales' that accompany recessions. A tax change in the USA accentuated this debt-deadening effect, delayed the recovery and deepened middle-class suffering. During the boom of the 1980s the high interest-rate payments on the swelling debt were all deductible from income before tax. After the tax reform of 1986, much of the interest consumers paid – and all of that on credit cards – ceased to be a deductible item. Even mortgage interest eligible for deduction became more restricted, now being available only for one's main home.
3. What happens in the market to the value of housing has an immense impact on consumer confidence and the propensity to consume. When your house value rises, you feel well-off. When it falls you are shocked, particularly if you end up owing more money on the mortgage than you can get for your house if you sell it in 'the buyers' market'. House values, like share values on the stock market, reached a peak by about the end of 1987. People began to feel less inclined to spend and borrow so much when the values of nearly everything they owned started shrinking.

Investors, their confidence and expectations

Business people – managers and business owners (investors and share-holders) – behave just like consumers. They too have ups and downs in their degree of confidence.[7] Similarly, they can raise or lower their expenditure and switch it in time and space: concentrating on minimal needs in a recession, taking on big purchases of durable goods in a recovery when there are prospects for the increased sale of what they produce at better prices. Thus the industries serving business buyers also fall into cyclical and non-cyclical categories.

In the non-cyclical category we have daily necessities like office supplies, fuel and power supplies, vehicle maintenance and replacement, and advertising. In the cyclical categories come big items like a new factory, new machinery, additional office accommodation, a new computer or automation system. Purchase and replacement of these can and will be postponed by business people who have unused capacity on hand and low confidence in business prospects in the short-term future.

It follows from this contrast between small perennial supplies and costly durable goods and facilities that business cycles – fluctuations in economic activity – can become more violent with the continuation of economic trends whereby the world becomes more heavily capitalised. Psychology as well as intellectual judgements, analyses and assessments can loom large in the swings from boom to bust and back to boom. All these factors add up to a heavy influence on the changing moods of the general public and of business people:

- consumer confidence
- investor confidence
- degree of confidence exuded by statements of public and business leaders;

- *facts affecting confidence*

- movements in markets for stocks, commodities (wheat, cotton), houses
- changes in the cost of living, the supply of and cost of credit
- the degree of stability in international affairs and in the (related) price of gold
- trends in international trade
- whatever is happening to the USA, Japan, Europe, Latin America and their big national markets.

The acceleration of downs and ups

We are grateful principally to J. M. Keynes and N. Kaldor[6] for showing us how it is that both the downturn and the upturn gather speed once they have started. They called it the *multiplier*. It is rather like a vicious circle (when down) and a virtuous circle (when up). The multiplier means that a change in spending can and usually will cause a larger change in income. It may not necessarily cause a larger change in real income (because prices may rise or fall while it is happening) but it certainly causes a larger change in monetary income.

It is easiest to understand in the upturn. When a consumer or business person spends more, the money spent passes into the hands of shops or other markets. The shopkeepers in turn spend some of it on ordering new stocks (their inventory). Producers spend more on manufacturing capacity and supplies. All of them, together with the raw materials and fuel suppliers, can make more profits and pay more wages. A large part of those wages go home to workers' families. The families in turn feel free to spend more than before. Thus the multiplier is a ripple effect like that caused by a stone thrown into a pond: little waves spread outward in concentric circles. They break when hitting islands or the shore. In the same way the economic multiplier does not multiply in the economy without limit: some of the new money is saved instead of spent and other parts are spent on imports instead of within the home economy.

When a downturn begins you have a vicious circle or, thinking of the pond again, a whirlpool sucking water toward it instead of a stone sending out ripples of water. (Do you remember Ross Perot's favourite frightener: 'that giant sucking noise' when jobs were being moved out of the USA into Mexico?) Each consumer or business person making a significant cut in spending means that all down the line, there is less money flowing outward. Similarly, recipients of the reduced flow of money are forced to make cuts in their spending – onward and outward the depressing effect is transmitted. At the edge are those who have been thrown out of work. Some of them in the USA have been reported to eat canned cat food (three cans a dollar) while still struggling to pay their mortgage to keep their roof over their heads.

Multipliers can be calculated. Finance ministries wishing to stimulate an economy by $100 million know they do not need to add more than $50 million to spending (e.g. building more roads) if the multiplier in their national economy is two. Obviously on further analysis the multiplier becomes a more complicated and variegated phenomenon. The most even effect may be obtained when the Central Bank simply increases the supply of credit that is actually drawn upon and spent by the borrowers. Building roads or raising teachers' salaries or constructing a new aircraft carrier are specific injections of government funds that might have localised ripple effects. They would be limited in time as well as space: we do not get a quick stimulating effect by deciding to start building an aircraft carrier that will take two or three years to complete. Most big construction projects have a spending curve like the back of a tortoise: the amount spent each week rises gradually to a peak and then curves downward toward the end of the project.

The acceleration and deceleration phases of downturns and upturns occur through the combined effect of the multiplier and changes in the same direction of consumer and business confidence. When explaining the business cycle, Keynesians linked up the multiplier process with the accelerator principle, which contends that the level of aggregate net investment in an economy depends on the expected change in output.[9] With the delay required for construction and with due regard to the changing cost of using capital, business people will have to build up capacity to produce the additional output expected to be required. They will postpone repairs and replacements if output is expected to fall and in the future will require less capital capacity to produce. (The accelerator principle also figures in the theory of economic growth, notably the Harrod-Domar model.)[10]

Why cycles are endemic to capitalism

While cycles do occur worldwide, affecting international markets and producing ups and downs in the rate of world economic growth, their origin and volatility are rooted mainly in the market-driven capitalist system of rich countries. This is largely because that kind of economic system is 'atomised': decision-making in the economy is in the hands of millions of different individuals – consumers, investors, traders, business leaders and company owners, bankers, government leaders, the major voices in the media and universities, in think-tanks and the like.

This character of capitalism stands out clearest when contrasted with the monolithic character of command economies. They are called command economies because nearly all decisions and orders come down through the economy from a highly centralised control at the top. In such economies, people make what they are told to make and they get what they are given. The all-powerful authority at the centre assumes it knows what they want and has the authority to give and deprive them of whatever it chooses. In this system there is little room for change; any which does occur comes about slowly. Hence there is little scope for instability and everybody can be employed – or rather, occupied and paid – simply by giving appropriate orders and, if necessary, printing money to pay them. Of course there is an endemic risk of inflation in situations of low productivity, restricted output and buoyant money supply.

Few countries today are willing and able to be independent of the rest of the world. But for a certain period of time, countries with centrally planned economies, by controlling economic activity and narrowing down the decision-making process to a few fairly well-coordinated national leaders, could stabilise the path of economic growth and the levels and patterns of consumption and investment.

The higher the actual or potential rate of economic growth and the greater the dependence on private capital and on a market-driven economy, the more likely the occurrence of instability, major cyclical fluctuations, unemployment and more rapid changes in the structure of the economy.

How recessions start

Recessions start in different ways at various periods of history. They occur less regularly when transcendental factors override them, such as wars, technological revolutions and major discoveries like oil or diamonds.

The Korean war started a boom in commodity prices that reverberated through the world economy of the 1950s, not least in developing countries exporting such commodities. First, the Vietnam war and then OPEC's shock increases in world oil prices ended the steady prosperity of the 1950s and 1960s. That prosperity had been launched by the accumulated purchasing power frustrated until the end of the Second World War, further propelled by the German economic reconstruction, the Marshall Plan and the Korean boom. The greater cost of fuel and power after the OPEC price-hikes in oil triggered off inflation, real estate and other speculation and a general overheating in the major national economies. These factors eventually induced the recession of the 1970s.

Apart from such transcendental shocks to the world economy as these, we can have a downturn starting independently in one country for reasons originating within its borders. The drop in demand in the home market and the consequent cutbacks in investment in productive capacity combine to reduce imports. That can instigate a downturn in the economies of countries from which the imports originate. Countries with large economies often impose instability elsewhere: when the USA sneezes, Europe can catch a cold.

The American boom of the 1980s was associated with a current-account balance-of-payments deficit. Foreigners provided the USA with the capital to pay for its excess of imports over exports, helped to create an offsetting surplus on the capital account of the balance of payments and at the same time helped to finance the American national debt. The trade deficit continued throughout the 1980s, rising from –0.2 per cent of national income in 1982 to –3.6 per cent in 1987 but falling to –1.6 per cent in 1990.

Another reason why recovery from the recession of 1990–1993 in the USA was slow was that the European recession (except in Britain) started later – and later still in Japan. Those are America's major customers. The USA was particularly anxious for Japanese recovery in order to reduce the extensive deficit in its trade with Japan.

Matters would have been still worse on the international trade front but for a surprisingly good recovery in some Latin American countries from the doldrums into which that continent had fallen under the weight of crippling indebtedness. This improvement in Latin America's standard of living occurred in tandem with advances in its democracy and its transition to market-driven, more open economies.

Errors of judgement

Generally speaking, the risk of a recession being set off is increased whenever big players in business circles make major errors of judgement. There are the over-optimists who make too much of a good thing. Often, for example, there are too many too hasty to get into the 'ground floor' of major new developments. The ground floor gets overcrowded and too many floors are piled above in their skyscrapers of hopes and dreams.

In the USA, Canada, Britain and Japan real-estate developers went off the deep end. Land values rose (most vertiginously in crowded Japan) and they were helped upward by much new building on urban land. It was thought that the rapid growth in services would call for a rapid expansion in office and other accommodation for managerial and professional staff. It was therefore seen as being clever to erect a great deal of new office accommodation, together with more shopping malls and other commercial real estate.

When the flop in real estate values came in the late 1980s, it was calculated that it would take ten years of future development in the USA before all the excess space created in commercial real estate could be occupied at profitable rents.

There was a genuine boom in industries using the new technologies. Notable were those in computers and informatics which sprouted in Silicon Valley in California and the (highway) 128 area west of Boston. Boston showed the economic stimulus of having a concentration of high-level research and innovation capacity through heavy private-sector investment in leading local universities and a careful nurturing of their relationship with 'high-tech' industry.

Whenever a new industry like computers develops, good, bad and indifferent performers jump on the bandwagon. At first, almost everyone makes money. But in time, performance separates the men from the boys and the boys quickly go bankrupt. The best and brightest grow into mammoth enterprises like IBM, Digital and Wang. Then all too frequently the mammoths themselves find that they too have made major mistakes.

The invention of the photocopying process took years before people – even its inventor – understood its enormous potential and applied it properly in the photocopy machine. The giant company Xerox could then grow up to supply its world market. Xerox has a large laboratory near Stanford University in Palo Alto (PARC), California. In a similar vein, some thirty years ago IBM and others were successfully supplying the world with massive mainframe computers. These were used mainly for mathematical calculations and for other large-scale figurework, such as corporate accounting operations and notably company and institutional payrolls that must be punctual and accurate despite the mass of detail and variation.

The Xerox laboratory, PARC, had a department called STAR which had the idea, as early as the mid-1970s, that small personal computers could be built for individuals in offices and homes to perform a variety of tasks. Nor would these computers need to be confined to tasks that mainly involve figure work. Letters, words, eventually pictures and diagrams (graphics) and even music could be recorded digitally, memorised, retrieved and rejuggled: we could have word-processing, computer-aided design and manufacture (CAD/CAM), trick photography and scenes from movies, and symphonies, operas, films and encyclopedias crammed on to digital disks.

Xerox's PARC got going and produced a small personal computer and software called 'Alto' and even showed that it could be further simplified for use by ordinary people: it developed the first 'mouse', which could move the cursor and manipulate words in word-processing. By 1978 Alto was working and in use at PARC and in the White House, at Washington. On the basis of Alto, a software programme called Lisa was then produced for use only on Xerox machines. BUT! . . . It was the Apple company which jumped ahead with the wider show and the nation's market when it introduced Mackintosh in the following decade.

Box 2.4: Birth of the Foundling Mouse

The author is grateful to Ms Maia Pindar of the Xerox laboratory – Palo Alto Research Center (PARC) – for the background to this and for finding the following quotation:

At times, Xerox was bizarrely generous with its computer inventions. For example, in late 1979 one of the company's investment arms contacted Steven Jobs of Apple Corporation about a possible deal. Jobs, who for years had heard about the fabled accomplishments of Xerox PARC, asked for and received a tour of the research center. According to Larry Tesler, who conducted a demonstration of the Alto for Jobs, the young entrepreneour immediately grasped what had eluded Xerox executives for more than half a decade. 'Why isn't Xerox marketing this?' Tesler recalls Jobs demanding. 'You could blow everybody away!' Ensuing discussions between Xerox and Apple fizzled. But within a month of Job's visit, Tesler left Xerox for Apple, and Jobs ordered an Apple team to design the 'Lisa', a computer introduced in 1983. The Lisa replicated many features invented at Xerox, and because of Apple's strong presence in the personal computing market, the Lisa seemed to steal a march on Xerox's Star. Office equipment analysts have started referring to PARC-like systems as 'Lisa-like', not 'Star-like', noted a reporter.' ('Fumbling the Future' Douglas K. Smith and Robert C. Anderson, New York: William Morrow, 1988).

continued

Box 2.4 continued

Within a year Apple's next computer, Macintosh, ripened into a commercial product and put the mouse all over the map. The present author received bad advice at that time (1984) – the mouse would take up too much limited memory space in the original pc's – and bought an IBM XT instead. We have since gone from 10 megabytes to 1 gigabyte and more on hard disks, even in a lap top. Now, the IBM Aptiva looks at least as attractive as Macintosh – the battle continues!

Until the mid-1970s computers were giants and used and understood only by PhDs in the sciences. IBM and even Xerox executives themselves, thought their PARC team had played a clever laboratory game and just left it at that. They were convinced that things as complicated as computers would never be used by anyone but advanced scientists, trained accountants and other 'high level personnel'.

For years, the PARC/STAR team were saddened and frustrated. Finally people came to appreciate what they had achieved at the Xerox laboratory. The Apple Computer company was inspired by Xerox's small computer and its mouse. Concerned with helping even small school children – our future adults – it soon leaped ahead with the mouse and the Macintosh computers. IBM, whose early computers filled a whole air-conditioned room, was slow to develop smaller 'mini-'computers. Digital Equipment Corporation jumped in first with its flexible VAX machine, one hundred or more of which could be bought for the price of one IBM mainframe. (In descending order of size, the jargon nowadays is 'main-frames . . . mini-computers . . . work stations . . . net-working desk-tops . . . personal computers:PCs . . . lap-tops . . . pocket organizers'.)

Word-processing (computerised type-writing plus editing) was pioneered by Wang. While for a long time people regarded desktop computers as new-fangled typewriters, they began to discover that PCs could do other kinds of work at home, including accounting and banking. IBM was very slow to introduce the first PC. Wang developed its system but confined itself to word-processing capacity. Today, they have many powerful rivals because their rivals' innovations were developed more rapidly and they promoted flexibility, diversity of use and additional facility with interfacing. The latter is most important today. IBM, Digital and Wang had for too long sought to work in an exclusive fashion making link-ups with other computer systems and programmes difficult or impossible. Late in the day they all tried to come closer together and even the giant rift valley between the IBM-compatible and the Apple-Macintosh worlds is being bridged. This came too late for Wang, which has stopped being a hardware producer altogether, and it was almost too late for Digital.

Digital was a jump ahead of IBM's monolith mainframes with its excellent VAX workstations, but it suffered from an uncoordinated, decentralised system of management by consensus and interdepartmental negotiation and in the 1990s it lost billions. It returned to profitability in 1995 by downsizing and succeeding with new technologies and good interfacing.

Now under new leadership, IBM is leaner and decentralised, and appears to have made an assured come-back. But IBM – one of the world's giant corporations – saw its market value fall to well under half its former glory. That can happen eventually to any new pioneer in the field of technology. Bill Gates, the world's richest man, an inventor-undergraduate who had dropped out from Harvard, heads his giant Microsoft, makers of operating systems for most of the world's computers.

IBM and Digital, both of whom proudly claimed for decades that they gave their employees security, had to lay-off thousands, including many fine workers, in order to survive. Digital's sales, which had soared from $6 billion in 1985 to $12 billion in 1989, tapered off to $14 billion in 1993 and then dropped to a $13.5 billion annual rate in 1994. Profits stopped in 1990 and annual losses plunged to a low of nearly $3 billion dollars in 1992 and were still 'only' $2.2 billion in 1994. The number of workers dropped from 126,000 to 63,000 over this period and is still diminishing.

Wang, whose headquarters had cost $50 million to build, had to vacate it when so few employees remained to be accommodated. They had the humiliation of seeing it auctioned off in 1994 to an astute buyer for less than $1 million. That mighty bargain in the history of real estate was a salient signal, visible across miles of countryside, of where over-investment in office space can lead. In these snakes-and-ladders games with new technology, players in an industry could rise and fall rapidly and considerably disturb the course of an economy whose other sectors were more traditional and quieter in their progress.

On the matter of major errors by business leaders, the examples selected include the three largest and most successful pioneers in the greatest new industry in the USA since the Second World War. They were once fine and courageous innovators and, in view of the needs they meet in the economy – information and business management – their leaders should have known how to position themselves in order to survive the business cycle better than any other American industry or business. Their problems were obviously structural, too, but it only took the 1990 downturn, which was less sharp and profound than the one in the early 1980s, to break their backs.

They, along with many other error-prone companies in more traditional industries, all share some of the blame for the downturn of the early 1990s. Such error companies include General Motors with its hubris and complacency; the giant real-estate speculators like Olympia and York,

Donald Trump, 8k-apartment Brown and the S & L, Continental Illinois and other companies in the over-extended banking industry.

The timing of the downturn was partly related to the Japanese capacity to compete with staples of the American economy and expose their inherent weaknesses. The Japanese also participated in the real-estate speculation, both in the USA and at home. The Japanese themselves experienced a recession in 1994 and had major problems to resolve. Speaking of mistakes, the Japanese have certainly made theirs. For example:

> *Japan's trade surplus is a reflection of the yen's rise against the dollar, not of real trade flows (measured in yen, the surplus is actually falling). America is the world's sole remaining superpower; Japan, riddled with corruption scandals and on its fourth government since the trade talks began (in 1993), seems politically chaotic. And those supposedly infallible Japanese turn out to make mistakes like anybody else. On one estimate, between 1986 and 1993 they lost more than $320 billion on their investments in American bonds, property and other financial assets.*[11a]

The next world recession may well be bound up with seismic shifts between the tectonic plates of the dominant North American, European and 'Asian Tigers' economic regions.

A study of the past is a source of strength to face the future. We now look at other factors in the working of the business cycle.

Under-consumption and over-investment

Speaking generally, we can have recessions arising from 'over-investment' or from 'under-consumption'. Over-investment appears when we have excess capacity with equipment lying partly idle, factories hardly turning-over, roads uncrowded, hotels and aircraft below the breakeven point in their percentage of room and seat occupancy.

Under-consumption is said to occur when many people have most of what they want, although they are perhaps still capable of being 'educated' about more things they might learn to want. However, the more we examine that explanation, the weaker it looks. People who have everything can often be induced to spend more on upgrading their existing possessions. Of course, many people do *not* have anything like all they want or need, even in the advanced industrialised countries.

What is really happening to cause less buying by people who still need many things badly? The obvious answer is that they do not have enough money to get what they want, even though a boom is in progress and there is spending, cruising and merrymaking on all sides. Recently, the president of Ford Motors observed that the world has the capacity to produce 56 million cars but, at current prices, people are only able to buy 45 million of them.

President Reagan cut taxes in a way that benefited the super-rich and the upper middle classes. The poor had no reduction at all in the cut taken by government from their meagre incomes: the small tax cuts and earned income credits they did receive were offset by increasing social security contributions. The cost of health care was soaring way above the rise in the cost of living; even large employers were crushed by the burden of premiums for medical insurance and insisted that their workers pay a larger part of them.

Thus, in the middle of the 1980s boom, we had high prices in the shops and less money in people's pockets. Retail sales eventually drifted downward and competition became more intense, leading to streamlining and lay-offs of thousands of workers. While banners held aloft at shareholders' meetings read 'Greed is good', we saw at personnel managers' conventions ('human resources directors' is the euphemism) the banners proudly spelling out the inspiration of the 1990s: 'Lean and Mean'.

Although it is constantly repeated in the USA that consumers represent two-thirds of purchases, little attention has been given as to how consumers' purchasing power is diminished by unemployment, by the flight of American capital abroad and by falling real wages under stiff competition for jobs and markets. Keynes pointed out 60 years ago that, while low wages may encourage employers to hire workers, higher wages give workers more money to spend on the things that employers make and sell. Even Henry Ford could understand some of that; he also paid the best wages around, not just to get and keep good workers but to increase the number of people who could afford to buy his cars.

An unsatisfactory answer has been given by a leading economist[11b] to the point that increasing economic inequality aggravates under-consumption and recession. He retorted that there cannot be any lack of purchasing power in a country, only a lack of willingness to buy, because there is a huge and unimpeded flow of international capital. If prices and economic opportunities are attractive, money will always flow in.

This is factually correct. More than a trillion dollars per day in world-wide foreign-exchange transactions are cleared nightly in the largest North American banks. However, in regard to retail shopping by consumers – the famous 'two-thirds' of demand – we see Japanese tourists on the West Coast gasping about how much more cheaply they can buy Japanese products in the USA compared to home. Similarly, we see European tourists in Florida and on America's east coast discovering how overpriced goods are in Europe's less competitive markets. They can buy European (and American) products in Florida's markets much more cheaply than in European markets. However, these tourist shopping-sprees are not enough to make up for the drop in spending by the USA's unemployed millions and their impoverished families.

The way recessions bottom out and recovery begins

Why and how do recessions end and recoveries follow?

First, in nearly all those cases we have noted where consumers and business people decided to economise and postpone major purchases, they have to buy replacements in the end. Our cars collapse, our clothes become threadbare, we've had more children, relatives descend on us, and we must buy a house with more bedrooms. The more prosperous will be the first to move and buy. Then, as recovery progresses, consumers and business people gradually regain their confidence. The ready buyers become more numerous. Some of the unemployed get new jobs and use their new earnings to buy the necessities they have been painfully waiting for.

Box 2.5: Job-creating in the USA

In defence of the American economic system there is a need to emphasise the point that unemployment anywhere is the product of both blades of a pair of scissors. One blade is the number of jobs offered (existing numbers employed plus job vacancies) and the other blade is the number of jobs wanted (number of workers, employed or not, seeking jobs or better jobs). A strong, dynamic economy such as the American one can create a lot of new jobs, speed recoveries and reduce the likelihood of long-term unemployment. *Bloomberg Business News* offered a chart of new jobs created in USA during the recent recession. By October 1993, 177,000 net jobs had been created in that year alone and a stronger economy was sensed. Salient points on the path of job creation are as follows (these are *net* figures – either losses or gains being the larger to yield the net figure):

1991:	November – nearly 150,000 jobs less
	December – about 10,000 jobs more
1992:	April – about 180,000 jobs more
	August – over 100,000 jobs less
	December – over 100,000 jobs more
1993:	February – over 350,000 jobs more
	March–July – jobs gained every month
	August – nearly 40,000 jobs less
	October – 177,000 jobs gained

Since 1991 the two blades of the scissors have combined to reduce the unemployment in USA to 6% – the lowest in the capitalist world and probably the lowest in the whole world if the truth be told. The only fly in the ointment is that history leads us to expect bouts of massive unemployment again and again in future.

Another major factor in the ending of recessions involves price changes. Before the turbulence of world wars and the collapse of societies, we were used to prices remaining more or less static. Money kept its value. The world wars broke that stability and thereby broke the very crust of society. Now, we are sensitive to the likelihood of major changes in prices and in the cost of living.

In a recession some prices may be 'sticky' but sooner or later there is cut-throat competition, sales in every store and bargains abound. Past history leads us to expect that there will be recovery eventually and that these bargains will disappear. If you don't snap them up while you can, you will regret it later when you are paying higher prices again. There comes a point in every recession where more and more people think that the bottom of the market has been reached, tempting them, at last, to go out and buy.

Box 2.6: Average mid-recession inflation rate: 1992

Ordered from the lowest to highest inflation rates, in mid recession.

1.	Belgium	2.3%	8.	Germany	4.3%
2.	Denmark	2.3%	9.	Netherlands	4.3%
3.	Luxembourg	2.8%	10.	Italy	5.7%
4.	USA	2.8%	11.	Spain	6.7%
5.	France	3.0%	12.	Portugal	8.0%
6.	Ireland	3.7%	13.	Greece	18.2%
7.	UK	4.1%			

Source: European Community

An excellent example of this 'bottoming out' occurred in the USA as the year turned from 1993 to 1994. There was a sudden spurt in house sales and new housing construction, which had been disastrously low for a long time. The cost of living had almost stopped rising entirely. Interest rates, in double digits in the 1970s and early 1980s, had fallen to their lowest level for three decades. Fixed-rate 30-year mortgages were barely above 7 per cent. Financial journalists noted high price-earnings ratios on the stock exchange and warned that the stock market would experience a major correction when interest rates started rising again. Suddenly – a movement began which became a stampede. Buyers rushed out to get a new house and a cheaper mortgage while the going was good. The central bank (Federal Reserve System) had, early in the recession, lowered interest rates to stimulate a recovery. This experience showed, once again, that lower interest rates take time to have an effect: confidence has to return and the psychological factor relating to a perception of the bottoming-out of prices has to be triggered.

A large proportion of families own their homes in North America and Europe. Their feeling of prosperity and financial security is sharply and sensitively affected by movements in house prices, both up and down. When they go up, spending is generally freer. When they go down sharply – as happened after 1987 – general spending gets throttled. For a while, the shops were eerily empty and quiet; car parking was no problem.

Box 2.7: Pace of American economic recovery 1993–1994.

Orders from manufacturers for machine tools are a notably cyclical item. They increased as follows in the US recovery:

	Value of orders (monthly figures $ millions)	Percentage increase	
		One year	One month
Jan 1993	175.55		
Dec 1993	330.35		
Jan 1994	356.05	+102.82	+7.8

The US economy in general expanded at an annual rate of 7% in the last quarter of 1993, always the quarter of the year when retail trade soars upward until the New Year. The winter was severe, there was a major earthquake in California and slower growth was expected in the first quarter of 1994 (but above 3%); in fact growth fell then to a disappointingly low figure, 2.6%. The question arose as to whether the central bank was correct in starting to raise interest rates in order to avoid inflation, running the risk of choking-off economic growth. In fact in the first quarter of 1994 spending rose on personal goods by 3.8%, on durable goods by 9.7%, on non-durables by 2.4% and on services by 3.1%. The implicit price deflator in GDP showed US inflation climbed by 2.6%, double the rate in the previous quarter, the highest since the 3.6% recorded in the first quarter of 1993. The help-wanted index rose in March and the number of workers filing first-time claims for jobless benefits fell by a steep 31,000 in mid-April.

Over the whole period of recovery the quarterly growth was jumpy. This demonstrates, as many economic statistics do, that it is wise to compare a month's figures with similar figures for the month the *previous* year:

Year	1991	1992	1993	1994
Quarter	IV	I II III IV	I II III IV	I
Growth % (GDP)	0.7	3.0 1.5 3.4 4.8	0.8 2.0 3.0 7.0	2.6

(Sources: US Commerce Dept. and The Conference Board, New York, 1994).

The 1994 recovery was strong and would certainly continue with strength. Plenty of people had money – but some no doubt remained haunted by daily newspaper headlines of major corporations' plans for dismissing thousands of their employees, in the USA and other countries. Workers were being hired, especially by small businesses and especially for jobs at low wages requiring little skill. Average wages and real wages were falling, though productivity of the labour force was rising and was about the highest in the world (Box 2.8). By September 1994 the nation's unemployment rate fell to 5.9 per cent, the lowest for four years. Job growth averaged better than a quarter of a million a month for each month of that year. There was a regional spread in unemployment rates: North Carolina 5.1 per cent, Massachusetts 5.2 per cent, Ohio 5.5 per cent, Michigan 5.5 per cent, Illinois 5.7 per cent, New York 6.2 per cent, Texas 6.2 per cent, Pennsylvania 6.7 per cent, Florida 6.7 per cent, New Jersey 6.7 per cent and California 8.3 per cent.

We had therefore experienced economic recovery in the USA and the UK by 1993, with the European Union claiming it had reached it in 1994. Nevertheless, many workers, including middle-class and salaried employees up to senior levels, suffered in the American recession of 1990 to 1992. Some of the older ones still remain in the ranks of the long-term unemployed, especially in Europe. Some Japanese, whose companies gave them the idea that they had a job for life with the 'company family', now find that idea to be a shattered dream.

J. K. Galbraith, author of *The Culture of Contentment*, suggested:

> *When one looks at the present scene, a further possibility emerges, one that is also rarely mentioned in our time. It is that in the modern polity, continuing unemployment is preferred by many (and especially by those with political voice and influence) to more vigorous employment expansion and especially to the measures necessary to achieve it.*

As examples of those with a relatively secure position as to income and earnings, he cites 'the large corporate bureaucracy . . . the large public bureaucracy . . . the very extensive professional class: doctors, lawyers, academicians, accountants'. They do not deeply feel or fear unemployment, whereas for many of them stable living costs in an era of low inflation are welcome. The many with fixed incomes, including the pensioned, would also wish to avoid inflation and are not directly threatened by unemployment. Employers also find some 'benefits' because with greater unemployment there is a more willing, more amenable, less assertive and more stable labour supply.[12]

While this is an important truth, economists and particularly politicians must identify shifts in the classes of people affected by unemployment. The recession of 1974–1976 was more serious than that of 1990–1992, because as unemployment reached 8.5 per cent of the labour force in 1975 whereas

Box 2.8: American worker productivity falls in advanced recovery

It used to be said by some economists that there will be a tendency for productivity per worker to rise in an economic downturn, and for it to fall as an upturn begins to appear. When laying off workers, employers will tend to keep their best workers and lay off the less experienced, trained or motivated. Eventually, however, productivity may start to fall as the remaining workers may have to work longer hours, reducing their average hourly productivity because output per worker falls off from fatigue beyond a certain number of hours, though they may be motivated to do their best in a downturn due to fear of lay-off.[13]

Michael Niemira of Mitsubishi Bank, New York, commented: 'We've seen a cyclical pickup in productivity in the last couple of years, which is normal in a recovery . . . we've now turned the corner and very convincingly.'[14]

Why is the increase in productivity 'normal in a recovery'? Two obvious reasons are: first, output is going up and yet employers delay taking on additional workers (meaning increased output per worker) until their confidence in recovery grows and until they are forced to recruit because the capacity of their existing workforce is fully stretched; second, at the beginning of the recovery there can be gains from economies of scale as output increases.

When productivity falls (or increases more slowly than wages) labour costs rise. In the first quarter of 1994 those costs rose by 3.1% (annual rate) and stepped up to 3.4% (annual rate) in the second quarter. Hourly compensation (wages) increased at an annual rate of 0.8% in the second quarter of 1994, the smallest increase since 1988.

About two-thirds of the total cost of a product in the USA comes from labour costs: that does not mean that American production is labour-intensive. On the contrary, it is more capital-intensive than in many other countries; hence, American employers, especially in high-tech companies, can afford to pay their workers relatively well. It is the high wage-level which pushes up American labour costs, despite relatively high worker productivity.

the peak for unemployment in 1992 was only 7.4 per cent. Yet the more recent recession aroused more anger in the public. Comparing the different occupations between 1975 and 1992, we find that executive, administrative and managerial staff suffered more in the recent recession, an increase from 3.0% unemployment in 1975 to 3.8 per cent in 1992. Similarly, sales staff experienced an increase from a peak of 5.8 per cent to 6.5 per cent unemployment respectively between the two years mentioned. There was also a big increase, from 3.5 per cent to 8.1 per cent, in unemployment between the two years for those in farming, forestry and fishing. For other occupations, however, mainly those usually hit worst by recessions, the unemployment in 1992 was *less severe* than in 1975.

In the future a major political threat may be posed by economic insecurity hitting large numbers of those educated to a high level, including college and advanced students. These are usually the most articulate and the most intelligent. They may be able to identify and articulate the faultlines in the USA's economic and social system. If sufficiently alienated, they would know how to inflame the masses against the super-rich and their defenders. The potential for violence in a USA facing high and persistent levels of unemployment is enormous.

Reducing the impact of cycles on workers

What can and should be done to reduce the volatility of economic changes and in particular to reduce the injury done to the social and economic well-being of the labour force (see Box 2.9)?

Box 2.9: Recession hits Hispanics in the USA

Of the 22.8 million Hispanics in USA, nearly 30% lived in poverty in 1982; this figure for poverty shrank to 26% by 1989, but rose again to nearly 30% by 1992. Poverty rates in the rest of the population were 14% in 1982, 12% in 1989 and 13% in 1992. Median income of Hispanic households in 1992 was $22,859, only some 68.5% of the median income of non-Hispanic white households. For men, fully employed year-round, the median incomes in the two groups of households were $20,054 and $31,675 respectively. For women similarly employed, the figures were $17,124 and $21,930 respectively.

Source: Census Bureau

Keynes' proposals wrongly applied for six decades

For the capitalist system, the stabilisation method proposed by J. M. Keynes in the 1930s can work well[15] and has never been given a fair and full trial. Do not be deceived by those who condemn it as disappointing, out-of-date and even misconceived. It was *never* properly applied.

The method is simple. In a recession the government should spend more money than it collects in order to make up for less spending by others. In a boom it should collect more than it spends to dampen down inflation when so many are spending and investing heavily. Another reason for running a surplus in the government budget in boom times is to be better able to repay any national debt caused by deficit-spending in the preceding recession.

Compare this last paragraph with the definition given on page 32 on how to achieve full employment. Recall the technical terms used. A government runs a deficit budget in the early period of any recession and spends enough to keep aggregate effective demand nearer to the full employment level. The demand for labour is derived from total effective demand, so government spending – particularly if favouring labour-intensive activities – will reduce much of the unemployment caused by the incipient recession.

When the boom comes, prices – and perhaps wages too – rise as money spent increases, to the point that demand may exceed full capacity output and stocks have to be drawn down. Inflation may only be avoided by the government collecting more than it spends and withdrawing some money from the economy. In both boom and bust, Keynes' formula can be a neat balancing act, involving compensatory moves between the public and private sectors. During a recession when consumer and investor confidence are falling it takes some nerve for the government to act in the opposite way, implying confidence in the future. Courage and sagacity are, however, required for the task of government and it is the hallmark of statesmen to exude confidence during difficult times, provided it is well-founded.

We have seen how business people and consumers postpone buying costly, durable goods when confidence is low. That is exactly when the government should buy more durable goods. For example, it might purchase heavy equipment for use in public works to build highways, buildings, public facilities or ports for both sea and air traffic. Confidence is then strengthened generally because expectations improve in a climate of supportive government intervention.

For Keynes' formula to work, however, it does not mean that the government has to go out and buy only those items that consumers and business people are buying in reduced quantities. Any expenditure, whether government or otherwise, may bring into play the 'multiplier' mechanism identified by Keynes and already mentioned. There is the ripple effect of expenditure whereby a part of each amount of money paid from one person or party to another as a price or as a wage, is in turn spent by the recipients of the payments; in this way total expenditure is sustained and demand for all goods and services is maintained by an increased velocity of the money in circulation. For example, workers find jobs in public works and buy loaves of bread; the baker pays an instalment on his new van; car manufacturers buy more steel; steel-workers buy loaves. This Keynesian formula of a counterbalancing, compensatory flow of public finance and expenditure was rarely followed through faithfully and on schedule by countries during the phases of successive business cycles.

The 1930s

As Keynes was presenting his advice in two great books in 1930[16] and 1936,[17] the world was undergoing the Great Depression and doing totally the wrong thing. Just when consumers and business people were panicky and gloomy, cutting their expenditure to the bone, governments in North America and Europe were doing the same thing when they should have been doing the opposite. It was terrifying to have everybody spending less at the same time. People actually starved in the USA, the country most blessed with food supplies of any on earth. Keynes wrote, 'It might be supposed – and has frequently been supposed – that the amount of investment is necessarily equal to the amount of saving. But reflection will show this is not the case.'[18] (See page 30 on Say's law.)

Governments acting in ways *opposite* to those advocated by Keynes made things so bad that world recovery hardly came at all before the Second World War. The exceptions were Germany and Italy where Hitler and Mussolini induced some prosperity through rearmament and strategic projects such as the first motorways (along which their armies could move rapidly). In France, political protests produced a United Front in 1936 which included economic stimulants (even relief measures can be stimulating). In the USA Roosevelt's recovery programmes and public expenditure staved off the worst of the appalling social distress but could not restore such a giant economy to capacity production. Major obstacles to American and world recovery were the Smoot-Hawley tariff and other protectionist policies which severely restricted international trade.

The Second World War and its aftermath

It took the Second World War to provide a substantial improvement in employment, through military mobilisation, rearmament and the provisioning of battles, bombardment and invasions, which kept factories (including those converted from civilian to military production) working at full tilt. In that worldwide conflict, almost all governments were overspending and piling-up national debts. Inflation inevitably occurred despite price and wage controls and forced saving schemes as the production of consumer goods faltered.

When peace returned, worries about a postwar recession were dispelled by the eventual release of the pent-up demand for consumer goods and by postwar social benefit programmes to reward returning soldiers and their families. Europe, lying in ruins, was further strengthened by the European Recovery Programme (Marshall Plan, 1948–1952) and by the reconstruction of the German economy after its currency reform. Postwar inflation was curbed somewhat in the USA by rapid cuts in military expenditure and by the reimbursement of much of the swollen national debt from current income.

In the UK, price increases were held back by consumer rationing, although rationing also discouraged production and reduced supplies as well as demand.

The 1950s and 1960s

In 1950, some worldwide inflation was triggered off by the Korean War and the boom in commodity prices it occasioned. The rebuilding of the South Korean, Taiwanese and Israeli economies, like the Marshall Plan in Europe, were genuine miracles of foreign aid.

The 1950s and 1960s saw economic stability: we look back to that period with nostalgia. Britain's Prime Minister Harold Macmillan said to the British people, 'You never had it so good!' Much of this stability and progress was linked to the restoration of market forces, to monetary stabilisation that held back speculation and avoided over-heating of the economy and to the stimulation of technological progress. That progress could be partly attributed to the cold war, involving competition in the arms race and in space exploration. Governments were not, as in the 1930s, choking back the economy with stringent cuts in public expenditure. The defence-related expenditures, however, precluded both the chance to improve government finances and to do more for the Third World.

The 1970s: oil shock, and 'the cycle returns'

Another contribution to the Western prosperity of the 1950s and 1960s was cheap oil. When the oil producers of the Third World revolted and formed OPEC, the huge oil-price increases OPEC forced through in 1974 and 1979 imposed an economic shock and an inflationary impulse in most countries, particularly in those like Italy and Japan who had to import their entire oil requirements. The USA produces plenty of its own oil but it consumes plenty more. In the 1970s it had strategic worries about its heavy dependence on oil supplies from countries that might not remain friendly. The USA already stockpiled immense quantities of strategic commodities and included oil in this strategic reserve. The mere existence of these big stocks give the USA considerable leverage in world markets: it could dampen price increases by threatening to sell from its own stocks.

Baby boomers who grew up in the two decades of easier times until the oil shocks of the 1970s were beginning to think that perhaps we had conquered the business cycle. It was a bad old dream that could no longer haunt us. In fact, it had continued in a muted fashion. Some of this stability could be attributed to institutions established at the end of the Second

World War. The 1944 Bretton Woods Conference set up the World Bank and the International Monetary Fund (IMF). Apart from the big devaluation of the British pound in 1949 (down from $4 to $2.40), the IMF had inaugurated a period of stable exchange rates between the major currencies. This continued until the New York 'Plaza' agreement of 1971, reached at the Plaza Hotel, ended that regime.

The fluctuating foreign-exchange rates since then have restored that old, familiar element of uncertainty for importers and exporters. They must continue to ask how much of their own money will they get in exchange for the money they earned in international trade? Since 1975, inflation rose substantially despite the dampening influence on economic activity of the recessions that made it difficult to stimulate the economy by running a budgetary deficit which might further fuel the inflationary process. Annual percentage price increases varied as follows:

Table 2.1

	1975	1980	1985	1990	1995–
USA	8.1	10.8	3.3	5.0	3.5
Japan	11.3	7.1	2.2	2.4	0.6
Germany	6.2	5.8	2.1	2.5	3.0
France	11.8	13.3	5.7	3.0	1.9
UK	23.7	16.3	5.4	4.7	3.6

Estimated by TENL, 1 July 1995.

The tight monetary policies at the end of the 1970s and the unparalleled increases in interest rates slowed down inflation but also induced a sharp recession in 1981–1982. A clear lesson was learned: inflation that is not nipped in the bud inexorably leads to recession and unemployment, as well as to losses for creditors and owners of assets. It explains the partial tolerance for strict monetary controls today on several sides. Not on all sides: you do hear people say, 'I lost my job' because they raised interest rates. There are some economists who think the stimulus of some inflation and a possible increase in employment justify taking the risk of permitting mild inflation. But will it increase employment only in the short term?

The Reagan–Bush 1980s: debt in a big way

In any event, despite the good sense of Paul Volcker, the American central banker who saved the sinking dollar, the USA under President Reagan made a foolish mistake. It was ironical that Reagan's Republican Party, which had cursed the Democrats for their party's 'tax-and-spend policies' and their espousal of Liberal and 'Keynesian' remedies, actually produced an economic recovery in the 1980s by what they called 'supply-side economics' when it was actually a Keynesian measure that led the way out of the recession. In effect, they spent more money than was being collected by taxation, which they had cut.

Reagan typically took the ever-popular half of Keynes' patent medicine and then stereotypically failed, like most of his predecessors, to apply the unpopular second half of the medicine during the ensuing speculative boom. Unfortunately that was a really roaring boom and speculative bubble. Both Reagan and Bush thereafter grievously failed during the upswing to collect by taxation more money than the government was spending. Such sound Keynesian action would have secured the recovery, reined back inflation and speculation and avoided or mitigated the stock-exchange and real-estate crashes which actually came in 1987–1989. It would also have put money in the hands of the government to spend again to ward off the recession – which duly set in once again, well before Bush's retirement. Thus Bush, like Hoover, had a recession named after him. They were both fine men in their respective fields, but both were out of their depth in economics. Before his election, Bush had said 'Read my lips, no more taxes'. He was then forced to increase taxes by the errors of his economic policy.

To stem the recession a tax freeze and additional government spending might well have been effective. But the Republican's previous tax cuts, their swelling of the national debt from $1 to $4 trillion (two-thirds of the GNP) in less than a decade and the uncontrolled speculation financed by heavy corporate and individual borrowing, put the government and the country in such an indebted position that tax increases were an urgent political necessity and perhaps the only remaining financial option.

Reagan and Bush hardly noticed what they were really doing even as they did it. They refused responsibility both for the over-heated boom and speculation and for the ensuing recession. Reagan prided himself on cutting taxes: in his view that alone was enough to stimulate recovery. The continued government expenditure and growing debt were, he thought, the fault of Congress and of the Democrats who went along with his costly military build-up to enable the USA 'to stand tall' again and to ruin the USSR when it tried to keep up with the arms race. Reagan argued that those Democrats who repelled his advice to cut most other government expenditure and programmes were most at fault, though he left it to them to do the dirty work and did not name where the axe would have to fall. He mumbled by way of example something about 'Queens of Social Relief' riding around in Cadillacs. Apart from speeches written for him, Reagan would say or explain anything by drawing on his stock of anecdotes. Some of them were less apt than the parables of Jesus.

It is possible that these two Presidents and certainly their handlers were pretty cynical about the whole process. Reagan was supremely vindicated in his arms race; his was the nutcracker that broke the 'evil empire' and brought the cold war to an end. With the wisdom of hindsight, people are now saying it could have been done less expensively: the CIA has a notorious record of incompetence and unreliable reporting on the USSR. There are indications that each side in the cold war failed to get through to the other earlier, to convey that a rapprochement was possible.

The Republicans knew that heavy expenditure on the military, combined with a massive public revolt against high taxes to finance that expenditure, would make it increasingly difficult to maintain the social programmes of the federal government. Most other programmes, together with the servicing of the national debt, were not legally open to savage cutting (Box 2.10). Hence the burden fell largely on those social programmes.

Box 2.10: The big chill on social relief

Time and again the issue of burdensome social relief and welfare pro-grammes come back to haunt Americans. As their patience grows thinner each time, so their traditional generosity and warmness of heart are further eroded by the feeling they are being taken for suckers by a swelling generation of chronically dependent and feckless people. This issue has gone beyond party politics. In the 1990s people were recalling the benefits of Nixon's plan for health reform and in early 1994 Democrats were wishing they had anything as good as Nixon on the table then. After mid-year, everyone seemed to have a different health plan, none acceptable; even magician Senator Mitchell's hope of Senate acceptance of his diluted plan appeared threatened by filibuster even before the pro and con abortion crowd could get their teeth into it. Clinton was universally blamed for naïve reliance on old 'big government'.

The tremendous lowering of interest rates by the Federal Reserve System, after the usual long delay to take effect, noticeably helped to promote recovery from the recession. As a valuable by-product, while the low rates lasted, that helped to relieve the cost of the national debt. Then, when they rose again in 1994, Clinton had to focus on cutting medical costs down and on reforming the social relief system to fit what the country could afford. He was obstructed by health and insurance lobbies. (In the 1980s, high interest rates failed to check inflation and speculation properly because the cost of almost all kinds of credit were tax-deductible until 1986.)

Recession opens the 1990s: how will they close?

It became clear that the American recession which began in New England as early as 1990 and ended late in disaster-struck and 'demilitarised' California by mid-1994, was not statistically as severe as previous ones. But it had novel and ominous aspects.

Box 2.11: Unemployment in rich capitalist countries, 1993–1994

Unemployment in fifteen countries as a percentage of the labour force in the first quarter of 1994 compared with a year before:

Country	1993	1994
Australia	10.9	10.3
Austria	7.3	8.1
Belgium	12.2	13.5
Britain	10.5	9.7
Canada	11.0	10.6
Denmark	11.9	12.6
France	11.1	12.2
Germany	7.0	8.3
Holland	6.0	7.7
Italy	10.8	11.2
Japan	2.3	2.9
Spain	20.2	23.9
Sweden	7.1	7.8
Switzerland	4.2	5.0
United States	7.4	6.5

This list shows clearly how the recession came earlier in Britain, Canada and the USA, where economic recovery was well under way in 1994, whereas Europe and Japan were in the depths of recession in 1994 and the terrible unemployment of one worker in four in Spain stands out. For Sweden and Switzerland major unemployment is a new experience. Eight countries – over half – have unemployment in two digits, over 9%. See also Box 2.1 regarding the underestimation of unemployment in Britain, France, Japan and USA.

First, it got a lot of media attention and political brouhaha for victimising not only blue-collar workers but also, almost for the first time, white-collar workers, including well-qualified professional, technical and middle-management staff.

Second, full recovery was much slower than recoveries from most previous recessions. That did not surprise me and a few other economists, in view of the heavy overhang of personal, corporate, municipal, State and federal debt, some of which had to be and was painfully whittled down by reimbursements from strained pockets. The sudden spurt in the economy in the fourth quarter of 1993 and the signs of a strong 1994 following through were surprising, although I would attribute much of that spurt to the realisation that bargain prices and interest rates would not continue for long and it might be wise to hurry, seize those bargains and not miss the bus. A wealthy capitalist economy has a lot of capacity and many occasions for spurts and delays. They can jolt its smooth operation and hurt people.

J. K. Galbraith likened interest-rate changes to a piece of string: you might have some effect by pulling on it (raising rates) to inhibit borrowing but less effect by pushing it (lowering rates) to encourage borrowing.[19] In both cases, there is a big risk of a delayed and only slowly beneficial effect. In favourable contrast, Keynesian budgetary policy directly and immediately changes expenditure levels in the right direction. Moreover, interest-rate changes by the Central Bank apply with equal force to all regions, whereas a budgetary pump-priming instrument can be directed at stimulating the regions needing help the most. For example, it was reported in January 1995 that the economic recovery from the 1991 recession had tapered off early in New England, where increases in employment levels during 1994 were minimal and lower than in other States. Another increase in interest rates, a step widely expected because of fears of renewed inflation with only 5.4 per cent unemployment in the whole country, might send New England back into recession. New England appeared to need a regional interest-rate policy (an impossibility under the Federal Reserve System, for legal and logical reasons).

Third, there were major ongoing changes in the structure of the economy and some of these coincided with and aggravated the cyclical recession. These structural changes and the resulting unemployment are discussed in Part (III).[20]

Boxes 2.11 and 2.12 overlap in subject-matter but they dovetail on a timescale, since the data in Box 2.12 have been compiled more recently and they focus on the recession in Europe which followed later upon the recession in North America. They underline the structural problem in Europe by showing the detachment of unemployment levels from economic growth.

The business cycle outside the USA

Europe's economies have major structural problems that differ from America's. These are taken up in Part III. Europe provides more social security and protection to workers than the USA, making the business cycle

Box 2.12: Unemployment and economic growth during the recession

In the European Union, with the exception of Britain, the recent recession came later than in the USA, which was well on the way to recovery by 1994 and got its unemployment rate down to 6% by mid-year. The following Table relates the rate of unemployment in March 1994 to the rate of economic growth in the years 1989–93 in Europe:

	GDP annual average % increase 1989–93	Unemployment rate (i) March 1994 %
Ireland	5.1	18.0
Luxembourg	3.1	3.2
Germany	2.9	9.0(ii)
Portugal	2.6	6.1
Holland	2.4	10.7 (iii)
Spain	2.0	22.9
Belgium	1.8	10.0
France	1.6	11.2
Italy	1.4	11.3
Greece	1.4	10.0
Denmark	1.0	10.5
Britain	0.9	10.0

(i)   EU standardised, except Greece
(ii) All Germany estimate not standardised
(iii) February

The countries are listed in descending order of rate of growth of GDP. If the countries are listed in order of GDP per capita, the order is not the same:

GDP per head	Countries
Over $20,000	Germany, Luxembourg
$15,000–$20,000	Belgium, Britain, France, Holland, Italy
$10,000–$15,000	Ireland, Spain
$0–10,000	Greece, Portugal

These figures underline the structural factors in unemployment, particularly the weak relationship between unemployment and economic growth.

continued

Box 2.12 continued

There is a slight connection between unemployment and personal wealth, since Ireland and Spain have disastrously bad unemployment and are not particularly prosperous, though progressing. The case of Ireland merits close examination since it had relatively rapid economic growth combined with massive unemployment. Ireland's joining the European Union induced large percentage GDP increases, starting from a rather low level. Ireland could have entered the steeper portion of the traditional S curve of economic development though this would be odd for such an 'old' country. A unique aspect of Ireland, possibly of help in the explanation, is its long-term shrinkage of population. An increase in unemployment could be partly associated with sharply reduced possibilities for emigration.

Sources: OECD, Paris; Eurostat, Brussels; present author

less socially serious in Europe while remaining – economically – just as wasteful as the American failure to sustain economic activity. European economic recovery emerged in 1994 and was forecast to continue in 1995 (Box 2.13). Forecasting is a part of the task of economic policy-making. Therefore forecasts cited here have not been replaced by current figures which prove them wrong. Wrong forecasts are facts.

Box 2.13: GDP in selected OECD countries, % change

	1992	1993	1994	1995
USA	2.6	3.0	4.0	3.0
Japan	1.1	0.1	0.8	2.7
Germany	2.1	−1.3	1.8	2.6
France	1.2	−0.9	1.8	2.9
Italy	0.7	−0.7	1.5	2.6
Britain	−0.6	1.9	2.8	3.2
Canada	0.7	2.4	3.7	4.3
Australia	2.1	4.1	4.0	4.3
Belgium	1.4	−1.3	1.5	2.6
Holland	1.4	0.2	1.4	2.8
Spain	0.8	−1.0	1.2	2.7
Sweden	−1.9	−2.1	2.7	2.9
Switzerland	−0.1	−0.6	1.5	2.5
Total OECD	1.7	1.2	2.6	2.9

Source: OECD forecasts

The lag behind the USA (except in the case of the UK) of the European recession is indicated in the figures for industrial production (Box 2.14). Note the lower volatility of industrial production in France, which has more state intervention in the economy than Britain, Germany and Italy. The UK, which devalued its currency and lowered its interest rates on withdrawing from the European Monetary Union in 1992, recovered more swiftly than the others.

Box 2.14: The European recession

Industrial production: 1990–94:
percentage change on year earlier

	1990	1991	1992	1993	1994
Britain	2.0	−5.5	0.0	2.0	5.5
France	2.6	−1.0	0.1	−3.9	3.0
Germany	5.1	5.5	−0.5	−8.0	2.8
Italy	0.0	−5.0	0.0	−0.8	3.0

Source: TENL, 27 August, 1994

PART III

STRUCTURES IN THE POPULATION, ECONOMY AND SOCIETY

Reducing long-term unemployment: population transcendent

We now focus on workers who have either already been unemployed for years or, though they lost their last job recently, are likely (and may expect) to wait years for another job – and perhaps never find one.

There are two overriding factors which, for a long time, have exacerbated all kinds of unemployment and transcended the boundaries of both structural and chronic unemployment. The first is the population explosion mentioned at the end of Part I. The current population increase, though slowing gradually, hopelessly outruns the capacity of the world economy to finance jobs for everyone. If it could be slowed down faster, the capital–labour ratio might improve enough to catch up with the demand for jobs by the end of the next century.

The second factor is also a novelty of recent history: the employment of women. The almost full participation of women in the labour force in the industrialised countries and in those other countries that had former Communist regimes which suppressed religion and traditional culture, has gone on now for so many decades that those countries have come to consider it normal to seek jobs for all women as well as for all men. In the USA, the percentage of each sex, aged 16 and over, at work or seeking work, has changed as follows:

Table 3.1

	1970	1980	1985	1990	1992
Female	43.3%	51.5%	54.5%	57.5%	57.8%
Male	79.7%	77.4%	76.3%	76.1%	75.6%

The drop within the male labour force was biggest in the group aged 65 and older. Note that in this period the total American labour force increased from 82.8 million to 127 million people, so numbers of jobs were substantially increased for males (51.2m to 69.2m : 35 per cent) and females (31.5m to 57.8m : 83 per cent).[1] When seen in proper perspective, with complete consciousness of the immense size of these two 'invasions' of the employment market, it is surprising that we do not have far more unemployment, bad though it is now. The progress of technology and the dynamism of the capitalist system have achieved an enormous expansion of the world economy and an increase of some billions of jobs and livelihoods since 1800. As far as further population is concerned, one wonders which of its several disastrous consequences will strike us first without any hope of escape.

If all women in the Third World tried to go out to work there would be far more catastrophic and overt unemployment than there already is. Those women will not try that, not only because their culture and often their own wishes preclude it, but also because they know well that such a quest for jobs would be either hopeless, or would simply be taking jobs away from men at even lower wages than those earned by men. When women enter the labour force, the number of jobs paying cash wages would have to be doubled. In poor countries that is an impossibility, except perhaps in the very long term.

Optimistically the 1994 world population conference in Cairo adopted a new UN plan. In twenty years, population growth is to be arrested through improvements in the status of women, to include the expanded and better employment of women. To put the issue of female employment in a more positive light, we must recognise the impressiveness of the economic achievement in those countries where most women have found jobs and made their careers. Those economies had to create huge numbers of additional jobs, roughly equal to half the population of working age, since there are more women than men in populations. Those economies also had to create additional jobs to replace a big sector of employment that almost entirely disappeared during this century because of changed attitudes and increased costs: namely, domestic service. Censuses in the nineteenth century did not count the numbers of servants working in private homes, but it is believed that in Britain then as many as one person in six of working age held such jobs.

If you travel and work in the Third World and notably in some Islamic countries, your attention is caught – particularly if you are a woman – by the number of so-called 'women's jobs' still being done almost entirely by men. They are nurses, secretaries, clerks, flight attendants, civil servants, hotel servants, police dealing with women and children, school teachers, chauffeurs and so on. On return to a Western country, you are perhaps even more amazed to see more and more women doing 'men's' jobs as well: driving taxis and trucks, piloting civil and military aircraft, going to the front line with fighting forces and collecting refuse.

Remember, then, that the physically light 'women's' jobs – most of which already existed in the last century – until recently were almost universally undertaken by men. This then gives us some idea of the magnitude of the structural changes in economic history that have affected employment, for better and for worse. They make even the replacement of jobs by machines look less significant.

Structural unemployment: the pain of adjustment

Structural unemployment includes jobs that are permanently wiped out by major trends and shifts in trade. This is one negative, particular and localised aspect of the impact of trade on a country's economy. In general and global terms, growing world trade is the important engine for big expansion of the economy and for some more modest expansion of employment and income for the poor. Admittedly, trade shifts that are ultimately beneficial do give us a bumpy ride on the way to paradise.

Primary, secondary and tertiary economies

The structure of any economy is made up of more or less inclusive branches within three main sectors or levels of the economy: primary, secondary and tertiary. The primary sector is like 'land': it is about obtaining natural resources to provide food, fibres, skins, leathers and furs for clothing, and minerals, chemicals and construction materials and fuels. The secondary sector makes heavy use of physical capital in manufacture and processing. The tertiary sector uses intellectual capital and allied equipment and supplies to provide services.

The primary sector includes agriculture, fishing, hunting, forestry and the extraction of minerals, oil, water, gases, etc.

The secondary sector includes manufacturing industry, often engaged in using and processing raw materials obtained from the primary economy: steel products from iron; textiles and clothing from cotton, wool and silk; oil-refining which provides fuels like petroleum, diesel and kerosene (used by jet planes), plastics, fertilisers, etc. The generation of power from oil, gas, coal and water is an important activity within the secondary sector.

The tertiary sector serves and controls the first two. It transports the products of the primary and secondary; it provides the content of and delivery mechanisms for information, management, coordination, planning, education and training, health care, entertainment and other social facilities; it assures the defence of the economy and society from attacks. The public sector, transport and communications, including modern information systems and the media, are clearly important parts of the economic structure (Box 3.1).

Interaction of economic and social structures

Laws, contracts, collective bargaining, social policies, labour laws and regulations, and the national culture are also a part of the tertiary economy. Social institutions are an element in humanity's intellectual capital. Their output is seen in their moulding of human behaviour. All

Box 3.1: The USA and the UK: Structure of GDP and labour force 1992 (in percentages of total gross domestic product and of total numbers in the labour force – LF)

	USA GDP	USA LF	UK GDP	UK LF
Agriculture	2.2	2.8	1.8	2.1
Mining	1.5	0.6	1.9	...
Manufacture	18.7	16.8	22.2	18.0
Construction	4.8	6.3	6.2	5.5
Public utilities	3.0	1.3	2.7	1.5
Transport,Communications	5.9	5.4	8.1	5.4
Trade	6.0	20.6	14.1	19.3
Finance	17.4	10.4	23.6	11.1
Public admin. and defence	12.0		17.3	
		35.0		37.1
Services	18.8		6.4	

Small miscellaneous categories excluded.

Source: *Encyclopedia Britannica Yearbook 1994*, p. 739

these things affect and serve the economic structure. When any parts of these things change – or, on the contrary, stubbornly refuse to change – in a way favourable to the working of the economy, economists refer to them as structural phenomena and any unemployment caused by them as structural unemployment. A lot of the long-term unemployment in Europe is structural unemployment attributable to these sort of social factors.

Governments cannot buy permanent reductions in unemployment by tolerating a higher rate of inflation. Ultimately, says *The Economist*, the level of unemployment will rise to a 'non-accelerating-inflation rate of unemployment' (NAIRU): the level of unemployment required to hold inflation steady. But the NAIRU is not a fixed number: it can change over time and it differs between countries.[2]

Sir William Beveridge, in a classic work on employment policy during the Second World War, foresaw that full employment without inflation would involve an irreducible minimum of 3 per cent of the labour force to be out of work because of frictional unemployment, shifts in foreign trade and the avoidance of inflation. However, he did not foresee how much structural unemployment would arise from postwar social policies and practices.[3]

One study puts Japan's NAIRU in the 1980s at a low 2 per cent, compared with 6 per cent in America and 8 per cent in Britain and France.

NAIRUs have been increasing and vary internationally for two main reasons, explained by *The Economist* and others.[4] First, the wage rate can get stuck above the level at which the supply of labour would equal the demand. The causes of wages staying above a level at which more people would get employment are:

● Labour unions: if employers hire non-union labour for a lower-than-union rate, closed-shop deals and strike threats may stop them from doing so. This depends on the power of the unions. The figures in Box 3.2 show unions losing membership, 1980–1990, and having membership today ranging from Sweden's extreme 80 per cent of workers, Britain with less than half that, the USA being below 20 per cent and France at the lowest level around 10 per cent. Nevertheless, French unions can be extremely aggressive and left-wing, in an effort to make their bite as loud as their bark. Despite their low union membership there is still high unemployment in France.

● Insiders against outsiders: insiders are employed workers who have the skills and experience their employers need. Outsiders are prepared to work for lower wages but firms do not want them because they would have to invest more in training them.

● Imperfect information: employers cannot know exactly the abilities of workers applying to them for jobs, so rather than take a risk of being disappointed with those hired they offer above-average wages to attract better qualified job seekers (among others). If supply exceeds demand at those wages, firms will not cut wages for fear of losing their most productive workers.

Box 3.2: Union membership in OECD countries, 1980–1990

As a percentage of all wage-earners, trade union membership in Sweden, Denmark and Finland (in descending order) remained over 70%, and in Sweden exceeded 80% in 1990 – the only country in the OECD where union membership increased rather than declined. In Austria, Ireland, Belgium and Norway, union membership was above 50% in 1980 but remained that high only in Norway by 1990 and was just below 50% in Belgium. In Italy, Britain and Australia, union membership exceeded 40% in 1980 but was just above 30% in 1990. In Japan, Holland, Switzerland and Germany it fell from 1980 to 1990 but remained above 20% in 1990. In France and the USA it was below 20% in 1980 and well below that figure in 1990. The biggest decline was in Spain, where it fell from 25% in 1980 to 11% in 1990.

Source: OECD

The second reason, says *The Economist*, why the wage rate can get stuck above the level equalising demand and supply in the employment market is the pervasive presence of government. Minimum-wage rules stop labour markets adjusting. Generous welfare benefits reduce the incentive for unemployed people to find work. Heavy taxation of your wages (the 'tax wedge') when you do find work can also discourage your efforts to work and to do more work. Payroll taxes (e.g. for health care) make firms less willing to hire staff.

Taxes together with social security contributions vary from more than 50 per cent of wages in Italy to around 25 per cent in the USA and a low of about 16 per cent in Japan. The challenge facing governments is to find ways to make labour markets work better and to limit the damage caused by tax and benefit systems.

Edmund Phelps, who pioneered the idea of NAIRU in the 1960s, in a new book[5] turns away from cyclical unemployment associated with variations around a relatively stable equilibrium (approaching full capacity production). He now sees that the equilibrium *is* NAIRU and since NAIRU changes we see a less stable picture with more residual unemployment after booms. Unemployment subsides in recoveries, but to a level above the level it had reached before the last recession. This growing level might well reflect the rising NAIRUs we have had until now. Phelps considers, among other things, public spending, debt, the aggregate burden of taxation, and investment as regards their influence over the structure of the economy. He expects that increased public-sector spending on capital goods will raise employment, whereas increased public-sector spending on consumer goods will lower it.

The Economist wrote in a similar vein under the heading 'Anxious about jobs', implicitly for the attention of labour ministers of the industrial countries who were attending the 'jobs summit' convened by President Clinton in Detroit (14 March 1994). *The Economist* derived this conclusion from the meeting:

> *The unpalatable fact is that the surest way to cut unemployment is to lower, or curb eligibility for, unemployment benefits. This was done in Scandinavia. But America, Japan and Switzerland also show that it works. In those three countries, unemployment benefit is strictly controlled and/or limited in duration, and next to nothing is spent on explicit 'employment promotion'. All three have an impressive record of low unemployment – as good as the Scandinavians at their best.* [A chart in *The Economist* article shows unemployment in the USA falling down toward 6 per cent in 1994 and in the European Union rising to 12 per cent.]
>
> *Europe's first priority should be to remove the barriers to jobs that it has already created. Beyond that, a mixture of threats (tighter control of benefits) and help (better placement services, limited use of subsidies for*

*the long-term unemployed, public employment for some) could further
reduce structural unemployment. A shift in this direction would certainly
raise output and average living standards, which in the end would help
even the unskilled and unemployed. But between now and the long term
there would be losers – those who remain unemployed, and some of
those working on very low pay. Would a Europe that looked, in this
respect, a bit more like America be a better place to live? In the end,
that is a question for voters, not economists, to answer.*[6]

Labour unions and employment

The Economist's unequivocal contention just quoted represents a kind of
thinking much disputed among economic theorists. Howard Sherman
recalls that Alan Binder, in his keynote speech to the American Economic
Association, attributed high European unemployment to the alleged fact
that 'intransigent trade unions and well-intentioned but unintelligent
governments have erected a web of microeconomic barriers to full employment that both make labor more expensive and transform wages from
variable into fixed costs. These include . . . high minimum wages, excessive
severance pay, heavy fixed costs of employment, restrictions on hiring and
firing, support for the closed union shop . . . heavy-handed workplace
rules.'

Sherman called this 'Blaming the victim'. He says it would appear from
this approach that the best policy to eliminate unemployment would be to
abolish all unions, end all safety regulations, do away with minimum pay
and allow plants to be closed on an hour's notice. Sherman goes on to say:
'it is important to understand that these policy suggestions are not merely
anti-worker bias, but stem from the neo-classical hypothesis that the system
would work perfectly without interference.' Moreover, the neo-classical
approach provides 'a bias toward assuming that all or most unemployment
is voluntary'.[7] (See Say's Law on p. 30.)

Let's be practical. It is obvious that most unemployment is involuntary
and always has been throughout the long life of neo-classical (pre-
Keynesian) economics. Many workers are laid-off who would prefer to
keep their jobs. Even those who do leave voluntarily hope or plan to move
to a better job soon. The unemployment pay they get meanwhile gives them
the courage to take the risk to seek an improvement for themselves.
Workers, once they find themselves unemployed, may quite understandably
use the support of their unemployment pay at least for a while to refuse
jobs offered to them at much lower pay and with vastly different work
content. Status rises and falls with our last job and it is hard to bargain for
pay much higher than the pay received in the last job we chose or had to
accept. Workers also have commitments to maintain, many of which have
been made for reasons which suit society: they borrow to buy a house near

their job so as to arrive at work each day fresh and punctual. They borrow to pay for a better education for their children than they had themselves because society is now relegating the uneducated to the bottom of the pile. It is to be expected that hardly any worker will take a job paying less than the unemployment pay he is getting: he can put his time to better use.

Sherman correctly emphasises the 'nutcracker' aspect of forces at work in the business cycle. Employment is likely to be increased from the supply side by low production costs and on the other side by the improvement in demand that occurs when wages stop falling and even rise: most wages are spent on consumption. When the unemployed get financial assistance (under social security) the demand for goods and services will fall less severely with the recession than it will when workers don't get any such support.

There are in fact a number of economic stabilisers of government origin. When earned income goes down, so do income taxes, while social benefits are maintained and the dole steps in, thus preserving some of people's disposable income and effective demand for goods. The nutcracker means that lower wages encourage employers to hire workers; social support in a recession and eventually higher wages indirectly increase employment because they are spent and increase demand for consumer goods. Both sides of the nutcracker have the stabilising effect of making total wage income go up and down less than the ups and downs in the numbers of people employed.

Union leaders, in their constant battles with economists, are happy to draw upon Keynesian theory as a basis for their argument that high wages generate additional demand for goods and hence more demand for labour. In practice, higher wages tend to confine employers' demand for labour to better qualified and more productive workers. Since union leaders are more concerned about their members than the non-members, they may not worry too much that higher wages can increase unemployment of non-members and push up inequality of incomes within the workforce. In fact, when and where governments tolerate monopolies, including labour unions, labour unions have the power to force capitalists to share their monopoly profits with the unionised workers. The consumer and the unemployed are the losers.

Conclusions

First, monopolies, including labour unions, have been combated and cut down substantially in the USA and the UK since Reagan and Thatcher. As a result, most workers (whether employed or unemployed) now have more economic interests in common. Also, they all share the current sad fate. All, even the skilled ones, are seeing a decline in their real wages (wages net of any value lost via an increased cost of living). There is less chance that high wages will boost consumer demand and employment (derived from demand) from now on.

Second, an indication that population growth is excessive can be seen when wages are declining and employers are in a 'buyers' market' for labour. Policies to protect workers' wages and various rights are appealing, but there is little hope of their being introduced and maintained, or of their having the power to help workers much under present-day conditions of over-population and surplus labour forces almost everywhere. In such circumstances, workers' welfare cannot be much improved by setting minimum wages. Exploitation of labour is inevitable with excessive population. Shortages of labour may be the most important catalyst for improving workers' welfare, even though it has an inflationary effect.

You may remember the students who rioted in Paris in March 1994 against the idea of discounting the minimum wage for those taking their first jobs, in exchange for receiving the on-the-job training they need. Here is what an economist might say to the students:

I am sorry, but I am afraid you will find that keeping up minimum wages does cause unemployment and young people will be especially hard hit. However much you riot, there will be lower incomes for workers, both from lower wages in some sectors and due to more unemployment in others. If financial assistance to the unemployed is high, there will be inflation and/or higher taxes and that also will mean lower incomes for workers. If workers and young people want a better material life for themselves and their children, they should have fewer children and they should seek to limit immigration.

That is a particularly hard saying for France, where there is an old political and anti-economic tradition of encouraging population growth by special tax and social policy incentives.

In this century, spectacular decreases in the birth-rate occurred in Italy and the Province of Quebec in Canada, showing that the Catholic Church need not be feared as an impediment to that achievement. France's birth-rate is not high but its rate of immigration has been.

Economic migrants

Countries with unemployment problems should obviously not make the mistake of importing more of the same problem from other countries by tolerating massive inflows of economic migrants. Economic migrants entering the USA legally or illegally are a heavier economic burden there than elsewhere because of the high cost of US standards of human rights and entitlements (Box 3.3).

Box 3.3: Hosting economic immigrants

It had been thought that total annual immigration in the USA was about half a million legal arrivals and a similar number of illegal entries. Figures for fiscal 1993 show that 880,014 legal immigrants arrived, going particularly to California (247,253), New York (149,564), Texas (62,777) and Florida (60,325) and it is probable that as many more or greater numbers arrived illegally. Gangs have been uncovered bringing in shiploads of their victims who arrive illegally and are employed in a status of semi-slavery while they complete paying-off the high fees they have paid to be brought to the USA. Nearly all these people come for economic reasons, hoping for a better life materially, with a few interested in and hoping for freedom and other intangible blessings. About 2.1 million illegal immigrants live in California, mostly Latin Americans and Asians. State officials say it costs upwards of $2.3 billion a year to provide them with public services such as schools, medical care and prison sentences as required. These may be cut off, except perhaps the prison 'service', probably the most expensive item per head. The Governor stated 16,700 illegal immigrants found guilty of felonies were costing $377 million for imprisonment. The SOS (Save our State) Proposition 187 would strip them of their rights to welfare, non-emergency health care and public schooling for their children. The Governor of California sued the Federal Government for requiring California to spend as much as 10% of its budget on social services for foreigners who are living in the state illegally. Other States badly affected (notably Florida) are also claiming financial compensation from the Federal Government, which holds the responsibility for controlling its borders and keeping people out.

The Third World countries experiencing tragic emigration for economic reasons (Box 3.4) should severely restrict their population growth until they have had time to accumulate sufficient capital to employ larger numbers of people. An average of two children per couple everywhere has been widely canvassed for such countries. More children may be thought necessary wherever bad health conditions cause excessive deaths when young, but less population density would be one step to improve health conditions.

There can be overpopulation in the short run even in countries with a low density of population on land. Land settlement and development takes a great deal of capital – more capital per acre than is required to increase the intensity of production on land already brought under cultivation. If the governments of Third World countries stopped pushing down the prices they allow their farmers to earn in order to feed their excess civil servants cheaply, they could grow more food to feed their hungry people and civil servants and mendicant city people could return to the land to help with

Box 3.4: International migrants

There are migrants and refugees – the categories overlap – and there are many of both who move mainly for economic reasons: to obtain a better life materially elsewhere. Economic migrants include major flows into Germany from Asia and elsewhere due to its lenient constitution concerning asylum; major flows from the ex-colonies of the UK (sharply stemmed in more recent years); similar flows out of North African ex-colonies into France, Italy and other European countries; a constant struggle by Hispanics and others from the Caribbean and Latin America to enter the USA legally and illegally, by land, sea and air; Indo-Chinese leaving for neighbouring Asian countries and quite a proportion since repatriated voluntarily or forcibly under the comprehensive Plan of Action for Indo-Chinese Refugees.

Figures on the refugee element are obtainable from the UN's *World Refugee Survey (1993)*. In mid-1993 there were 18.2 million refugees worldwide (a jump from ten million when I served as a consultant to the UN High Commissioner for Refugees toward the end of the 1980s). As a potential source of further exodus in future: a further 24 million persons were thought to be displaced within their own countries. One-third of the refugees – 6 million – are in Africa. Out of 6 million Afghan refugees, 1.9 million have been repatriated to their country since the end of the civil war.

Numbers of refugees by area of origin in 1993 relocated abroad are indicated below (with places where they settled shown in brackets):

Yugoslavia	1,767,800	(around Europe)
Palestinians	2,658,000	(North Africa, Middle East)
Afghanistan	4,286,000	(India, Pakistan, Iran)
Mozambique	1,725,000	(Southern Africa)
Ethiopia/Eritrea	746,700	(Other Africa and Yemen)
Somalia	864,800	(Other Africa and Middle East)
Sri Lanka	185,700	(India, Denmark)
Myanmar (ex-Burma)	333,700	(Thailand, Bangladesh, etc.)
Angola	404,200	(Zambia, Zaire, etc.)
Liberia	599,200	(Ivory Coast, Guinea, etc.)
Sudan	263,000	(Uganda, Zaire, etc.)

the farm work. When agriculture becomes more prosperous, new investment and employment in rural development can be afforded and will occur with adequate profit incentive.

Vigorous policies to increase food consumption in poor countries might usefully be pursued including, in the short run, free food aid from food-surplus countries abroad. It would permit the expansion of agricultural employment in the food-surplus countries and increase productivity in the food-aided ones.

Free food imports should be sold at market prices and not be allowed to dampen down the earnings of local farmers. An increase of money supply by governments to enable hungry people to buy food need not be inflationary. The free food aid being imported can be sold by the government on the market to meet the stimulated demand at a rate that maintains (rather than depresses) market prices. Government could encourage employment by paying part of the employees' wages during a period when businesses and farms are just starting up and struggling to survive.

Age and sex structure and skills

Situations in which unemployment hits particular groups harder than others, such as youth, ethnic, the old, either males or females, are examples of structural unemployment problems. They are *not* discrimination problems: other, more powerful, factors will cause structural unemployment problems even where racial discrimination disappears (as it almost has in Brazil, for example).

The incidence of unemployment can hit either men or women worse, according to where we live, what work we are qualified for and the period of history in question. Times have changed from when it was exceptional for women to leave home for work, to when it was exceptional – and quite an affluent privilege in 'rich' countries – for women to stay home, care for husband or children and not work. This socioeconomic factor has had a massive influence on the labour-supply/job-demand side. On the job-demand side, in big cities there is a heavy demand for women in secretarial and office work but rather less demand for 'male-type' jobs (other than for the well-educated). Men are in greater demand in situations that involve traditional heavy work: agriculture, mining, transport, heavy industry. Thus men suffer in the 'industrial' countries from the employment decline because of their increased productivity, while women benefit more than men from their flexibility when the pattern of demand for labour is rapidly changing and in recent times when the services sector looms large.

The employment of children and youth changes on both the demand and supply side. Relevant factors here include the rising age at which employment and training are completed, growing legal restrictions on child labour, changes between periods when populations are expanding rapidly (having a large proportion of children) and periods when populations are stabilising or shrinking (having a large proportion of old people).

An increased birth-rate and immigration both tend to increase (within fifteen years) the proportion of the population of working age. They also tend to increase the proportion who are unemployed, especially where the economy is not expanding and where the immigration and birth-rates are caused by 'push' rather than 'pull' factors. People feel pushed out of poor, slumping and tyrannous countries and pulled toward rich, booming, freer ones.

At the end of 1993, the unemployment of school leavers up to the age of 25 (a year when there was a bunching of children of the post-Second World War 'baby-boomers') was seen by many in the rich countries as appalling, except perhaps in Japan and Germany. This may be seen in the following data involving proportions of the specified categories unemployed.

Table 3.2

Country	All workers	Youth
Italy	10.5%	30.0%
France	11.0%	25.0%
Canada	11.5%	17.0%
Britain	11.0%	16.5%
USA	6.0%	12.0%
Japan	2.5%	5.0%
West Germany	3.5%	4.0%

At the previously mentioned international 'summit' on unemployment in Detroit, the difference between youth unemployment in Europe and the USA was described by Lester Thurow of Massachusetts Institute of Technology:

> In Europe you get unemployment insurance; in the US you get a low-wage, dead-end, part-time job.

In fact, in 1994, 22 per cent of employed Americans were either part-time or temporary workers: the highest proportion ever. Since 1989, median full-time earnings for American workers aged 20–24 have fallen, in real terms, by 7 per cent. School-leavers expect to earn little more than the minimum wage of $4.25 an hour. The gap between the earnings of university graduates and high-school graduates doubled during the 1980s and in 1994 those with degrees earned 77 per cent more than others taking their first jobs. The gap continues to widen.

This is fortunate for American college graduates in so far as they typically enter the labour force about $10,000 in debt, from loans taken out to pay for their soaring tuition fees. In Massachusetts, the American State probably better endowed with higher education facilities than any other place in the world, an education at the State universities, all expenses included, costs about $12,000 a year ($48,000 for the four years to a first degree) and at private universities from $20,000 to $30,000 ($80,000–$120,000 per degree). This is in sharp contrast to Europe where the State finances much or most of university education.

In a sense all students are subsidised, since hardly anywhere do tuition fees cover the entire cost of educating a university student. Where that cost is highest, all students admitted, including the wealthy ones, are being rewarded for their high academic prowess by the handsome endowments and subsidies that make highly 'capitalised' universities financially possible.

Earnings in the USA are tied ever more tightly to skills. When hiring young workers, employers look to their education level as the first indication of their skill level. Although about half of American youths enter higher education, many drop out early. Three-quarters of Americans do not have a full university degree. They face a grim future of stagnant or falling real wages and the picture is worst for those 40 per cent of school-leavers who receive no higher education at all. In the centre of Detroit, where the international meeting on unemployment took place, 18 per cent of people were out of work and 47 per cent of black people aged 16–19 were out of work at the time. The centres of other big American cities also show the heavy burden of joblessness among young black and other minorities even though they earn less when employed. Young men in cities can have more difficulty than young women in finding jobs: women are more versatile, flexible, cheaper and, arguably, more law-abiding.

More training and education are the obvious remedies being studied and acted upon in rich countries, but they are not the whole solution. The number of unfilled vacancies, together with business and employment opportunities lost due to lack of qualified applicants, would not provide jobs for all the unemployed, even if they were given the requisite skills.

Now we return to further description of the economic structure and the history of its evolution and impact on employment. There is much ground to cover but we can do so in two parts: first we look at the 'exogenous' factors and then at the 'endogenous' ones.

As we might guess from the first two letters in each of these words, the first one, starting with 'ex', refers to changes and events occurring *outside* the economy but having an important impact on it. The second, starting with 'en', refers to changes occurring *inside* the economy and involving its structure, sometimes occasioning unemployment.

Exogenous factors include:

● wars and other man-made disasters and natural disasters;
● the rise and fall of different religions, cultures and ideologies (quite different in kind and in degree from economic ideologies or business aims, which are endogenous);

- shifts in fashions, changes in sources of enthusiasms and in value systems; and, important in our earlier history at least;
- new inventions and discoveries, facts and information which change the behaviour, directions and motivation of human actions. A major element here is technological progress.

Money has been described as an exogenous factor by those who think that its supply is entirely under the control of the government. Actually, money, like the government itself, is greatly influenced by the economy. We might expect to find that there are fewer purely exogenous factors in rich countries, where interest rates are highly sensitive to sentiment in financial markets (notably, their assessment of the risk of inflation in the short- and long-term) and that sentiment bends the will of government.

Endogenous factors, for example, are economic events such as shifts in the pattern of international and interregional trade, and population growth. The economy basically affects how many people can live and when and how they will die. Population is comparable to the discovery of oil or other mineral wealth, which increases the supply of 'land' – the economists' name for natural resources: another factor of production. A discovery of gold – almost money itself – is like a direct increase in capital, the third major factor of production in economists' equations. Gold-mining played a major part in the supply of capital in the USSR. Oil is almost as monetary as gold, although, unlike gold, it varies in quality and price and is not as easy to sell immediately.

Exogenous factors in structural change

This section is about the fact that nothing in life stays still. After 1950 people began to say that world weather patterns seemed to be becoming much more violent and abnormal. Meteorologists and historians then pointed out that we were actually returning to normality! What had been abnormal was the unusually calm weather conditions in the first half of the century. Records showed that in preceding centuries there had been greater extremes in our planet's weather. However, there are changes that could radically affect life and the economy even when we only look forward one century: for example, the widening holes in the ozone layer over Earth's polar regions are already killing off some species; more carbon dioxide in our atmosphere might warm up our planet, melt the ice caps and raise sea-levels. Many major ports and cities are only a few feet above sea-level: indeed much of Holland is below it. Most of Florida is less than 500 feet above sea-level and much of it could be swamped by a massive tidal wave or 'tsunami' caused by seismic shocks under the Atlantic Ocean. Such shocks are more likely to happen in the Pacific, which could endanger Baja

California, San Francisco Bay and Japanese and Chinese ports, notably Hong Kong and Shanghai.

The weather profoundly affects agriculture. It can certainly upset the insurance industry. Floods have cut communications, destroyed stocks and hindered trade. The recent hurricanes in Florida, the floods in the Mississippi watershed and valley, floods and droughts in California, together with earthquakes, and forest fires during dry periods, are among costly disasters which helped to seriously undermine Lloyds' great insurance market in London. (Lloyds also had internal problems.)

A worse risk is being hit by a meteorite or an asteroid such as the one that killed off the dinosaurs, and the several 'fragments' that shook Jupiter in 1994. The risk of being struck by spatial objects, heavier than those that hit southern Arizona and Eastern Siberia during this century, is calculated on average to be about once every 300 years.

Box 3.5: Defence industries after the cold war

The end of the cold war brought slower and smaller cuts in military expenditure in the USA (down 29% since 1985) than were hoped for and smaller transfers of expected 'savings' to social needs occurred. (US defence spending was 6.5% of GDP in 1986; 6% in 1989; around 5% in 1991–92; falling toward 4% in 1994 and expected to reach 3% by 1997). Both the government and the defence industry paid-off debts and profits were maintained in the industry by imaginative conversions to 'peace-time' production and by cost-cutting, the brunt of which fell chiefly on the workers. For example, in 1993 Raytheon Co. laid-off 5100 workers and raised its earnings in the first nine months by 9.1% over 1992. It used the same division that makes radars for the Pentagon to build satellites for commercial cellular phone networks, while a unit making missiles also worked on a new high-speed 'tilt-train' – but said that job growth may take time. Martin Marietta Corp. eliminated 10,000 jobs in 1993 and increased earnings 23% in that year. It bought General Electric's aerospace division and closed ten plants in order to become more efficient. McDonnell Douglas Corporation, which has the largest sales under defence contracts of any company in the world, has shed 14,000 workers since January 1993 and earned $528 million in the first nine months of 1993 compared with a loss of $7 million in 1992. Profits in the last quarter of 1993 were the best ever. Hughes Missile Systems Co. bought General Dynamics Corp. missile business and said it would consolidate five missile manufacturing plants into one and eliminate as many as 6000 jobs. In 1992–93 about 3000 workers lost their jobs at the Electric Boat division of General Dynamics, which makes nuclear submarines.

In his Princeton lectures in 1947[8] Professor Jacob Viner maintained that capitalists do not instigate wars for the sake of profit. Capitalists lose from wars like everyone else. Where they do profit, said Viner, is from costly *preparations* for war, above all from arms races such as went on for so long during the cold war. It also seems that they may gain or lose when there is disarmament (Box 3.5).

The spreading of diseases – old and new – is another possible exogenous factor. The risk is heightened in some countries by economic distress which, coupled with civil war or the breakdown of authority, is causing regression in terms of standards of hygiene and other civilised arrangements. On the other hand, the Black Death in mediaeval Europe reduced the size of the labour force and temporarily improved wages and the lot of the surviving poor. These kinds of disasters affect a country's economic and social structure. They can call for massive reconstruction which, ironically, creates expansion in employment.

Apart from disasters there is also, in the normal and gradual evolution of both the economy and the natural environment, a process of interaction and even conflict which has major implications for employment (Box 3.6).

Box 3.6: Production in the biosphere

Is production the primary theatre for posing the issue of social change? Professor R. W. Cox writes: 'Consciousness of the biosphere . . . frames the dilemma of late-twentieth-century humanity. In the biosphere, a thin envelope encompassing the world, humanity interacts with other forms of nature. Nature is not just an object of human activity; people are just as much objects of the responses of nature. Global warming and the hole in the ozone layer are actors in world politics. The dilemma is how human and non-human nature can survive in this identity of subjects and objects. Indeed, the modernist mentality that places human subject as dominant over non-human object is challenged (just like the domination of economics over society) . . .

'The problem of the biosphere has to be attacked at the level of consumption as well as that of production, especially the consumption model of the affluent parts of the world. George Bush was reported as saying (at the Rio de Janeiro environment conference June 1992): "Our lifestyle is not open to negotiation." This can be read as a recognition of the problem, together with a recognition that politicians (because of the short-term thinking essential to their profession) are unable to face it. The same short-term thinking pits maintenance of jobs against maintenance of the biosphere. How could an effort to make consumption compatible with biospheric survival be made also to change production practices so as to give meaningful work to all who need it?'[9]

An extreme example of biospherical conflict is to be found in north-west USA. There the logging industry is of vital importance to the country as well as to the workers in it. Most American houses and their furniture are made of wood, still cheap but rising in price because of its dwindling supply. Most of the communications we do not see on a screen we see on paper. American newspapers often run to more than 100 pages, which visibily chews up softwood. An entirely obscure bird, the spotted owl, has become an 'endangered species' because of logging operations. Production and employment in logging have been severely cut back for the benefit of this bird, suddenly raised to a privileged status rarely accorded to human beings. The massacre of hundreds of thousands of Rwandans, or even the unemployment of American loggers, cause less practical concern than some spotted owls being put at risk. It is easier for Rwandans to reproduce themselves than spotted owls. What should loggers do instead – move metal furniture or build brick houses?

Government legislation, regulation and deregulation are far-reaching. They can be seen as exogenous factors in changing the economic structure with impact on employment (Box 3.7).

Box 3.7: Book box: Regulation and deregulation

'Contrived Competition: Regulation and Deregulation in America', by Richard H. K. Vietor, Harvard University Press, is a history of regulation in the USA since the Depression. Vietor is a Harvard Business School Professor. He traces the history over 75 years of four companies in four different sectors: airlines, natural gas, telephone and telegraph communication and banking; and also traces the co-evolution of the various bureaucracies that arose to regulate them. He shows why the New Deal experiment with top-down regulation died of natural causes.

De-regulation of airlines changed and increased the numbers of the people employed as well as of passengers carried, but it hit profits (Box 3.8), and may have reduced total employees' earnings.

Consultants, trouble-shooting chief executives and top investment bankers specialising in mergers and buyouts hinder and help, as do government officials and departments, in the process of corporate reorganisation and restructuring in the face of economic vicissitudes (Box 3.9).

The Economist paid close attention in 1994 to corporate restructuring[10] and mergers.[11]

On restructuring, the unemployment angle looms out of the 'downsizing' process. In 1993, seeking lower costs, higher productivity and fatter profits, American firms announced 615,000 job cuts, an all-time record. In the first

Box 3.8: America's airlines

Big losses are suffered by enterprises where the State steps in with massive assistance. American airlines, on the other hand, illustrate an industry where the government has not helped; in fact it initiated the more intense competition and shake-out of ownership structure by de-regulating airlines and, notably, opening up competition by price. The only public sector help has been American bankruptcy law, which some say does too much to keep in existence ailing companies that cannot be salvaged.

Net profit or loss in all US scheduled airlines, 1978–92:

1978–80 From a billion dollars down to nearly zero

1981–83 Losses during this recession period reached a peak of minus one billion dollars in 1982

1984–89 Loss occurred only in 1986 with a peak of $1.75 billion of profit being reached in 1988

1990–92 Huge losses – around $4 billion at the beginning and the end of that recession period and nearly $2 billion in 1991.

The total losses of $10 billion, 1990–92, exceeded all profits of the industry in the past 55 years.

De-regulation occurred in 1978. For ten years the airlines accumulated large debts, bought new aircraft and redesigned operating systems to increase competition and fill more seats in each plane at a lower average price. Then came the recession and the Gulf War to compound the losses.

Employment in the airlines 1978–93 grew till the recession of the 1990s but total earnings probably grew less as companies went under and staffs were rehired and replaced at lower wage and salary rates. Employment was just under 300,000 in 1978, reached a peak of 452,000 in 1990 and dropped to 425,225 by June 1993. Number of passengers carried grew more, so that the ratio of staff to passengers fell. There was an obvious cut-back in services as well as fares, particularly in the regional airlines: no on-board meals, limited baggage and terminal services and no readily accessible reservations service. Travel agencies have had to work harder for less money and their staffs have had to work late at night revising tickets during the severest price wars.

No frills carriers have also restructured their route systems. Instead of following the hub-and-spokes pattern that many airlines set up in the 1980s, no-frills flights hop from stop to stop in more or less a straight line like a bus service.

Further cuts in staffs are expected. American Airlines alone were to lay off 4000 to 5000 by the end of 1994.

Source: Air Transport Association of America

Box 3.9: Book box: Transforming threatened businesses

The Phoenix Agenda: Power to Transform your Workplace, John Whiteside, Oliver Wight Publications, Essex Junction, Vermont, 1993. The author worked for Digital Equipment and consulted to Volvo, Intel, American Express, General Electric and Schlumberger. He proposes a 12-step programme for transforming threatened businesses – or for individuals trying to survive those transformations.

seven months of 1994, according to a Chicago consultancy, Challenger, Gray & Thomas, a further 319,000 workers suffered the same fate. (Figures in previous years had shown a steeply rising trend through the recession: 100,000 in 1989; 300,000 in 1990; 550,000 in 1991; 575,000 in 1992). Corporate America now spends $10 billion a year on restructuring. A major part of that sum relates to the cost of compensating laid-off workers.

An American Management Association study (1994) found that one-quarter of the companies it studied had undergone three or more episodes of downsizing in the previous five years. Fewer than half of any that had shrunk during that time subsequently raised their profits. Those that did, did not begin to see real benefits until three years after the cuts. Only one-third reported higher productivity. A new book on business strategy[12] alleged that managers' obsession with downsizing could reflect a lack of imagination. It may be easier to increase returns on investment by cutting assets or jobs, rather than by raising profits.

By sector, in the first seven months of 1994, out of 319,000 lay-offs, one-third were in computers and telecoms. The lay-offs in aerospace and transport was almost one-fifth. Next came oil and utilities: about one-tenth. Another fifth was divided roughly equally between financial services, health care, consumer goods and retailing. The remaining fifth come under the heading 'miscellaneous'.

In the 1980s cars, defence, computers and others needed to be slimmed down. There was less need for so many similar American cars when many more foreign models were coming on to the market. In newer industries such as computers we start with more companies than we finish with, since the weakest are weeded out in the competition – especially after the onset of a recession. Telecoms and computers were also grappling with price wars and technical change.

'The answer to such points is not to abandon downsizing, however. It is to do it better. Finding new economies is as difficult in practice as it is desirable in theory. It is easy for bosses to become obsessed with cost-cutting and forget about both strategy and the well-being of their workforce, both essential if downsizing is to succeed.' Professor Mike

Useem (Wharton School, University of Pennsylvania) said 'companies underestimate the personal cost and grief to employees' and Joe Galerneau (of AT&T, which shrunk its 300,000 workforce by 20 per cent) thought his firm was typical: 'In the past we said to employees: "Do as you're told and you have a job for life." Then we betrayed them. Trust levels were devastated.'[13]

Managers themselves who carry out sweeping dismissals on orders from above become demoralised and troubled. In some cases, economies from job cuts are simply used to pay higher dividends to shareholders.

The Economist concludes: 'One reason why firms begin cutting back is that their competitive environment has changed. Preoccupied with their restructuring, too few firms give enough thought to adapting their products as well.' They 'should rethink how they compare their products and processes with those of world leaders – a practice known as "benchmarking". Shrinking companies too often benchmark old enemies. Better to benchmark future rivals.'[14]

On the question of mergers, *The Economist* plunged into the deep end: the 10 September 1994 issue had on its cover a colour picture of copulating camels under the title 'The trouble with mergers'. The opening paragraph of the 'cover' article evoked Cole Porter's titillating song:

> *Camels do it, birds and bees do it, even companies do it: all over America firms are falling in love and settling down together. So far this year, more than $210 billion-worth of corporate mergers have been announced ... Even bigger deals are said to be on the way ... They are portrayed as intelligent adaptations to a changing business environment, caused variously by shrinking markets (defence), government reforms (drugs, medicines and health care) or technological change (media and telecoms). Unlike the hostile takeovers of the 1980s, most of 1994's mergers have been friendly. Entailing true romance rather than shotgun weddings, tempting synergies rather than financial opportunism, no rash of mergers has ever seemed more benign, or better calculated to boost corporate profits.*

There are good and bad mergers. J. K. Galbraith has referred to a merger disparagingly as a 'deviance'. Many mergers in the 1960s (forming diversified conglomerates such as ITT and Beatrice) were disasters caused by faddish management theories. Those in the 1980s often freed potentially robust businesses from unwieldy conglomerates created two decades earlier. The value of mergers hovered around $200 billion a year in 1986–1987; approached $350 billion in 1988 and $300 billion in 1989. It then dropped back in the recession to a low of $140 billion in 1991.

'Much depends on the quality of managements', wrote *The Economist*, to be able to meld firms with different cultures, to avoid distracting top management with acquisitions and neglecting their core business. If a takeover does not install a fresh management, the justification in terms of synergies or economies of scale needs to be all the stronger. A high price is usually offered to persuade shareholders to accept the offer for their shares That price may be too high to 'pay for' later, in the view of shareholders in the buying company who may find that their share prices do not retain their value.[14]

The new wave of mergers may not repeat all these earlier mistakes. Recent relaxation of the anti-trust regime allows firms to achieve rationalisation in industries such as defence and banking. Greater trade freedoms also help. A sole supplier in a country is no longer a monopolist if imports of the things he sells can enter freely and compete with his prices.

Endogenous factors in structural change

We could treat technological progress more as an endogenous factor than an exogenous one. A purist might argue that pure science is an exogenous factor because it is the pursuit of knowledge for its own sake. However, applied science might be regarded as an endogenous factor because its aims are usually to improve life, promote efficiency and save money. Its origin is more likely to be embedded in the developments and prospects within the economy itself.

Developments in technology are crucially important to economic growth as well as to changes in structure and structural unemployment. In a study focusing on economic growth and technology, the ILO, has published detailed statistics (Box 3.10).

We now travel over the geographical and industrial landscape to see endogenous factors at work. The path of development and growth of each of the economic sectors should be in chronological order: primary, secondary, tertiary. When the economy does not proceed like this, we have a major flaw. For example, Latin America – unlike Africa – had major cities *before* it had much broad-based wealth. The cities were sustained by tertiary activities such as government and the armed forces. Like all public sectors and in slightly developed countries with hardly any secondary sector, they tended to employ more people than they needed at a crippling cost. People who are employed but have little to do are not only a burden on society but they tend to obstruct people who do have work. Latin America now limps through to prosperity, its secondary economy expanding as best it can when not over-suffocated by its premature, over-developed tertiary economy.

Canada presents a special case of being out-of-step. The entire Canadian economy would look more like a mistake were it not for its abundant natural resources and valuable oil and minerals by which its primary economy can flourish. Canada's problem, which it shares with Latin

Box 3.10: Employment structure in G–7 countries, 1920–1990

The pace of social change has accelerated in the last quarter of the century under the combined impulses of a major technological revolution and of worldwide economic restructuring. A major indication of structural change is the transformation of employment and occupational structures. Indeed, the theories of 'post-industrialism' and 'informationalism' use the strongest empirical evidence in support of their argument that a new social structure has emerged, characterised by the shift from goods to services, the rise of managerial and professional occupations, the demise of agricultural and manufacturing jobs and the growing information content of most jobs.[15] Implicit in many of these theories is a sort of natural law of economics and societies, according to which they will follow a single path along a trajectory of modernity spearheaded by American society.[16]

An article published by ILO in early 1994[17] sought to examine the empirical evidence for the transformation of employment and occupational structure over the past 70 years in the so-called G–7 countries (those industrially prominent industrialised countries whose leaders meet periodically to discuss and occasionally try to coordinate their economic policies: the USA, Japan, Germany, France, Italy, the UK and Canada). Those sufficiently interested may read the article, which is accessible in all countries in several major languages.

American countries, is its vast, thinly populated territory. That is fine for separate tribes of Indians in a subsistence Garden-of-Eden type of economy, but it can prove to be a massive burden for an integrated polity and economy. Canada needs immensely extended and expensive lines of communication and transport to service government and trade. To exaggerate the truth, it has almost as many railways stations and petrol pumps as people and longer distances over no-man's-land than anywhere else in the world. Thus Canada began with a structural problem: not of too much land – which was an *embarras de richesse* – but of not enough capital and labour to develop its natural resources.

In the 1930s, Argentina was as rich (per head) as Canada until Argentina was ruined by destructive politics. The Argentine rail network was so intensive that nowhere in Argentina (except Patagonia) was more than 25 miles from a railway station. Argentina had a higher population density and incomparably less land than Canada. If it had been blessed with better government and made good use of the better climate and soils than in Canada and of as much oil per head, Argentina today would arguably be a rich country.

Economic mistakes mean land misused and capital wasted, but both survive and can be used better later. The worst aspect is that economic mistakes cost many people the loss of their jobs and cost others a lower standard of living than they might have had. Economic mistakes, as much as wars, kill people prematurely.

Asia, the Middle East and North Africa have major cities and large cities. The major ones usually reflect healthy economic growth. The large ones tend to accommodate the overspill of excess population growth. Cairo is an extreme example: an enormous surplus population makes it one of the world's largest cities in the crudest numerical sense. Egypt's population is growing at one million every nine months. In a decade or so, it will be so big there will either have to be a massive famine or an explosion outward of desperate people from a country bursting at its seams.

In all human history before the last century and this, world population grew very slowly.[18] Changes in that population, more or less, reflected wars, diseases and major migrations. In fact, those factors did not produce very big population changes and most serious migration occurred in the nineteenth century.

Americans are well aware of the potato famine in Ireland and the great emigration of Irish people, mainly to the USA, in the last century.[19] In 1800, Ireland had a population of 6 million and Britain of 14 million, so Ireland mattered quite a bit to Britain. After Ireland gained its independence in this century, its population had dropped to 2 million – a third of what it had been – whereas Britain's population (including a fair number of Irish) had become four times as large as it was a century before. Ireland's economic decline has been partly arrested by entry to the European Union, though unemployment remains a major problem.

The great inflow of foreign immigrants to the USA in the nineteenth century, many of working age when they arrived, swelled the American labour force who were looking for jobs. Most immigrants arrived with little or no money, many with almost as little education and training, but the American economy managed to absorb them and to grow because of two key structural factors.

First, there was an abundance of land and other natural resources. Millions of acres in a temperate climatic belt could grow cereals and other storable and transportable food to feed the world. Minerals were there to be mined and processed in new basic industries. Unlimited wood was available to build houses and make furniture and vehicles. The world's largest fresh water supply – the Great Lakes – lies at the heart of the USA. Even before the railways were built, the Great Lakes made it possible for Chicago and Toronto to trade worldwide.

Second, its abundant capital: financing was available from Europe. Britain and France were then the world's richest countries. Their wealth had been amassed from industrial and agricultural revolutions and technological advance already under way. It was augmented by revenues from their empires which considerably exceeded the costs of imperialism.

Much money was sucked away from London and Paris across the Atlantic by the thrilling investment opportunities in both North and South America: opportunities that grew out of the combination of plentiful raw materials, cheap labour and abundant natural resources. Today a lot of capital is being sucked out of North America in search of the exciting investment opportunities in the so-called emerging-market countries. In 1994 the booming stock-markets were in Brazil, Chile, Portugal, South Africa, South Korea, Taiwan, India, Hungary and Singapore. Downturns in the stock-markets of countries such as Thailand, Malaysia, Indonesia, Hong Kong, Israel and China (in ascending order of gravity) have not driven away massive American and other rich countries' capital invested there. Fingers burned in Mexican investment between 1994 and 1995, temporarily threatened to imperil investment in Latin America. Many immigrants, their backs to the wall, were motivated to work hard and to learn quickly. Those with intelligence and the earlier settlers of the New World readily adapted, adding to the inventions and scientific advances transmitted from Europe.

Today about half of all the immigrants entering the USA yearly do so illegally and stay illegally despite a campaign to step up defences against illegal residence. These immigrants are mostly poor and ill-educated, bringing little or no capital with them. Immigration laws mainly seek to enable American residents and citizens to have their relatives join them from abroad. It hardly caters at all any longer for the encouragement of investors to enter and to settle.

International displacement of workers and jobs

How can these additional million or more settlers from abroad every year be given jobs? The law restricting migration for employment and economic gain induces them to squeeze into the ranks of those living on relief, who thus become a liability instead of a labour asset. As for the rest, the figures in Box 3.11 indicate that it is difficult for the USA to create enough jobs for hundreds of thousands of legal (working-age) immigrants a year as well as all those school and college graduates who are entering the workforce for the first time.

The problem may be worse because new figures are being mentioned about an increase in legal and illegal immigration rising from 1 to 1.5 million a year. Such an inflow can take many jobs from American citizens – and even college places from American students – because some of the immigrants, notably those from Asia, are still as highly motivated as their predecessors were in the nineteenth century. Newcomers from Eastern Europe and the former USSR include, notably, well-educated, skilled people.

To create more jobs for everyone in North America, there is not the same inflow of foreign capital as there was in the nineteenth century. New

Box 3.11: Job-creating in the USA

In defence of the American economic system it is sometimes emphasised that unemployment anywhere can be viewed as the product of both blades of a pair of scissors. One blade is the number of jobs offered (existing numbers employed plus job vacancies) and the other blade is the number of jobs wanted (number of workers, employed or not, seeking jobs or better jobs). A vast flood of immigration can create serious unemployment anywhere and place an enormous social relief burden on those employed. Contrariwise, a strong, dynamic economy, such as that of America, can create many new jobs, speed recovery and reduce the likelihood of long-term unemployment.

Bloomberg Business News offered a chart of new jobs created in the USA during the recent recession. By October 1993 177,000 jobs were created and a stronger economy was sensed. Salient points on the path of job creation may be of interest, as follows (these are net figures, either losses or gains being larger to yield the net figure):

1991:   November – nearly 150,000 jobs less
         December – about 10,000 jobs more
1992:   April – about 180,000 jobs more
         August – over 100,000 jobs less
         December – over 100,000 jobs more
1993:   February – over 350,000 jobs more
         March–July – jobs gained every month
         August – nearly 40,000 jobs less
         October – 177,000 jobs gained

Since then, the two blades of the scissors have combined to reduce the unemployment to 6% – the lowest in the capitalist world and probably about the lowest in the whole world if the truth be told (e.g. 'hidden' unemployment in Japan). The only fly in the ointment is that history leads us to expect bouts of massive unemployment to recur in the future.

York and other American financial centres obviously have massive financial resources. But there are major outflows from them into new foreign investment opportunities worldwide. The US government also managed to raise its national debt from 1 to nearly $5 trillion (80 per cent of national income) in a few years. Much of that money mountain was sunk in the armaments race and used for purposes that do not yield a direct economic return. And it heavily reduced supplies of capital for investment in the American economy to more fully employ the swelling workforce. The increase in labour supply may be moderated in the next century by a modest natural rate of population increase and an ageing of the USA population. If it had not been for Washington's success in conquering inflation and lowering interest rates, this national debt burden was on the way to becoming crippling. Future inflation is feared particularly for this reason and for others.

Much foreign capital does come in but it arrives and leaves by itself: telexed in and out. Much of it is fickle. It is attracted on a fairly short-term basis by interest rates when they are high in the USA, as they were in the 1980s, and by the stock exchange and real estate capital gains readily made in the 1980s. By 1992 those chances for quick gains had disappeared, and interest rates had fallen to new, historically low points; much foreign money deposited for short terms has gone. Increases in interest rates occurred gently in 1994–1995, while the dollar's weakness on the foreign exchange market also chilled foreign investors.

There is some long-term foreign direct investment (FDI) in American production facilities, by the UK, The Netherlands and Japan respectively, in descending order of importance. (A larger part of Japanese investment in the USA is in bonds and other 'paper'.) The huge American domestic market is an attraction, but recently has been less so during recession and, since 1990, with the overhang of consumer debt. By 1994 the loss of confidence in the dollar occurred for political, often Clinton-related (exogenous) as well as economic (endogenous) reasons. China and other countries now have huge domestic markets, too, and much capital is being sucked into the resuscitation of Eastern Europe and the current renaissance in Latin America (Box 3.12).

Box 3.12: Multinationals' Foreign assets 1992

According to the *World Investment Report* published by the United Nations Conference on Trade and Development, at the end of 1993 multinational companies held worldwide foreign assets of $2.1 trillion. The largest ten held, in 1992, the following foreign assets:

Company	HQ Country/ies	$billion
Royal Dutch/Shell	Netherlands/UK	69.4
Exxon	USA	48.2
IBM	USA	45.7
General Motors	USA	41.8
Hitachi	Japan	35.0*
Matsushita Electric	Japan	32.0*
Nestlé	Switzerland	28.7
Ford	USA	28.0
Alcatel Alsthom	France	25.0*
General Electric	USA	24.2

Source: UNCTAD, *The Economist*: (*estimated)

There is a welcome and significant compatibility and collaboration between the US and Mexican economies which can be reinforced and facilitated by NAFTA. This includes the notorious Maquiladora: foreign-owned factories built slightly south of the US border which receive considerable Mexican-granted privileges as well as cheap labour. They are suspiciously viewed by Ross Perot and the American labour union movement as devices to take away jobs from American workers.

The American industries and plants most likely to benefit from a transfer of their production capacity to Mexican soil are those that still need to be comparatively labour-intensive. Irrespective of the existence of Mexico, inherently labour-intensive American plants are an endangered species and will probably be replaced by foreign or American producers in the many other countries with cheap labour.

NAFTA offers the opportunity for the American companies – threatened like this by Mexico – themselves to move to Mexico and be in full management control of the Mexican outposts of their production. The Maquiladora at the Mexican border, unlike foreign companies elsewhere in Mexico, are, under the pertinent Mexican programme, permitted to have 100 per cent American ownership and control of their Mexican plants. They can also repatriate 100 per cent of their profits back to the US in American currency and are obliged to export most or all of their output back to the US.

A certain portion of the American companies' total output, specified in the Mexican maquiladora programme, is to be produced in Mexico. This means the remaining portion of the companies' output will continue to be produced in the USA. The total output will be sold in the USA with little or no reduction of prices to the American consumer. Cars, for example, will be sold in the USA at the same price as before. Yet the cost of producing them will be far lower in Mexico than in the USA. This will yield extra profits that can help to cover the excess labour costs in the USA and maintain the American part of the companies' total work-force. American employment, threatened by extinction by high labour costs, can be subsidised and continued by virtue of the savings on Mexican labour.

That is the social benefit of NAFTA to the USA. Mexico benefits by having American capital, advanced technology and manpower training. Mexican labour can achieve a level of productivity way above that ever achieved before in Mexico. This prospective benefit to Mexico was temporarily and famously reduced by its government, which wrongly kept its currency overvalued. That over-encouraged imports to the extent of causing a disastrous, confidence-shaking deficit in its international account by 1995, when the peso had crashed. In all economic changes, there should be more effort to respect the necessary speed limits. Without Mexico and the Maquiladora, strengthened by NAFTA, the whole of the output of the goods doomed by high labour costs in the USA would soon be displaced by a foreign producer not controlled at all by the American companies concerned. Those companies and all their American employees would be totally and permanently displaced from employment in that sector.

It is inevitable that there will always be change. Whether there will be progress is less certain. Changes will continue in the economic structure and they will speed up. First, they will be accelerated as part of the greater speed and stress at which we now live our lives, because of technological progress. Second, changes in economic structure will accelerate if we maintain and develop our efforts to achieve free trade.

Trade that endures and prospers is trade that exchanges goods and services between those specialising in making them well. The best specialists command the best price. Monopolists keep prices up if they can. De Beers of Johannesburg controls the world market in diamonds by always being ready to buy and store them when too many come on to the market. In a sellers' market, there is an excess of buyers until prices rise. In a buyers' market, there is an excess of sellers until the prices they ask fall to the level at which they can sell.

OPEC spectacularly raised oil prices in the 1970s, but its members developed high-spending tastes and some now feel they can no longer afford to hold off supplies from the market to get a better price. There have been similar schemes to protect and stabilise the markets for commodities such as sugar, cocoa, coffee, tin, copper and cotton. However, it is difficult to withstand the strong winds that blow in the world marketplace.

The United Nations' efforts to apply economic sanctions against offending countries reveals how difficult it is to stop a healthy backdoor or below-the-counter trade induced by major price differences. Smoothly functioning, well-informed global markets can be effective in evening-out price differences worldwide (except irreducible differences caused by transport costs for delivery of items sold to long-distance buyers). Low-cost producers can thereby prosper and grow, at least until their production costs become higher than those of their competitors.

The key initial 'secret' of the economic miracles of Japan, Hong Kong, Singapore, Taiwan and South Korea – the Asian Tigers and the recently born tiger cubs (Malaysia, Thailand, Indonesia and Vietnam) – was cheap labour. High profits gained from low wage production, if ploughed back in more capital-intensive production and products, raises worker productivity and, after a delay, even raises wages, resulting from the higher value of output per worker achieved from the capital investment.

Japan as a problem for the USA

In Japan, many new industries launched by its investors have, for years, been expanded by them in other countries. This was not only because labour abroad became relatively cheaper than labour in Japan. The Japanese, stifled by population and urban density and by industrial pollution, arguably preferred to go and pollute somewhere else when seeking to expand.

In South Korea, several new cities, starting with Ulsan (which I saw being launched in 1973), were built from scratch by Japanese investors down to the last temple and tennis club. The Japanese also built abroad to satisfy the USA and other countries by employing those countries' workers to produce many of the Japanese goods that had conquered major segments of their home markets.

To some extent the USA is retaliating by improving its own efficiency. An example is the recent improvement in efficiency and quality in its car production. World dominance from 1950 to 1975 had made General Motors, Chrysler and Ford (in descending order of culpability) complacent and second-rate. By the late 1980s they started producing better cars at lower prices than German and Japanese car firms. The American car-makers and other industries had also learned to join their enemy as well as to seek to beat him. Joint ventures were set up in both Japan (e.g. Sharp TVs) and the USA (e.g. the Saturn car). BMWs and Volkswagens are now built in the USA as well as in Germany. BMW and Rolls-Royce are gradually merging. Ford bought Jaguar and it was rumoured that Jaguars may eventually be assembled in the USA, even though the cost of British labour is regarded as reasonable. All the new 1996 Mercedes models were produced in the USA. There is a significant boost to American employment resulting from other countries building assembly plants in the USA. They establish those plants to be close to the massive North American market. European car-makers also wanted to take advantage of less onerous social charges in the USA than in Europe.

Japan seldom played fair in international trade. It invaded other countries' markets, but kept its own market almost closed. There are exceptions, however: some American companies managed to penetrate the Far East. The American firm 'Toys R Us', whose huge warehouses, highly visible on Hong Kong's waterfront, demonstrate the international character of modern corporations, has successfully begun to sell to Japanese children.

After a major American diplomatic onslaught, Japan stopped reneging on its contract with Motorola and let it develop its incursion into Japanese urban markets for cellular phones easing American access to the Japanese market. In any event, economic stimuli in Japan to counteract the recession were urgently required.

Japan's economic turmoil has caused major reverberations in its culture, which some believe needs modernisation and internationalisation for its own good. On the other hand, Japan's competition is a healthy corrective factor for the old complacency in American industries. It has benefited American consumers and – through price competition – it has helped to bolster real wages in the USA against further decline.

Some historians see Japan's attack on Pearl Harbor partly as revenge for their being discriminated against by American trade-protection policy in the

1930s. They lost the war, but succeeded in trade forty years later. We hope there will not be another trade war between the two countries in this century (see Box 3.13). In 1995 it was absurd for the USA to threaten trade war with Japan to force an entry of more American cars there without showing a willingness to change the side of their steering wheels (as the Japanese do for the USA). The next world recession might be triggered off by Japan. Reduction of large US trade deficits with China and other emerging Asian economies would reduce the supply of dollars they need to buy Japanese goods.

Box 3.13: USA trade with Japan

At their meeting on 11 February 1994, President Clinton and Japan's premier Morihiro Hosokawa failed to come up with a way of cutting Japan's $60 billion trade surplus with the USA. Clinton blamed the lopsided picture in large part on a closed way of business in Tokyo that fends off foreigners, even when Tokyo had pledged in writing to level the playing field. In 1991 both sides agreed to a plan that set 20% as the expected market share for foreign companies that compete in Japan's lucrative semi-conductor market.

The US trade deficit progressed to reach the following levels in mid-1994:

Balance (millions)	May	June
Japan	−$4,388	−$5,518
Canada	−$ 831	−$1,285
Western Europe	−$1,430	−$1,824
OPEC (oil exporters)	−$1,026	−$1,671

These large US deficits represent a major boost to the economies of the other countries and regions named; without such heavy US imports their economic recovery from the recent recession would have been all the more difficult. In May 1994 the US trade deficit widened by 11.6% to $9.517 billion. It fell 1.5% in June to $9.368 billion, reflecting strong gains in US exports to offset record merchandise imports whose growth reflected continued US economic growth and higher prices paid for imported oil. Nevertheless the US government considered that the Japanese trade surplus was intolerable and the risk of a trade war loomed nearer. (Some relief came when the yen stopped rising against the dollar and the dollar recovered past the 100-yen threshold in 1995.)

According to the US Department of Commerce, China's annualised trade surplus with the USA rose above $5 billion in 1989, reached $10 billion in

1990, exceeded $15 billion in 1992, passed well above $20 billion in 1993 and reached about $28 billion in 1994. The head of the department, Ron Brown, visited China and reported that China's leaders would soon resume the 'dialogue' between America and China on human rights. This issue has repeatedly threatened their bilateral relationship, but did not in fact prevent the renewal of China's most-favoured-nation trading status with the USA in 1994. Even so, duties were raised to 100 per cent on $1 billion worth of China's imports to the USA in retaliation for China's failure to respect copyrights and pay royalties.

The rise and fall of industries and countries

The powerful trends in interregional and international trade brought massive visible changes to the landscape. The old manufacturing cities of New England shifted first to Birmingham, Alabama, and to other places in the South where workers, many of them black, earned much lower wages. US employers then crossed the Mexican border and went still further afield to obtain even cheaper labour and other costs.

The European single market, with almost 400 million consumers (Box 3.14) began to feature still more prominently in the consciousness of global 'players'.

Box 3.14: The European Union

With the admission of Austria approved by voters on 12 June 1994, and subsequently Finland and Sweden, the European Union was composed of fifteen countries:

Austria	Germany	Portugal
Belgium	Greece	Spain
Britain	Ireland	Sweden
Denmark	Italy	
Finland	Luxembourg	
France	Netherlands	

Switzerland remains so strictly neutral it still does not take part in many United Nations operations outside the sphere of charity. Enthusiasm for a federal United States of Europe has waned for some time. European voters in each member country elected, in June 1994, a European Parliament of 567 members. It will meet monthly in Strasbourg and is largely an advisory body. The highly bureaucratic secretariat of the EU, headed by the European Commission, is based in Brussels.

Old England also saw a massive loss of manufacturing industry. It had been one of the world's largest ship-builders. That honour passed first to Japan and then to places like Ulsan in South Korea, where Hyundai builds ships as well as cars. Similarly, there has been a long-standing decline in Western economy ship-building. Shipping has long had to be subsidised (with some military justification) for its continuation to be assured.

Arguably such patterns and trends reflect the long canvassed 'de-industrialisation' of the mature Western economies.

Box 3.15: Employment in manufacturing 1962–1993

During the past 30 years, jobs in Britain's manufacturing sector have shrunk at a daunting rate of 2.2% a year, faster than in any other leading industrial country. Employment in that sector also fell in Western Germany and Italy, but at much lower rates. In Japan, on the contrary, manufacturing employment grew at an annual rate of 1% during 1962–93, making a total increase of nearly 40% over the period, well above the modest annual rate experienced by the USA (0.2%) and France (0.1%). The economic crises of the mid-1970s and the early 1980s dealt a hard blow to manufacturing employment which many countries have found hard to overcome. Only in Japan and Western Germany has manufacturing employment increased since 1986; only in Japan did it stand much higher in 1993 than in 1962, while standing only slightly higher in the USA and France.

Source: *The Economist*, 2 October, 1993, p. 111: see chart

The ports of London and Liverpool were once teeming with the world's shipping. Where now would they be, were it not for gentrification, tourism and the Beatles? Anything to do with international transport plunges owners into the freest world markets as their vessels and planes enter international waters. The same now applies to international communications. Texts can be faxed; digital data can be beamed by satellite; newspapers and books can be printed worldwide the same day where ever the net costs of printing and delivery are lower. The sons and grandsons of unionised printshop workers in Britain and the USA can no longer hold the trade to ransom, paid in guaranteed employment at maximised wages. Links between unions and organised crime in American ports, the sheer vulnerability to theft when loading and unloading of ships' cargoes worldwide: these were among the factors adding to the cost advantage of a shift to using containers and truck flatbeds on ships and shifting to new ports and fresh docks facilities and labour where containers could be handled. These changes can be seen near Calcutta as well as in Britain's Felixstowe; in Djibouti as well as in the old and new ports of the USA.

Rotterdam, the world's greatest port at the mouth of Western Europe's largest river, has equally managed to adapt to such changing patterns.

The USA, with its amazing capacity to make constant and courageous changes in its economic structure, can still challenge the world's tigers. In fact, change is the order of the day in the USA. The average American family moves to new address once every five years. They think nothing of hiring a removal truck and driving it with their furniture, towing their car at the back, three thousand miles from one city to another, such as from Philadelphia to Los Angeles, to take a new job. Much of the movement is away from the north-east and westwards toward the sunbelt, and from the centres of big cities to suburbs or small country towns (Box 3.16).

Box 3.16: Getting away from New York City

Some bravely wear buttons to say 'I love New York' but big cities as places to live are losing both their attraction and their employment capacity. New York's problems are symptomatic. Its gross city income of $278 billion is roughly equal to the whole GDP of Australia. Though it contains only 3% of the USA's population it had 40% of the country's net job losses during the recent recession whereas in the recovery it regained by 1994 only 12% of the 342,000 jobs it lost. New York's cost of living and doing business competes with San Francisco for summitry. Local taxes per person in New York are three times as high as in Chicago. Taxation declines by city in this order: New York, Boston, Philadelphia, Baltimore, Seattle, Los Angeles, Chicago, Detroit, Houston and Phoenix. Apparently to discourage people staying in its expensive hotels New York charges four varieties of tax on top of each other and shoppers face heavy retail taxes. Vacancy rates in downtown Manhattan property remain close to 20%. The 60 million square feet of property empty in New York is equal to the total additional space built during the 1980s. There are 200,000 New Yorkers HIV positive; those with full-blown AIDS are likely to double by 1998, and the population is ageing.

Statistics from TENL, 25 June, 1994

Structural changes in the USA can also be a problem: no institution, however fine its tradition and place in history, is sacrosanct. Woolworths were in every American and British town, reliably serving families of modest means. Today Woolworths are sinking. The word now is Walmarts: an immense cost-cutting chain which is wiping out Mom and Pop stores all over the USA and, in just a few years, made the late head of the Walton family, its founder, America's richest man – with eight billion dollars. There are now 136 billionaires in the USA, including more than one of

Walton's heirs. Another, Bill Gates, the founder of the Microsoft company, its DOS and other software, built his fortune from nothing to billions before he was forty and became the world's richest man in 1995. Even his deputy made several billions. Sears have had trouble: they have stopped publishing and selling from their famous catalogue, a mere soft-bound book that once made Russians gasp with amazement, but they have been managerially rejuvenated.

Well-known landmarks, symbols of historic companies, disappeared over-night in the feverish and turbulent 1980s. The world's largest, and almost the tallest, office building, erected in a year over railroad tracks kept open on Park Avenue, New York, was built by Pan American Airways as their headquarters before they went bankrupt. Where the PAN AM sign stretched across the top, visible forty blocks down Park Avenue, a new and unknown owner's name now glows at night. Helicopters no longer land on the roof and the Pan Am planes, once familiar worldwide, may never be seen again. The RCA building in the Rockefeller Center also has a strange new name on its summit. The parents of airlines and of radio-television have been decapitated. Televisions were once made nowhere but in the USA and in Britain, the country of Baird, their inventor. Now they are nearly all made in Japan. All eleven skyscrapers built at the Center by the Rockefeller family were sold to the Japanese. All the world's farmers had learned to respect America's Caterpillar, maker of farm machinery and tractors, so the news that they might be turning the corner after difficult times came as a relief.

Boeing, whose factories include the largest building of any kind in the world, has been having some trouble competing with Airbus and trying to win the argument as to which of them gets the largest government subsidy. America's airlines – and indeed some of Europe's – impoverished by the cut-throat competition between them, can no longer afford to replace their old stock with new air liners or even to lease them. Then we had the spectacle of Boeing and McDonnell Douglas executives almost in tears of relief when Saudi Arabia eventually turned down Airbus and placed a $6 billion order with Boeing. This mattered enough to the whole country for the USA's President himself to receive the Saudi Arabian and American signatories to the White House and be seen with them on national television. The order, though big, will not lead to an expansion in the Boeing labour force, but only forestall the massive lay-offs that had to be envisaged.

London and Liverpool, once the centres of world commerce, became almost like ghost towns in the docklands. The Royal Navy's ports have been cut to the bone; a navy which at the beginning of the century had twenty full-scale battleships capable of firing shells as heavy as cars now has to import its few nuclear submarines in order to have something in which to go to sea. Clydeside, where the great Cunard liners including the QE2 were built, is almost forgotten. When the QE2 was damaged recently in the USA, neither Boston nor the Clyde were capable of repairing it: that had to be done in Germany. The subsequent public relations disaster of disgruntled passengers on an only partly refurbished ship possibly exemplified management decline in senile corporations, although today it is not difficult to succeed in the cruise business due to the growing wealth of the wealthy and their need for security.

In the port of London, modern developments like St Catherine's docks are quite decorative and pleasant for tourists, but it was hardly reassuring to find Canary Wharf going bankrupt before it was finished. There was long delay before money was found to build an extension of the underground rail to the docklands, while the matching by Britain of France's high speeds on the rail service through the Channel Tunnel to London may not be attained for some years. The London underground transport system, the world's first and largest, is now about the world's least well-maintained. Britain now shares the USA's reluctance to subsidise public transport.

More encouraging, early in 1994, were reports about an economic revival in Lancashire and north-west England. The old textile and other factories were being replaced by high-tech companies attracted by the lower costs, including well-skilled workers at moderate wages. Lancashire was doing as well or better than Massachusetts, with the end of the cold war shifting major military production to more peaceful applications of advanced technology. The economic gap between north and south Britain, decried by Benjamin Disraeli, may continue to narrow.

Americans, including former Senator Paul Tsongas (Massachusetts' highly regarded politician with statesmanlike qualities), are deeply worried to see the withering away of the manufacturing base of the American economy. Academic, financial and other opinions are often more sanguine about such developments. Trade economists said in the 1950s that India should specialise heavily in iron and steel production. Although US plants in Pittsburgh and elsewhere were more efficient, America's efficiency in wheat production (based on huge-scale production and unlimited cheap sources of fuel, power and capital) was greater still: both the USA and India would be best off exporting wheat and steel respectively.

The history of the American steel industry illustrates the structural drawbacks of the lack of competition. It had a pricing system for steel products called 'Pittsburgh plus', which effectively eliminated price competition in the American steel market and reduced the incentive for the industry to keep itself up-to-date. Pittsburgh eventually achieved a remarkable turnaround. The city itself cleaned up its act and converted itself from a notoriously polluted centre of 'smokestack industry' into a handsome, clean city, now considered an agreeable place to live. The city's steel mills were fully modernised and, albeit at a lower level of output, can now supply the world steel market at the world price and still make an adequate profit.

There is current talk in Washington about the Third Wave – the coming information age – and scorn is often poured on those who weep and worry about the decline of manufacturing and other monuments of the old and receding Second Wave. Great confidence is placed, probably misplaced, in the promise of prosperity offered by further rises in the share of the national income gained by the services sector. It is true that the service sector may, in future, provide more employment. However, it may well offer falling earnings: if education development is adequate and the exemption of the medico-legal monopolies from anti-trust suits is ended, there may be a reduction in the scarcity value of high-level manpower in service-type activities.

The American economy has proved itself vigorous and innovative enough to grow at a pace that generates new jobs at a higher rate (as a percentage of total jobs) than in any other major and mature economy. The failure to cut back unemployment as much as is desired is caused by the fact that, though employment is rising relatively fast, the labour force seeking employment is growing still faster. Economic growth that fails to reduce unemployment has been called 'growth recession'. We have to act on both sides: on the demand for labour and on its supply (see Box 3.11, p. 92).

What is positive and what is negative about the course structural changes we are following? In the main, they have the virtue of necessity: they are adjustments made to stay in business so far as possible in the face of stiff international competition, which is being maintained by trade agreements, the most recent being the completed Uruguay Round of the General Conference on Trade and Tariffs (GATT) and the establishment of the World Trade Organisation.

In the USA, competition in the domestic market, always pretty vigorous, has been intensified in the last two decades by a number of developments. First, by 1970 the USA had lost some temporary privileges it had enjoyed in the prosperous 1950s and 1960s (due to the pre-eminence of its economy and the relatively smaller strength of other industrial countries) which have subsequently withered away. For example, they had permitted a relative overpayment of American auto-workers which can never happen again. Some of the other industrialised countries, notably Japan and Germany, have become economic superpowers; China and others are not too far behind. Second, particularly since the preponderance of Republican Party Presidents, many protective regulations of parts of the American economy have been stripped away and competition in those areas has become intense. A notable example is the airline industry; another is telephones. The cost of air travel, per passenger mile, has fallen in North America far below the high costs still prevalent in Europe. The same applies to telephone charges per minute per mile, which are far cheaper in the USA. Some prices in the USA are much lower, not only because of lower costs and reduced profit margins, but because of lower taxation there than in the rest of the world. For instance, gasoline and diesel fuel in the USA is only about a quarter of the cost in Europe, where more than half the price goes in government tax.

Also, in the USA, anti-monopoly policy and legislation has had a longer history and has developed sharper teeth than in Europe. Indeed, there are few examples of the cosy monopolies still present in Europe – and even in Japan – that hold back intense competition. Thus the USA economy has been forced to restructure itself so as to be more efficient and competitive. Workers – and employers – in positions still protected in Europe and Japan have already lost their jobs in the USA.

The degree of monopoly power is reflected in market shares and in the level of difficulty in entering certain occupations and of becoming established as a new firm entrant to an industry. It seems that if you can open a shop in Sweden, relatively high shop prices and the modest degree of competition permit you, like nearly all Swedish shopkeepers, to prosper without difficulty. By way of contrast, in the USA shops are continually opening and shutting, rising and falling; the competition is so intense that only the fittest survive. Many mergers of US corporations, both vertically and horizontally, are motivated by the need to cut costs and preserve profit-making.

Some occupations, normally rather precarious, do seem to survive because the nature of their business requires or permits the bulk of transactions being conducted in cash. This facilitates tax evasion by those who could not otherwise make a profit. Many American business leaders complain that they have difficulty in competing with foreign companies in the world market (and even in the US market) because they bear heavier taxes and labour and other costs. These must involve government regulations on such things as safety and hygiene, occupational health and safety, fair employment practices, medical and other insurance, the reduction of pollution and protection of the environment, reporting require- ments and so forth. The truth is that several of the other rich countries are even more burdened than the USA in exactly these ways. Although the poor countries are less burdened in these respects, they are arguably more burdened in others. Judged and measured by the benchmarks, conceptions and ideals of the rich countries, many of the poor ones are just plain backward. The USA is a giant in a world of pygmies and beggars and a few solid and stolid burghers!

It is frankly a paradox, almost a parody of self-pity, to hear American business people so often and readily complaining that they have such a hard struggle to compete with the rest of the world and to give their workers as much as employers elsewhere, when they live in a country with unparalleled advantages and a comparatively unblemished history. When US minimum wages are lower in purchasing power than they have been for decades, business people today say they cannot afford to pay any more.

Japan's economic success is believed to partly reflect the quality of management there. Notable is their paternalistic, 'happy family' policy in large corporations which generated team spirit and fidelity to the company and to its aims and policies. In a more limited way, something similar once happened in the USA. Lester Thurow, Professor of Management and Economics at Massachusetts Institute of Technology, put it this way when speaking about a post-Second World War 'social contract between employers and employees' which 'was never offered to everyone'. Nevertheless:

> employers implicitly offered 60 to 70 per cent of the workforce lifetime employment with career ladders at good wages in exchange for workers who agreed to work hard, willingly accept the training and hence career picked out for them by their firms, and agreed to disruptions in family life that frequent geographic transfers required. Firms wanted more profits but active effort to lower wages were not a permissible route to higher profits unless the firm was going broke ...
>
> In many ways, this implicit social contract was unique to the postwar period. It certainly did not exist in the 1930s. After the war American economic dominance was so huge that foreigners could only compete in those markets where Americans chose not to compete. Foreigners did not have the technology to directly compete with Americans. Military strategy dictated that defense procurement was an American monopoly. Military contractors were among the most generous of employers.

His latter point looms large today when we think of the blow to the current economy of the big reductions in military procurement post-cold war and the end of the Pentagon's cold war generosity to research, development and innovation. Professor Thurow continues:

> With the Cold War over and telecommunications and transportation making it possible to make anything wherever costs are lowest and sell it wherever prices are highest, economic activity is going to move back and forth around the world at a pace never seen before ... The political climate has changed and it is now 'all right' for even profitable firms to explicitly cut wages to enlarge already large profits. The first wave of downsizings in the late 1980s and early 1990s occurred among firms facing economic oblivion. But in the mid-1990s were mostly occurring among firms that were profitable before the downsizings began ...
>
> Younger workers are going to see the world very differently. For them there will be no point in working hard, accept in training that benefits only the firm or in agreeing to be transferred. They know they are going to be downsized regardless of whether they contribute to the firm's success ... Yet no employer can create a learning organization and a high-productivity environment if employees are simply working to rule (doing exactly what the employer asks them to do – no more; no less) and unwilling to make those extra voluntary efforts that are the difference between excellence and mediocrity ... Esprit de corps is the essence of any successful corporation.
>
> Workers without tenure in their company, expecting several job

changes in a lifetime, will decide for themselves what portable skills they will acquire to help them build their own career. 'Firms can no longer unilaterally make human investment decisions' and mould their workforce to their own requirements . . . [Thurow hopes] government would use its training grants and the tax deductibility of training to force a faster adjustment.[20]

Mention should be made of two items left out of Thurow's picture. One is that younger as well as habitual older workers may try to satisfy employers out of sheer fear of job loss. The other is this. The disappearance of any reason to feel morally obligated to the employer, or to sympathise with and emulate them, could produce another political change among both employed and laid-off workers, parallel to the political swing Thurow mentions as making employers unashamed and aggressive in their greed and opportunism. That political swing could swell to a majority of voters in the USA antipathetic to 'business as usual' as well as to 'politics as usual'. After all, there are many more workers than employers and each has only one vote.

Foreign trade

Prominent among factors which have both positive and negative effects on employment are international trade and technological progress. They are obviously allied. It is said that 'necessity is the mother of invention'; it is indeed true that growing trade across the world is economically stimulating and challenging. It calls for increases in productivity to be able to compete; and technological progress is the principal motor of productivity improvement.

A basic distinction should be drawn between countries that are heavily dependent on international trade and those that are not. The extreme case of the former group are such city states as Hong Kong and Singapore. They have large imports and exports, each constituting a major part of their national income. They are also major examples of entrepôt traders – they are like wholesale traders with huge warehouses. They import and re-export goods and serve as regional distribution centres as well as markets placed strategically on major trade routes, shipping lanes and airline paths. Trade has made them hugely prosperous so that they constitute prolific growth points of the world economy, stimulating through their trade employment at home and overseas.

At the other extreme, there are countries that are large in area, or large in relation to their population, that gain much from trade but would not be crippled if trade were almost extinguished (as happens during world wars). With the resumption of trade after the Second World War, Britain's international trade constituted a quarter of its national income; it would have starved without it, as in the early postwar period it could only produce enough food locally to feed one person in twenty in Britain.

In the case of the USA, international trade in the early postwar period was only 4 per cent of national income. Since then, trade has grown faster, especially since the USA has for long been the main supplier of goods and services to the countries whose economies have grown rapidly since 1950. However, since 1975 the USA has failed to increase its net national income from trade. In the 1977–1978 recession years and in every year since 1982, the USA's balance of payments current account has been a negative percentage of national income. At its worst, it was some –3.6 per cent of national income in 1987; that was at the peak of the boom, when Americans flush with money were heavily importing foreign goods. Since then the negative percentage has dropped, but it is still a cause for anxiety. There is believed to be some link between this deficit and the deficit in the American government's budget, so that reducing the latter might help reduce the former.

In due course German, Japanese and, to a diminishing extent, British industries became major suppliers of the growing industries overseas and ended US predominance of the 1950s and 1960s. France was and still is much less heavily populated than Britain. It is blessed with good natural resources, excellent agricultural land and has little fear of starving in the event of a closure of foreign trade. French farmers, however, especially those with large farms, became spoilt by a changing array of factors – first 'natural' and then 'artificial' – which supported their prosperous lifestyles. The 'artificial' element relates to the bias of the Common Agricultural Policy in supporting high prices for EU food items.

On balance, what does an expanding and freer world trade do for incomes and employment? Before my conclusion, three main viewpoints should be summarised.

First, there are the sceptical, the cautious and the outright *protectionists*. This group includes people across the whole spectrum, including individuals such as the American Ross Perot and the Anglo-French James Goldsmith, both right-wing billionaires, as well as more left-leaning union leaders and columnist economists such as Robert Kuttner. Indeed, arguably the communists who, when in power, practically excluded their countries from the open world market and from conformity with free-trade agreements, could be regarded as participants of this group. For practical purposes, they primarily care about the economic and the social welfare conditions of their *own* country. They think that foreign trade may be worthwhile as a rule if it is carried on with their traditional trading partners, liaisons with whom, from experience, can be regarded as being of net value. But when it comes to *new* trading partners, their attitude to trading liaisons is more hostile. This is so whether they are dynamic, emergent economies (probably the economic giants of the future) or, *a fortiori*, whether they are much poorer countries 'blessed' with cheap labour and freedom from irksome environmental, health and safety regulations and from burdensome social security and other social obligations. This group wants trade with such countries to be tightly controlled and eventually excluded. They are not appalled at the prospect that the world economy might end up being divided into separate trading blocs, having much more trade within blocs than between blocs.

Second, there are the *free traders*. Historically and with due respect we might include among the leadership of this group *The Economist* magazine, which has long engaged in an eloquent and well-reasoned free-trade promotion as its *raison d'être* during one-and-a-half centuries. Others in that camp include the majority of academic and practising economists, together with more worldly wise politicians, major newspaper editors, successful business people and international officials (except some in the regional international organisations). They argue that, overall, world trade expands world income and employment, although admittedly it causes major changes in the location of industries and shifts growth points for employment from shrinking to expanding regions and national economies.

Third, there are a few realists in a *'don't care group'*, who just go fishing when it is time to vote on the matter. They are joined by the *'don't know'* group, with whose ignorance we can sympathise because of the complexity of the issues and the passion of the respective advocates. For example, there are a few economists, led by the eminent Paul Krugman (until recently of Massachusetts Institute of Technology and now of Stanford University), who see less need to get excited about foreign trade one way or the other. Krugman relies less on economic theory and abstract reasoning or emotion than do the debaters. He takes great care to examine the statistics and empirical evidence about where and why expansions and contractions of employment and business activity have actually occurred.

Krugman looks mainly at the United States economy. He points out that international trade is only a tenth of the USA's national income, so whether it is in surplus or deficit makes little difference because the main source of income and employment in the USA remains its huge domestic economy. Krugman says: 'Even though world trade is larger than ever before, national living standards are overwhelmingly determined by domestic factors rather than by some competition for world markets.'[21]

Regarding the concern about US companies laying-off workers in high-paying manufacturing jobs in America and moving work offshore to take advantage of cheap foreign labour, already discussed above, the more general case is different. Krugman's co-author Robert Lawrence notes that US-based multinational corporations cut US payrolls by more than 8 per cent between 1977 and 1989. But the job cuts in the USA have not turned out to be job gains in those companies' foreign affiliates. Quite the opposite: the same companies cut their overseas payrolls by 14 per cent.

It may be added to Krugman's remarks that although many factories lay-off workers, some are even producing greater, not smaller, output because technological progress permits the replacement of workers by machines, with major productivity gains. The *value* of industrial goods in total production shrinks because technological progress and productivity improvement means that prices can be reduced. By way of contrast, the prices of services which are produced less efficiently are rising so that their total value relative to the total value of industrial output is also rising.

Economists distinguish between value in exchange (*exchange value*) and value in use (*utility value*). *Exchange value* simply reflects observed costs and market prices. In so far as we can measure *utility value*, it would be higher than *exchange value* for industrial goods and lower than *exchange value* for services.

According to Krugman, American wages are stagnating, not so much because they have been driven down by foreign competition but because the growth rate of US productivity – the amount workers can produce per hour of effort – has slowed with the rising importance within the economy of less efficiently produced services. 'The nation's plight would be much the same even if world markets had not become more integrated', write Krugman and Lawrence. 'Our trade plays at best a small role' in explaining the nation's problems.

I agree with the free-traders: a world which maximises its income will certainly be and can only be one in which trade is as free as possible. When everyone is encouraged to concentrate on doing what they can do best, output is bound to be higher than it can be when a lot of people are making things that could be imported more cheaply. There will still be frictional and other types of unemployment due to the shifts and growths caused by trends in trade. While free trade by itself will certainly never guarantee full employment, it will in a general and aggregate way reduce the amount of unemployment we would otherwise have under protectionism.

Nevertheless, there is a risk that free trade will, in a particular way, cause major and intolerable levels of unemployment, much of it long-term, in certain places and over certain rather long periods of time. Similarly, it will cause serious losses of income and prosperity in particular places and times. It is politically – and no doubt morally – difficult to expect those places to accept increased hardship for the sake of net gains for world economic prosperity and growth in world employment.

The free-traders say: why worry that much? A prosperous world can afford to provide a social safety net for the victims of progress and somehow to rehabilitate them. It is a partial problem, limited in time, which will ultimately pass. I hope you are right and that I prove to have been unduly pessimistic. But as long as things – mainly capitalism – remain as they are and always have been, there will continue to be substantial unemployment caused by all the factors discussed in this chapter and the previous one. This amount of joblessness is already socially explosive and yet is growing. If, in certain major areas, we allow the free rein of trade to create still more jobless and hopeless on top of the existing total, we may see the start of systemic destruction. Indeed, we may have major rebellions and wars on our hands. Almost nothing restricts free trade as much as war.

For the politicians, the footnote is this. Capitalism and free trade are the ways to make the rich not only richer, but the richest possible, and at the same time to provide bread and circuses for the vocal poor to keep them quiet. Capitalism and free trade do not, for any inherent reason, restrict the increase in the numbers of the poor or the depth of their poverty.

Baumol's disease

The relation between men and machines is ambivalent. On the positive side, machines enhance the status and earnings of workers by raising their output per head and reducing their drudgery and discomfort. On the negative side (socially though not economically) a rapidly increasing number of machines – the robot types – can do the work better than the workers who did it before and can do it alone. So the workers lose their jobs, although some better qualified workers might be needed indirectly to design and operate these machines.

However, there are areas of work where technology has not, as yet, contributed useful equipment. Speaking specifically, it is striking that any symphony orchestra member has had nothing more than their instruments for centuries (some of them were better made in the past) to enable them to increase their output per day. Speed-up is out of the question with music. Top-rate orchestra players earn $50,000 a year and it costs $5,000,000 a year to employ a hundred-piece orchestra, even before any other expenses. But the cost of artists – even of a Pavarotti – does not matter much in so far as technology makes music readily available under every roof and inside every form of transport by means of recording and reproduction equipment. The quality of that equipment has risen so rapidly that many now question the superiority of live performances before live audiences. The Canadian pianist Glen Gould gave up his worldwide concert tours and said that in future he would only produce recordings of his work. He argued that they were of better quality than his 'live' work and he considered the pre-recorded process of diffusion and entertainment to be more economic and efficient.

The superiority of live performance remains a more compelling argument in acting than in music-making; theatre performances are different from watching films and surfing videos at home. Sports performances, though, come through quite well on worldwide television. The price gap between seat tickets and cable TV continually widens.

Nevertheless, a majority of professional workers using mainly knowledge-based skills have had their productivity increased enormously by computers. Many can use computerised databases more quickly than libraries and librarians and can cover larger volumes of knowledge.

Librarians themselves use them, as do lawyers to trace case law. Doctors use them to help with diagnosis and currently available treatments. Indeed, computers may soon be available with built-in safety checks and foolproof devices, to reduce human failure in communicating prescriptions and dosing the medicines. A major study revealed that for every hundred admissions to the Massachusetts General and Brigham and Women's Hospitals, there were 6.5 life-threatening, serious or significant medication-related injuries.[22] At a more manual, paper-shifting and sifting level, there are office staffs with automated processes and procedures and banks with automatic teller machines, helping to conquer much of the drudgery of operations in such environments and raising output per head.

Professor William Baumol of Princeton University has made a major contribution by identifying the significance of the service sector (and a few other occupations) being inherently and inescapably labour intensive in operation. Perhaps to Dr Baumol's irritation, this costly and inescapable labour intensity has been called 'Baumol's disease'. Parkinson was no doubt also a good man, but his 'disease' came down to us with a name as bad as cancer, though perhaps mellowed when blended with our memories recalling the good humour and telling truth of Parkinson's law. Parkinson's law was a cousin of Baumol's disease. It recognised the tendency of work to spread over the time available for it and for work supervisors to proliferate. We will return later to Professor Baumol's citation of the health care sector as exemplifying the problem of expensive labour intensity.

In a letter to me, Professor Baumol pointed out that 'the US is not losing its place in manufacturing. The data I have gathered indicate that the US share of the world's *industrial employment* has exhibited a marked upward trend throughout the postwar period. Moreover, while it is true that the share of the US labor force engaged in the services has risen sharply, taken as a percent of the labor force, it has risen far more sharply in every industrialized country except New Zealand.'

Such facts have to be established on the basis of those countries providing valid statistics of their total industrial employment, such as the selection in the ILO's *International Yearbook of Labour Statistics*. Unfortunately, data from some sources must be treated with some caution. (In 1988, I visited an iron and steel plant in Ainshan, Liaoning Province, China, where the manager claimed to have some 400,000 employees in that plant. It appeared no more than two or three times the size of a modest Stewarts and Lloyds iron and steel plant I visited in Corby, England, in 1936. The latter closed down entirely, decades ago.)

New Zealand once had a strong safety net, generous social policies and a considerable public sector. More recently it has swung over to incorporate major cuts in its national budget and public employment, reining back its economic interventions in favour of a freer and larger private enterprise sector. It achieved this, rightly or wrongly, well before other countries emitted much rhetoric pointing in the same direction. It may also prove to be ahead of the pack in having some second thoughts as to whether it has thrown out the baby with the bath water!

Agriculture and industry in the USA are so efficient that they are cheap, largely because of advances in technology. Services are inefficient and expensive, despite all their self-promotion, largely because of Baumol's disease. Their main 'blessing' is that they provide a lot of today's employment. To do so in future, they will arguably require a better educated workforce. Brain-intensive work has more value in production than manual labour and it may be more difficult to displace by machines; pure human brawn is readily displaced by machines. Education, even if Baumol-diseased too, must be expanded and improved.

Fine minds can do applied research into problems where there are millions of possibilities or factors. Going still further, fine minds engaged in pure research have no single problem which needs an answer. They just roam around the shop, trying everything for taste. They can surprise themselves and us by coming on penicillin and other useful novelties. Try inviting a computer to engage in pure research. A cast of thousands would soon be pouring more data into the computer at its own request, but with little creative outcome.

Any human mind is a miracle of nature and a fine one is unparalleled in the physical universe. People possessing such minds can be worth paying heavily in money or honour to perform as they can. They will excel even when they only have the clothes they stand up in; even when as paralysed as a Stephen Hawking. The incidence of Baumol's disease may be expected to vary inversely with employees' level of education and their intelligence quotient (IQ). The challenges to education and technology are imposing. T.S. Eliot wrote:

Where is the Life we have lost in living?
Where is the wisdom we have lost in knowledge?
Where is the knowledge we have lost in information?
(T.S. Eliot, Choruses from 'The Rock')

Wisdom cannot be computerised. Analysis – *maybe!*

The mixed blessings of machines

The substitution of machines does not matter so much in occupations in which the volume of work is rapidly expanding. Again, a favourable impact occurs where the use of computers and word-processing software removes much of the drudgery and repetition in secretarial work, releasing the more intelligent secretaries to move upward to the point of becoming personal assistants in various ways. Some secretaries, originally below middle-management level, are now constantly increasing their productivity and widening their scope. They are closer to their bosses, know their minds and requirements and come to be more trusted than middle-management cadres. Under the contemporary 'mean and lean' approach in corporate life, the staff side has been thinned down between top management and line supervisors. These super-secretaries first-draft and deliver orders approved by top management down the line, with dwindling assistance, advice or impediment from intermediate 'managers'.

Other 'staff' or advisory personnel, such as economists and PR folk, are often replaced by cheaper, *ad hoc* consultant services as and when needed. In some instances they might eventually be replaced by machines. Long ago an expert produced a computer programme. It could replace his company's entire accounting department, including its vice-president. The expert was given a prize and transferred by his company to a foreign branch. The vice-president stayed, having advised that the programme was inadequate to replace him and his people.

In the 1960s, J. K. Galbraith argued in a major treatise that in large corporations (though not in small 'entrepreneurial' corporations) there were large staffs below the top management level who really ran the corporations, with top management rubber-stamping their actions and decisions. He did not call these middle managers but 'the technostructure', consisting of specialists in the different branches of modern management and technology. They were so powerful as to usurp the power of share-holders and reverse the interaction between producers and consumers, so that instead of consumer sovereignty the producers brainwashed the consumers about what they really wanted. Competition was largely muted, except in the small-scale retail trade and outside manufacture. This was necessary to achieve the steady long-term growth required by industrial planning and applied technology and suggested a rather secure and stable economy.[23] In fact, it was the sort of economy the USA had in the 1960s. This view may seem rather dated given the growth of global corporations and the expansion and increased intensity of international trade which has tended to restore consumer sovereignty, promote vigorous competition and inject more instability into the economy. Much of the 'technostructure' has been replaced, in terms of employment opportunity, with more highly skilled personnel aided by high-technology equipment.

Nevertheless, if we care to open our eyes and look around, there are numerous menial jobs that must still be done, cannot be mechanised and few people willing to accept menial wages to do them. Offices are filthy, computer screens dusty, keyboards splashed with last week's coffee; office-cleaning is reduced to a quick run over the wall-to-wall carpeting with vacuum cleaners. Poor, old immigrant women may still scrub the marble floors in the most elegant entrances at dawn, so that they may bear the elegant shoes of top management and VIPs skimming through. On their way out, the top crust may notice a tailored lawn and a regiment of flowers saluting them between the great door and the limousine.

Millions of homes need household help. Millions of children return from schools to empty, run-down homes, waiting for the return of their tired, edgy parents. Millions of old, sick people lie at home dreaming wistfully of the days when people called at the door to serve them. When the bell rings now, they quake in fear.

Labour-intensive, highly (socially) valued activities await an imaginative policy matching the unemployed to these unstaffed vacancies. The underclass should be mobilised to do some of these jobs. Welfare-reform programmes are beginning to seek out means of linking benefit receipts to the provision of much-needed services of a labour-intensive variety.

Chronic unemployment: too many workers, fit or not

At the beginning of Part III, emphasis was laid on two overwhelming factors in long-term employment: the population explosion and the entry of almost all women into paid employment. These factors are much at work in chronic unemployment. The shifting of unemployed workers from short- to long-term unemployment, thereby adding to the ranks of chronic

Box 3.17: Unemployment 1993–1994 in Western countries

Annualised growth in GDP, percentages and unemployment (percentage of labour force not working):

	GDP 1994	GDP 1993	Unemployment 1994	Unemployment 1993
Australia	7.7	5.0	10.0	11.1
Austria	1.4	3.0	6.7	6.9
Belgium	na	−1.3	13.1	12.1
Britain	3.6	3.3	9.4	10.3
Canada	4.2	3.4	10.3	11.3
Denmark	1.7	5.0	12.4	12.2
France	1.9	0.8	12.6	11.7
Germany	2.2	1.6	8.4	7.3
Holland	4.0	1.9	7.2	6.2
Italy	0.3	0.6	11.6	11.3
Japan	3.9	nil	2.9	2.5
Spain	2.9	0.8	24.6	21.7
Sweden	0.6	1.5	8.5	9.0
Switzerland	1.3	1.1	4.6	4.4
USA	3.7	4.0	6.0	6.9

TENL, 6 August 1994

unemployment is a major problem for many governments, as is the decoupling of the previous link between rises in GDP and rises in employment (falls in unemployment). This can be seen in the experience of the major economies since 1993 (Box 3.17).

Note that in Belgium, Denmark, France, Germany, Holland, Italy, Japan, Spain and Switzerland unemployment got worse, though GDP was increasing (except in Belgium, where it actually shrunk). The two columns for GDP indicate where its growth was accelerating (Australia, Britain, Canada, France, Germany, Holland, Japan, Spain and Switzerland) and where it was decelerating (Austria, Denmark, Italy, Sweden and the USA).

In 1994, France, Germany, Holland, Japan, Spain and Switzerland were the countries that were having worsening unemployment even though their GDP was not only growing but growing at an accelerating rate. France and Spain were the most chronic cases, with unemployment as high as one worker in eight and one worker in four respectively. It has been reported in the press that some of the 'unemployed' in Spain are not admitting to their employment.

In statistics, an important distinction is drawn between short- and long-term unemployment. For example, OECD gives the following proportions of unemployed people in Europe out of work for more than a year. The problem is more evident there than in the USA, where it would be hard to get unemployment insurance payments for such long periods:

Table 3.3

Country	Long-term unemployed as % of all unemployed in 1992	
Spain	50.1	(1993)
Finland	8.2	
Ireland	60.2	
France	34.2	
Italy	58.2	
Denmark	27.0	
Belgium	59.0	
Greece	49.7	
Britain	35.4	
Holland	44.0	
Sweden	10.9	
Portugal	30.9	
Austria	16.9	(1993)
Western Germany	33.5	
Norway	27.0	
Switzerland	20.6	(1993)
Luxembourg	17.6	

For all these countries, long-term unemployment is a grave problem. It is most serious in many of the countries at the upper end of Table 3.3, since the countries are named in descending order as regards the percentage of total unemployment in their labour force in the year indicated. Thus nearly a quarter of all workers in Spain were unemployed and more than half of them – one worker in eight – had been out of work for more than a year. In Ireland, one person in six was unemployed and nearly one person in ten were long-term unemployed. Altogether, more than 40 per cent of the 17 million unemployed in the European Union had been out of work for at least a year; indeed, a third had never worked at all. In the USA only 11 per cent of the unemployed had been looking for work for more than a year.

Another aspect of the unemployment situation was chronic, too: namely, the far higher levels of unemployment among youths (workers under age 25) than among workers in general. In France, Italy, Greece, Sweden and Norway the unemployment rates among youths were at least twice as high as the general rates for all the unemployed. In Spain nearly one youth in two was out of work. The trend in overall unemployment in Europe has moved steadily upward, from about 2 per cent in 1970 to more than 10 per cent in 1994 (Box 3.18).

Box 3.18: EU unemployment

The unemployment rate in the European Union hovered just above 2% till the oil shock of 1974, when it soared upward to over 4% in 1976, slowed off at 5% in 1978, then gathered speed up to 10% by 1982: a recession year. It dropped to 8% in 1988 and then, before the next European recession, it went up to around 9% in 1992 and reached nearly 11% in 1994.

Source: OECD

With a sense of the gravity of the matter revealed by these figures, we now elucidate what are the facts that lie behind them.

There is a category of would-be workers nastily named the 'unemployables'. This can be taken to mean many different kinds of people in a variety of situations. In the strict sense, the 'unemployables' are those whom no employer would take on wherever they are located and whatever the situation. We should exclude the genuinely disabled and retired people from this category. The ageing process may cause people to succumb to some of the following difficulties: get tired too easily; have a weak short-term memory (though keeping a strong long-term memory); difficulty in learning and readapting; perhaps a dwindling gift for teamwork; less openness of mind; diminished readiness to accept and build on innovations.

Nevertheless, many disabled and retirees can perform a range of jobs and perhaps do them better than anyone else, because those jobs require a kind of concentration and depth of experience which go with the focused minds and bodies they have developed.

Unemployables might more realistically include people who prefer to be free and live on a lower income on the dole or social relief. Nevertheless, they may be obliged to say they are looking for work even though they are not.

When the difference between the incomes of the employed and the unemployed becomes too small, incentives may be created for non-workaholic people to choose a life of idleness. This unemployment is caused by the net income differential in favour of being unemployed, when we take account of the other benefits that they receive because they are unemployed and what they would lose in benefit should they move into gainful employment. If you are offered a job only at low pay, it is not easy to give up immediately such benefits as help with your mortgage payments; a credit on your income tax return payable to those with little or no earned income; social relief due to the family members when the breadwinner is unemployed and the medical care and medicines you receive entirely free. In contrast the employed have to pay taxes or contributions in order to obtain all these benefits.

These flaws in the system which put an unfair burden on employed workers are a festering cause of resentment. They have led to a strong political backlash, as well as having an impact on the structure of the economy. In a similar way, there are other well-meaning gestures which become targets for backlash and retribution:

- assistance to refugees which is more generous than that given to citizens, whether employed or unemployed;

- the costs of incarcerating each criminal in prison exceeding a nation's average *family* income; and

- other arrangements seen by some as putting more 'passengers' on the back of working people and tax-payers.

The ranks of unemployables certainly include people unfit for work though not classifiable as disabled. They have problems similar to those of a large fraction of homeless people: drink and other addictions; mental problems, sometimes associated with rejection by their families or simple loss of relatives and any friends; rootlessness, restlessness and an inability to stay fixed to any obligation like regular work. Finally, there are the totally uneducated and ignorant. From UN experience I know that the informally educated (e.g. by relatives) in some poor but cultured countries are better informed and more highly skilled than formally educated workers in the more disadvantaged rural areas and inner-city localities of the the USA.

Those with a low IQ could also have trouble finding and keeping a job in an increasingly technocratic age. But they are not necessarily unemployable; perennial trouble-makers make the worst trouble when they have a high IQ!

These factors are not, in total, a large enough reason to think of unemployable people as unworthy. More than half of them in the more advanced countries and more than three quarters of them in poor countries are unemployable simply because they are utterly surplus. There are not enough jobs to be done to employ all the world's huge population and there is not enough land or capital for everybody to have the means to employ themselves if there is no employer who can take them on.

Those who join the world army of economic migrants may not find a job even if they manage to move to a better place than their country of origin. Arguably they are eminently employable in the sense that they have courage and initiative and know they must try very hard to compete. They often speedily learn the local language and bring some useful skills with them. Nevertheless, they suffer from many problems and impediments. There are too many of them and not enough jobs, especially if they arrive when there is a recession in their host country. They are not welcomed and admitted by the local labour unions and professional associations. They may be more skilled than the locals; all the more reason to exclude them or oblige them to repeat all the studies and training they had abroad. Many jobs are closed to people who do not have citizenship.

Theoretically, no jobs at all are open to illegal aliens who got into the country without a proper visa and work permit. If illegal aliens get jobs, they tend to be the least well-paid – and they are savagely exploited.

People easily distinguishable for their race and religion are often discriminated against, not only by employers but also by other antagonistic ethnic and religious groups. An employer cannot risk mixing them in the workplace with others, even if he has himself no prejudice. Some nationalities have a bad reputation because of the perceived behaviour of their national leaders: a clear case of the sins of the fathers being visited onto the sons.

A few nationalities are welcome to employers because of their good reputation as workers. Notably, they include some Asian countries, whose people are hardworking and reliable, learn quickly and do not have customs, cultures and habits considered awkward or hostile. American university people today are heard to say 'Thank God for the Asians'. They are high-performing students regarded as valuable acquisitions to faculties and research groups who are often less demanding than complacent citizens accustomed to expecting and often receiving high incomes and social status on graduation or advanced degree status.

Among the millions of the chronically unemployed are those not counted in statistics because they have given up looking for a job altogether. They have simply lost any hope of finding one.

When counting the unemployed, it is hard to differentiate between all the causes. There are people who never had a job and will never find one. Hundreds of thousands of school-leavers in the USA in the 1930s found no job until the Second World War and they could join the army in 1941. When this happens today to some young people, and no war comes along to save them, they drift into the 'outer-class': those who have abandoned society, ignoring its benefits, obligations, laws, customs and ethics. Other chronically unemployed people may eventually end up in the outer-class.

We noted above in connection with business cycles that unemployment rises in a recession and fails to fall during the recovery to a level as low as it was before the recession. It is possible that some of those people who lose their jobs during a recession and do not find another during the recovery are destined to join the ranks of the chronically unemployed. The risk of that happening appears to be greater in Europe than in the USA.

Lay-offs attributed to the economic situation ('it's the economy') are, in the case of some workers, a way in which the economy purges itself of its least productive employees – at whatever level they aspire to work – and of employees who are regarded by their current employers as not worth their pay.

Part-time employment

Until the slump of 1991, it was on the workers' side, especially among women workers, that we heard more complaints about inadequate opportunities for part-time employment in the USA. Today it is employers who mainly want part-time workers and their strong demand often brings into this category workers who would prefer full-time jobs.

Governments effectively discourage part-time work by piling on the backs of employers the same burdens of bureaucracy and social policy interventions applicable to the legal employment of full-time workers. Little official or corporate help is given to childcare facilities for infant and pre-school children. Women's organisations would do well to help the setting-up of more practical assistance to women in working life, especially working mothers.

So now we have two apparently contradictory requirements, which can be complementary if well-coordinated. On the one hand, part-time employment requires official encouragement for the sake of women, child-bearing and family life and for legitimate work-spreading wherever serious unemployment is chronic; on the other hand, there is a need for official combating of the abuse of 'part-time employment' as a device for undercutting minimum standards in working conditions and terms of employment.

Contractors and consultants

In recent years, employers have shifted much of the cost of doing business to employees through such measures as wage concessions, health benefit reductions and temporary worker status. Now there is a new wrinkle – one that rids employers of employees altogether.[24]

A recent Congressional report called the practice of wilfully misclassifying employees as independent contractors is arguably a 'pervasive and serious problem'. Workers are paid in cash and the employers duck expenses such as the witholding of federal and state income taxes, FICA taxes (social security), payment of unemployment compensation and payment of workers' accident insurance.

These costs can be substantial. In the case of a contractor who hires carpenters, for example, they amount to 58 per cent of the basic wage rate. In construction, therefore, the powerful financial incentive to misclassify has pushed the cash-based practices of the underground economy from the margins to the mainstream. Work forces of independent contractors are building multi-million-dollar projects today in Massachusetts.

Under these conditions, how can a legitimate employer who, in President Clinton's words, 'plays by the rules' compete? In today's world of work, the constant drumbeat to be competitive is not the concept of fair competition taught to school children. It is a myth that all players follow the same rules so that hard work, talent, persistence, ingenuity are rewarded. In many industries today, there is no such level playing field. Instead such players compete on the basis of the greatest willingness to undermine working people's standards . . . Under these pressures, non-union builders rarely provide health insurance, pension benefits or training programs for young workers, let alone decent wages. And with the independent contractor scam, these employers flout legal as well as social obligations to employees . . . Employers in a host of industries, from blue-collar to professional services, are fleeing legally mandated financial obligations in order to cut costs and be competitive. If mandated national health insurance is ever introduced, even more employers will pursue the employee misclassification route.[24]

This is one side of the picture. The other is that there are working people who prefer to serve as 'contractors' or as 'consultants' because they do not like having to handle all the payments and paperwork of taxation and benefit schemes any more than regular employers do. They prefer to reduce the taxation on themselves and arrange their own social security. In the USA if you are registered as self-employed you have to pay heavy income taxes on your earnings, plus a 15 per cent 'self-employment tax' in lieu of the social security contributions you are not making.

Under-employment and low productivity in poor countries

'Unemployment' – living without a job – is only possible where there is some insurance or relief scheme. In poor countries these do not exist. People work desperately at whatever they can to earn their subsistence. But they cannot use much of their time productively for lack of one or all of the following: land, capital, tools and training. The main way to help them toward full and productive employment is through economic development, which will bring increased access to capital and training. More land can be provided to the landless to cultivate, but not much cultivable land still remains, ready to be cleared, settled and brought into production. Cleared 'retired' land in rich countries might be brought back into production when world food shortages occur in the next century.

I had twenty years' experience with the UN World Food Program organising projects to do these things in poor countries. Many of them were food-for-work schemes: we provided food in lieu of wages and there were many hungry people ready to work for food alone. (It was not agreed by donor governments then that the food might be sold to finance job creation and wage payment.) With more food we could have done much more. There were 'mountains' of surplus food in storage and going to waste in Europe – even 'lakes' of surplus wine. The main problem is that the cost of transporting the food to the poor areas of the least-developed countries is expensive, especially when overland transport is required, and our cash was limited. It is easy to give surplus food. It is hard to give scarce cash. It costs a lot of money to store food for years and that money could be used to transport it, but government accountants don't or won't work that way. The full solution to the problem is like a pair of scissors: one blade stands for economic development; the other stands for birth control, to reduce the number of destitute babies being born to destitute people whom no one can or will help.

A separate book needs to be written about the two faces of economics in poor countries because the situation is so different. Few can have the chance I had of seeing one hundred and twenty countries in a lifetime, many of them several times. Our image of poor countries in the West depends on hearsay, tear-jerking pictures and an array of statistics. But then, how do we imagine a family living on an annual income of no more than what some people pay for a single night in a hotel of a major European or American city? The under-employment, the poverty and other ills are subsumed in various, rather impersonal, statistics (Box 3.19).

Poor countries, like others, need imports. They also need to borrow money, which is only easily done if they have a record of paying off old debts. How can these countries pay for even vital imports when the following percentages of their income from exports in 1993 have to go to pay off principal and interest on old debts: Ecuador (57 per cent); Bolivia (47 per cent); Peru, Nigeria and Argentina (each about 45 per cent); Brazil

Box 3.19: Economic and social indicators for poor countries

According to the United Nations Development Programme (UNDP) over two-thirds of the 1.3 billion people in the world recorded as 'poor' live in the following ten countries:

(in brackets: poor people, and their share of total population)

Bangladesh (93 million, 80%)   India (350 million, 40%)
Ethiopia (60%)   Nigeria (46 million, 40%)
Vietnam (just over half)   Pakistan (28%)
Philippines (just over half)   Indonesia (25%)
Brazil (72 million, 49%)   China (105 million, 10%)

(over 40 per cent); Colombia, Mexico and Ivory Coast (just under 40 per cent); Uruguay, Morocco and Venezuela (around 30 per cent); Chile (25 per cent); Philippines (20 per cent). (Source: Morgan Guaranty Trust Co.)

UNDP produced its 'human-development index' for 173 countries as an alternative measure of relative living standards.[25] It combines life expectancy, adult literacy, average years of schooling and Gross Domestic Product per head (measured at PPP: i.e. at purchasing power parity, bringing dollar value differences between countries into conformity with cost of living levels rather than with market exchange rates). This index gives quite another picture of the different degrees of wealth or well-being than that given by figures of gross national product (GNP) per capita (pc). Out of 173 countries, China is 143rd in GNP pc but 94th in the human development index. On the contrary, Gabon is 42nd in GNP pc but 114th in the index. Similarly South Africa, Saudi Arabia and the United Arab Emirates also rank lower in the index than their wealth would suggest. For rich countries the difference in ranking tends to be smaller. In 1994 Canada, though it came 11th in GDP pc in the world, stood at the top of UNDP's index. Switzerland, the world's wealthiest country (top in GNP pc), also came second only to Canada in the index. Japan had topped the index in 1993 but fell back to third place after Canada and Switzerland in 1994. France, USA, Britain, and Germany, in that order, were close to the top of the index and well up in GNP pc. Clearly GNP figures do not always give an accurate picture of the true standard of living.

Women in the poor world get the wrong end of the stick, as usual. Girls spend fewer years at school than boys. The differences are the greatest in South Asia and the Middle East, but rather small in Latin America. In Uruguay, for example, girls spend 10 per cent longer at school than boys; in Pakistan only 25 per cent as long. Ranking 112 countries according to the educational status of women. Argentina ranks highest among developing countries, with a score of 93 (not far behind America's 98); but India scores only 50. Families in poor countries often see less point in paying to send daughters to school, assuming that they will marry rather than earn. Girls often stay at home to do domestic chores. But educated women are healthier and produce healthier children. Educating girls is three times more likely to reduce family size than educating boys. (Source on women: Population Action International.)

There is ongoing growth of national incomes in the Third World (Box 3.20) and related, but slower, growth in employment.

Box 3.20: Economic growth in the Third World

Average annual growth rate of GDP

Category of economy	1965–1980	1980–1990
Low-income economies*	4.9	6.1
China	6.8	9.5
India	3.6	5.3
Other low-income	4.8	3.9
Middle-income economies**	6.3	2.5

* Under $580 per year per person in 1989
** Between $580 and $6000 per year per person in 1989

Region		
Sub-Saharan Africa	4.2	2.1
East Asia and Pacific	7.3	7.8
South Asia	3.6	5.2
Latin America and Caribbean	6.0	1.6

Source: World Bank: *World Development Report*, 1992

The World Bank and the International Monetary Fund reported to their fiftieth annual meeting (Madrid, 1994) that the world economy, after struggling through a painful recession and extremely sluggish recovery, is poised to enjoy the strongest growth since the late 1980s. Growth in the industrial world would be 2.6% in 1994 and 2.7% in 1995.

Employment policy and human resources planning

Part III has shown that the reduction of unemployment depends on promoting prosperity and the most rapid rate of economic growth consistent with an acceptable level of inflation. If economists are providing sound guidance and promoting the right policies over the whole range of economic affairs, unemployment should subside considerably. Further help will still be needed from other social scientists.

Training and the education which forms its basis are expensive activities, especially when they are organised to be comprehensive. In poor societies we can be less ambitious: perhaps we can make do by giving workers specific, tightly focused modular training and adding more modules later when required. This means we just teach a man about hammers and nails if that is what he knocks in; later he can also learn about screwdrivers if screws are being introduced into the job. And the process goes on, from wheelbarrows to horse and cart, from carts to tractors, from tractors to trailer trucks and so on.

All the things produced in the world are not put together from raw materials and inputs which start out from something flat, smooth and homogeneous. Our natural resources, as we find them where they lie, come in many shapes and sizes; weights and densities: gas, fluid or solid; and, above all, in many mixtures. We can and sometimes do, break down mixtures – process mineral ores and chemicals – to obtain the basic elements assembled in their molecules. We can then 'reassemble' those elements in the form of the molecules we need, such as plastics and petroleum products.

Otherwise, it is often simpler and cheaper to 'take things as they come'. For example, certain medicines are extremely costly to manufacture in a laboratory: a few may even require weightlessness in the making, calling for production in space shuttles and stations. In contrast, other medicines can be made more easily from animal and plant life. An easy one is the insulin needed to treat diabetics, which can be taken straight from pigs without any processing. A more difficult but still relatively cheap one is to produce medicines from 'in-house farms' of minute organisms, bacteria, etc., which can be induced to provide what is needed.

Our present question relates to one of the most complex natural resources, one that springs to life very cheaply all over the world and becomes capable within two or three decades of making a wide variety of substances and accomplishing the most intelligent work in the universe. I am talking about human beings. Human beings – the 'supply of labour' – must eat, must work and will search relentlessly for work.

Human beings, given the chance, prove how adaptable they are. When young, they are at the best age to learn quickly and retain knowledge and skills. They can undergo years of education, training and concentration. Much of what they study now is chosen and organised by society on the basis of habitual thinking about what 'an educated person' should know and be able to do. For centuries before the present one, this habitual thinking about education gave little attention to what makes people suitable to earn a living. More attention was given to providing them with character, social graces and manners and the qualifications believed to be necessary to please God and be admitted to heaven.

Education is necessary in a more complex and technocratic era: but how broad and general, how specialised and focused on job requirements? Not too narrow: if we educated people only for job performance and filled most of their time with work, society would become dull, uncivilised and possessed with a circularity of birth, work, materialist consumption and death, pointlessly repeated *ad nauseam*. In the proper balance, it is vitally important for all educators and trainers to have a clear-minded, constantly updated picture of which human abilities are required to best equip individuals for the world of work. It should not neglect the qualities of character and spiritual values embodied in character formation and the development of personality. Those qualities give point, vision and direction to the work that needs to be done and the leisure that needs to be enjoyed in a sane and civilised society.

Nevertheless, some part of any framework for those who design and implement education and training – the pragmatic, opportunistic part – must encompass what economists call 'manpower planning'. We now talk about 'human resources planning', as a basis for 'human resources development', which stands for upbringing, character-formation, education and training. In addition to employment planning (foreseeing and arranging to supply the skills required), it is obviously of basic importance to have employment information.[26]

Box 3.21: Career-planning

The Massachusetts Department of Employment and Training reports the fastest growing careers in the next few years will be computer service technicians, medical assistants and systems analysts.

Ellen Goodman observed, when students were graduating in May 1994 that, compared with the motto of the class of 1968: 'Make love not war', the aspirations and expectations of the class of 1994 were expressed by 'I don't know'.

She recalled 'the class of 1984 headed lockstep for Wall Street', whereas 'the class of 1994 is warily wandering into the real world of McJobs and McTemps. Their laser-printed resumes, updated on computer programs that didn't exist when they were born, bear a good strong fear of the future. They carry a recognition of reality's bite. This is the generation born to and bored with the baby boomers. They were raised in front of the tube by unravelling families in an unravelling economy. Some look back on the 1980s as good old days and others look back on the 1950s, studied in endless sitcom reruns, as a child's Eden. But the Nirvana of the 1990s was destroyed by the suicide of Kurt Cobain.'

Source: BG, 29 May 1994

Some indicative economic planning needs to be medium- and long-term for a variety of reasons. The focus on shorter time periods needs to emphasise adjustments in the demand for labour to the supply, while the focus on longer time periods can emphasise adjustments of the supply of labour to the demand for it.

There can be:

● full or part-time training;
● institutional or on-the-job training; and
● 'sandwich training'.

The last of these, perhaps the best for many jobs, is where the training is part-time, contemporaneous and coordinated with the part-time per-formance of the job. Such jobs may later be done full-time with full use of the pertinent skills that the training has provided.

One benefit that technology in information science should aim at is to provide a worldwide and constantly updated database on the demand for human labour and services.

Box 3.22: Supply and demand for PhDs: 'Eggheads unite'

Adlai Stevenson, the most brilliant and the baldest candidate ever to lose in a US presidential election, once cried out during his campaign: 'Eggheads of the world unite: we have only our shells to lose.' It is more timely than ever, by now, for PhDs to put their eggheads together to defend their market and career opportunities.

First, the evidence. The job market for graduate students with new doctorates in philosophy, English and modern languages is the worst it has been in decades, say new PhDs and their mentors as they scour the academic landscape. In many other areas of the humanities and history, the situation is slightly better. Academic jobs in English and modern languages dropped to the lowest point since records were kept from 1975, while the supply of PhDs has spiralled up since the late 1980s. Philosophy PhDs out-number jobs available to them 2 to 1; 1994 is 'the tightest year ever, including the late 1970s, which we called the academic recession' (Warren Goldfarb, Harvard University). Unemployment among 1993 PhDs in mathematics reached 8.9%, a 15-year high; among those in chemistry it reached 17%. Since 1992, new PhDs in history, not counting earlier PhDs, outnumber available jobs in that field.

Prospects are generally better in fields with direct application to industry, such as economics and engineering. But even in some applied fields such as chemistry, where industry is the largest employer, the slow recovery from recession has not completely whittled down the job shortage.

continued

Box 3.22 continued

For the majority of students who had counted on careers as professors the culprit appears to be the forced contraction of State universities due to taxpayer revolts and the attempts of private colleges to hold down costs and, with them, tuition fees. Meanwhile there is no reduction in the supply of new PhDs.

If the situation does not improve soon, some professors suggest, the scholars of the 1990s will become the second 'lost generation', closed out of academia like the numerous graduates of the late 1970s. With academia, the main growth area has been part-time and temporary teaching jobs, as colleges seek flexibility and cheaper ways to do business.

Source: BG, 5 June 1994

Meanwhile the government and other leaders are stressing America's needs for high-level manpower; students and their families are going heavily into debt working their way up to levels as high as PhD in the desperate search for job and economic security. Up to Master's degree level the advice given and income levels attained by graduates suggest higher education is not being overdone, but full PhDs do risk to become narrowly specialised, over-qualified for many jobs, and miserable if these are the only jobs they can get.

The implementation of human resources planning invariably involves *employment market organisation*. This embraces the bodies and arrangements which actively bring recruiters and seekers of work together and help them to take all the steps facilitating the filling of jobs. That includes a chain of employment offices and various forms of assistance to find out about vacancies, to get appointed to the jobs and, if necessary, to move house and home to where the jobs are. Sweden successfully pioneered what was called active employment market policy because it went well beyond information, embracing incentives, the subsidising of removal and job creation projects and guidance for training and trainers. It is no good to have all the policy ammunition directed towards improving the supply of labour and enabling workers to look more attractive and available to employers. As much as possible must also be done on the demand side (Box 3.23).

If it is not profitable to employ everybody, they won't all be employed. However, a lot of things can be done to make employment more profitable. For example, some workers in some situations may not be worth hiring at the going wage; it can be made profitable to hire them by subsidies which make them available at lower cost to the employer (Box 3.24).

Box 3.23: JOBMAP

Recently an American company described a public service activity it was undertaking, as follows.

'An information management system and process provides continually updated data on career fields to help steer dislocated workers into productive and growing industries. JOBMAP lists the requirements that must be fulfilled to secure positions in particular fields and can be used to match individual skills to the requirements of demand occupations – occupations that need people. Among its various functions, JOBMAP compares individuals' background and skills with demand occupation needs and identifies good matches; evaluates a person's readiness to enter a demand occupation by comparing current versus required skills; and provides a tailored plan for fulfilling skill needs by defining training requirements. JOBMAP is being implemented at our company and may some day form the foundation of a national skills information system.'

Box 3.24: Subsidising wages

Instead of receiving a dole or welfare benefits, the unemployed might get a voucher promising that the State would pay part of their wage if they found a job. This would reduce the cost of labour for employers and add nothing to the government's expenses – just transfer its money through another channel. Unfortunately, two decades of trying such schemes led to only a small net increase in jobs. Some workers would have found jobs even without the subsidy. It is thought that two-thirds of the unemployed helped in this way in Australia and Ireland would have got their jobs without subsidy. A wage subsidy can tempt an employer to fire existing workers in order to hire subsidised ones. If some, but not all, unemployed workers are qualified for subsidies, then those qualified have an unfair benefit over the rest: this was true of three-quarters of those helped under a Dutch scheme. Employers may dump subsidised workers when their subsidies cease, as did some American employers.

Dennis Snower (Birkbeck College, London) argues that better targeting of subsidies is the key to success of such schemes. He proposes vouchers directed at the long-term unemployed; the value of vouchers could increase with the length of time the workers to be subsidised were unemployed; then their value could be allowed to decline in proportion to the length of time workers are employed. Such vouchers could be more

continued

Box 3.24 continued

generous to firms which use the subsidy money for training since that will make those workers more valuable to keep by the current or future employers. The vouchers could be restricted to situations where there is a net addition to the employer's work force and not simply a replacement of full-wage workers by those subsidised. Mr Snower considered his scheme most worthwhile in Europe, where benefits to the unemployed are high in relation to wage levels. The nearest approach to his suggestion so far is the job-subsidy programme announced in 1994 in Australia (which will cost $5 billion).

Adopting such policies might make the labour market work more efficiently while also delivering social benefits such as reducing crime and preventing the long-term unemployed from getting too rusty.

In conclusion, readers wishing to refresh their memory about conditions for the attainment of high levels of employment may turn back to page 32 in Part II.[27]

PART IV

'THE POOR YE HAVE ALWAYS'

Justice in a policy of income and wealth

Large differences of wealth look ugly and cruel – and worse when the poorest are sick and die from their dire poverty. Wherever denial of vital needs causes pain and undermines human dignity it is better for the well-being of a society to reduce the glaring differences in wealth which add insult to injury, even if some consequent reduction of total wealth cannot be avoided.

A median personal income is the amount received by a person whose income is less than that received by a half of the population and higher than that received by the other half. A country which has a national income of $10 bn and can *sustain* a median personal income of $20,000 is arguably 'better off' than one which has a higher national income, such as $15 bn but a lower median personal income of say only $10,000. A person living in the USA today on $10,000 a year or less – and it *would* be less for half the population – would be seriously deprived and would be unable to pay for a doctor unless insured. The median family income in the USA reached $40,000 in 1989; that would be equivalent to $10,000 per person in a family of two parents and two children. It gradually declined during the ensuing recession years and by 1993, at $36,959, the median family income was back at the level of 1985 in real terms.

Please note carefully the word *sustain* in the preceding paragraph about targeting a reasonable sharing of wealth. There is no gain from redistribution in the end if the higher median personal income of $20,000 in our example eventually drifts down to a much lower level. This would happen – and has happened in too many countries – because the measures adopted to reduce inequality also reduced the efficiency and prosperity of the economy.

The recent distributions of income in the UK and the USA are compared in Box 4.1.

In the world as a whole, the median income is pitifully low due mainly to the vast global population outweighing the planet's resources. The proportion of crushingly poor people is too large to permit effective redistribution; redistribution alone would only have a modest impact on world median income. The only solution is to increase world income and then to make room for still more improvements.

An indication of how much global income distribution became still more unequal in the thirty years up to 1989 is given in Box 4.2. As indicated, this largely reflects excessive (relative to resources) population growth in poorer countries still further diminishing the absolute income levels of the disadvantaged.

Box 4.1: UK and USA: Distribution of income

Reference is to disposable income (income after payment of taxes); there, and to a varying extent elsewhere, taxation reduces the inequality of disposable income. For both the UK and the USA, figures show the percentage of total household income going to each quintile i.e. to each of the five groups from the lowest quintile (bottom 20% of income receivers) to the highest quintile (top 20% of income receivers).

Quintile	1	2	3	4	5
Percentage in:					
USA	3.8	9.4	15.8	24.2	46.9
UK	6.6	11.2	16.3	23.5	42.5

Source: *Encyclopedia Britannica Yearbook* (1994), pp. 739, 741

Box 4.2: Global income distribution 1960–1989

Year	Share of global income going to		ratio of
	Richest 20%	Poorest 20%	Richest to poorest %
1960	70.2	2.3	30 to 1
1970	73.9	2.3	32 to 1
1980	76.3	1.7	45 to 1
1989	82.7	1.4	59 to 1

Source: United Nations Development Programme, *Human Development Report 1992*, New York: Oxford University Press, 1992

If some low national incomes cannot be increased, then arguably the populations in the countries concerned should be reduced. It would be a miserable and unlikely human failure if world income does *not* continue to increase. Nonetheless, the world population will probably have to stop growing and maybe shrink a bit before the problems of poverty can be solved and associated environmental impacts be mitigated.

Even in 'rich' countries, the majority of people work for modest wages. Within those countries there are still huge contrasts of wealth and poverty. Within the wage-earner majority there is a big gap between the less and the better paid. In the USA between 1984 and 1994, the number of wage earners paid at poverty levels rose sharply. By 1994, nearly one in five full-time employees were counted among the poor (Box 4.3).

Box 4.3: Poverty-level wage-earners and other poverty

The Census Bureau (of the US Commerce Department) published *The Earnings Ladder* in March 1994. It showed 18% of Americans with year-round full-time jobs had earnings less than $13,091 in 1992. In 1979, only 12% of all full-time workers earned comparably low wages. The official definition of poverty in 1992 was a family earning $14,428 a year (under £10,000 p.a.). The report revealed that, especially for younger workers, and for those who did not go to university, the job market is a much more forbidding place than it was in the 1970s. The nation was moving away from higher-paying manufacturing jobs in the car, steel, chemical and other industries and toward lower-paying service jobs in everything from health care to retail stores to fast-food restaurants.

A more recent census report of October 1994 looked at all poor Americans, wage-earners or not. It found 39.3 million Americans (15.1% of the population) living in poverty in 1993. In 1993 a family of four with an income below $14,763 would be 'poor'. Children, who are 27% of the population, make up 40% of the poor. Among ethnic groups, 33.1% of blacks were poor, 30.6% of Hispanics, 15.3% of Asians and 12.2% of whites. Poverty is found among 14.2% of urban populations and among 17.2% of rural populations.

Wages

What are wages, as distinct from salaries and other forms and sources of income? Both wages and salaries are most accurately and comparably expressed as amounts of payment per hour. A 'weekly' wage of $100 is not the same for a forty-hour week as for a sixty-hour week. Wages should not only be expressed by the hour but also be payable for every single hour worked. If you are asked to carry on working for longer on one day, you must be paid for the extra time. Some workers or their families object to 'unsociable' hours involving nights and weekends and succeed in getting overtime rates paid for working at such hours.

Aside from calculating payments by the hour, there is the matter of how often the payments are delivered. Wages are usually paid at the end of each week or more often, as for day-labour.

Salaries

A salaried worker, on the contrary, is usually distinguished from weekly paid wage-earners by being paid less frequently: for example, after every two-week period in the USA or each month in European countries. Salaried personnel are characteristically expected to work overtime on occasions without any additional pay at all. Reducing inequality in incomes should perhaps take account of 'qualitative' factors, such as the numbers of hours needed to be worked to achieve such incomes.

Paid holidays, enforced idleness, workaholism

Wages are payable on public holidays without requiring the worker to work on those days. However, some American workers are forced to work on some public holidays without compensatory overtime pay or time-off another day. Regular annual holidays for wage and salary earners are commonsense for the employer, who would have his people going on sick leave or taking another job if he did not grant them. Unfortunately, employers lose commonsense and employees lose holidays under cut-throat competition. The ensuing situation often involves tired and sick people being quickly replaced.

Holidays seem like a rightful release in a society that values family and community life, giving the chance for repose and reflection. Oddly, annual holidays vary in length between countries and between occupations from one week to six or more. These differences may reflect occupation. A farmer is always on the job, for example, whereas a teacher has months of school vacation. Holidays may grow longer with the length of service. As between countries, the variations often reflect differences in the political and economic system, in the culture and value system and in geography (such as human 'hibernation' in the depth of northern winters, with little or no daylight).

Generosity with holidays certainly does not go in line with the wealth of countries! For example, Sri Lanka (formerly Ceylon) offers all its workers 174 public holidays every year: that is the world record. Sri Lanka's economy is poor but growing: gross domestic product was up 4.3 per cent in 1992 and 5.5 per cent in 1993. Employers in a few of the wealthiest countries, usually so proud of their prowess as 'the nation's only genuine creators of wealth', nevertheless complain that they cannot compete with employers in other countries, who can apparently afford to give their workers much longer holidays. In the USA an annual holiday of only two weeks and no holiday at all for the first twelve months on the job, is quite normal and indeed is thought to be so.

As for the employers themselves, it has been put this way by an observer whose profession requires close study of human personality:[1]

You look at people in business. Anyone who's obsessed with work is going to sacrifice a great deal. Every day, men die of heart attacks because they're just working and don't have time with their families. They're not evil men, it's just that they're rather naïve to think that work is everything.

Equally odd are the workers in wealthy countries who explain they do not want longer holidays because they could not afford them: they would then have more time and more need to spend money. Such workers, when given longer holidays or when finding a job with limited working hours, are likely to take a second job or engage in other forms of 'moonlighting', because they prefer more income to leisure.

This illustrates how inhabitants of wealthy countries have a problem of materialism and consumerism and a weak or withered capacity for leisure, rest and tranquillity. Oscar Wilde suggested that work is the refuge of those who have nothing better to do (Box 4.4).

Box 4.4: Workaholism in the USA

'America once led the rich world in cutting the average working week, from 79 hours in 1850 to less than 40 hours by the 1950s. Since the 1970s, however, hours have risen to an average of 42 hours in 1994 in manufacturing. Executives and lawyers boast of 80-hour weeks. Yet working times in Europe and Japan continues to fall.' In the German engineering industry the working week will be cut from 36 to 35 hours in 1995. 'Most Germans get six weeks' paid annual holiday; even the Japanese now take three weeks. Americans still make do with just two . . . The puzzle is why America, the world's richest country, sees things differently. It is a puzzle with sinister social implications. Parents spend less time with their children, who may be left at home alone for longer.' American economists Richard Freeman and Linda Bell were quoted as saying that Americans, when asked, say they actually want to work longer hours.

This is true whether their recent real earnings are trending upwards or downwards and irrespective of the fact that lower income taxes do not discourage efforts to earn more. They are offset by increasing social security and health insurance contributions.

Source: TENL, 22 October 1994

Individual workers often find that sport offers a change as good as a rest, but tend to prefer sports which are more costly to perform. Walking, jogging, bird-watching and other cheap activities are devoid of glamour. The slight amount of jogging in the USA has so far failed to reduce average body weight. The remaining solace for many is spectator sports, especially when excitement is heightened by the possibility of injury, even death, for the performers and by chances of winning a bet on successful and surviving performers. There is growing demand for the suspense and thrills associated with such entertainments as cinema, novels and amusement parks.

In sharp contrast to the increasing overwork of employed people is the long *compulsory* holidays of the unemployed. Theirs is the pure pain of being banished from normal society. They are unloved and find it increasingly difficult to love themselves. All the lost production represented by leaving millions of people unemployed could be partly salvaged by employing a number of them to compensate for workers already employed being given longer holidays. Similarly, retirees – especially those who are better skilled and experienced than today's newcomers to the labour force – might be employed part-time to replace workers given leave for further study and training.

More of those studying full-time, but financially strained, might make each year a 'sandwich', combining some work-for-pay with the solid 'bread' of some study. Indeed, there are colleges which already adhere to this educationally sound principle: study is sandwiched with practical experience doing work relevant to the field of study chosen.

Arrangements for spreading more evenly the burdens and benefits of work in Western countries would be more feasible if both full-time and part-time employment were rendered less costly to employers. Ways of achieving these employers' cost reductions depend on factors such as deregulation, changes in taxation systems and the financing of health care.

The meaning of real wages

Most workers care most about the level of their wages in relation to the level of the prices of things they have to buy. In economic jargon: workers care about their 'real' wages and the amount of 'wage goods' they can buy. For example, the US median incomes during 1985–1993 quoted above were expressed in the *real* terms of what they could buy at the cost of living existing in 1993.

To convert nominal into real wages, a *cost of living index* is used. This tells us what it costs today to buy a basket of the things most people regularly buy, as compared to what it cost in some base year such as 1960. There will be a change in that cost, probably upward rather than downward. This change is expressed as a percentage, with the cost at the base year being taken to equal 100.

A distinction should be made between three things. First, there is **the public cost of living**. The cost-of-living index measures the cost of what most people actually buy. Each cost is weighted according to the proportion of income spent on that item. Food, clothing, rents or mortgages and transport are the largest items.

Second, there is **the individual cost of living**. The choice statisticians make of the items they put in the basket to measure changes in 'the public's' cost of living is based on the things that most people spend most of their money on. However, many people who are very different from the average family in size, age, education, income and culture, buy a completely different basket of items when they go out shopping. They have their personal order of importance and preference about what they want in their home and in their life. They have a harp instead of a TV, for example. They may be well aware of what their way of life is costing them and how that cost is changing over the years. Although there are no indexes of the cost of living of one particular family, there are indexes of the cost of living of separate groups of people, such as civil servants, military forces, students, officials of international organisations, business people and the elderly, who have spending patterns which differ from the 'typical' individual or family.

An interesting example of the latter is the index published by the *Financial Times* of London which shows differences in the cost of living for travelling executives visiting all the major cities of the world. The United Nations has a similar system for measuring the cost for its officials of staying in different cities when they are travelling. There is a third such list of *per diem* allowances for US officials travelling abroad, based on regular check-ups of costs. Data are also gathered by the UN, major countries and corporations on the cost of living. This is used as a basis for fixing the salary and allowances of officials, diplomats and executives stationed for long periods in countries other than their own.

Third, there could be an index of the changing **cost of a traditional standard of living**. People who calculate cost-of-living indexes noticed that the indexes tended to show the cost of living rising more rapidly than is actually the case. The truth is that if certain items, such as kinds of food, rise in price more rapidly than other prices and become more expensive for modest pockets, people shift to *substitutes*. For example, the cost of fish has risen because of scarcity, so people buy more of other foods such as meat or pasta, which are now more economical, and foods made with soy bean products which make up the protein we think we need. Another example is the theatre. Going to a play was not so expensive when there were many local theatres, but now most people can rarely afford a trip to a Broadway theatre and buy tickets at $50 each. They get their drama at the cinema and at home from the TV or from video films. Books might be an even cheaper source of fun and satisfaction, such as the new dollar classics from Dover Books, and the 60p Penguins from Penguin Books. Thus, statisticians say that to make their indexes more accurate they should modify the items included 'in the basket' more frequently. When they do that, they measure the cost of living the way people are *obliged* to live.

However, it would be interesting to know what is happening to the way we would *like* to live if 'things weren't getting so expensive'. This index would embrace the list of things we think ought to be put 'in the basket' when measuring the cost of living. We personally may not actually buy today all the things we put on the list. The list may be strongly influenced by what we and our parents either bought, or thought we ought to have bought if we could.

Retired Americans became incensed in 1995 when Congress members and officials found they could cut the government budget deficit by billions of dollars simply by revising the official cost-of-living index. It was found to overstate cost-of-living increases, triggering corresponding increases in pensions and other social security benefits tied to the cost of living. The official index took account of some items now bought less often because they had become relatively costly. It left out major new consumer goods, such as computers, whose prices are falling and they could pull down the cost-of-('correct')-living index. The retirees' point is that items less often bought are not less wanted if they are bypassed only because they became expensive. Water in the desert is expensive but still wanted and needed (and drunk and bathed in liberally by the rich in places like Las Vegas). Medical care is wanted and needed, but one American in three is denied it by its prohibitive cost. Moreover, older and retired people have less need or taste for new items most likely to appeal to and serve the needs of younger, more active people.

Working and living conditions

'The pay for the job' should take account of all aspects of the job and of the workplace. The actual characteristics of job conditions may differ from those given in the official job description. Account should be taken of the actual work-pace and pressures; 'ergonomics' – the degree of comfort, convenience and adequacy of tools provided to do the job; feeding, washing, changing, parking and other facilities; job satisfaction and the possibility of taking pride in work achieved.

Akin to this is a consideration of the needs of women workers, such as the provision of childcare facilities and working hours compatible with family responsibilities. Some of women's problems in work, such as sexual harassment, are becoming well-known and combated. But how many men (and male architects) have noticed in some public places the long lines of women waiting at the doors of toilets? Obviously it takes women more time and space than a man requires to urinate. Toilets for women should be double the number of those for men. More economically, let both sexes share them all. The South Korean company Daewoo daringly set up a workplace in Belfast, of all places, and treated its Catholic and Protestant workers on a basis of 'daring' equality. Unfortunately this paradise of work and welfare was rather blemished by a cultural quirk: the management warned women workers not to spend much time in the toilet!

Other elements in British and American working conditions are shown in Box 4.5.

Box 4.5: The UK and USA: The quality of working life

Data on items which do not change rapidly are presented for 1992 and 1991 and for a few earlier years, in both countries:

	US	UK
Average workweek (hours)(% overtime):		
Male and female	34.4 (9.6%)	
Male	42.2 (8.6%)	43.3 (8.6%)*
Female	37.4 (2.1%)	30.2 (2.1%)*
Annual rates per 100,000 workers:		
a. – injury or accident	1700	752.6
b. – death	9.9	1.5
c. – % insured for a. and b	56.6%	100%
Average days per 1000 workdays lost to stoppages	0.1	0.2
Average journey to work (minutes)	22.5	
principal means of transport		
Public transport	5.9%	81%
Private automobile	85.7%	15%
Other	8.4%	4%
Rate per 1000 of discouraged (unemployed, no longer seeking work)	8.1	

Source: *Encyclopedia Britannica Yearbook (1994)*, pp. 739, 741.
Encyclopedia Britannica Yearbook (1996), pp. 739.

Public squalor amid private affluence

The ironic anomaly of public squalor amidst private affluence in the USA was eloquently depicted by J. K. Galbraith in his book *The Affluent Society*.[2] Some comparable ideas about Britain were expressed earlier in R.H. Tawney's classic *Equality*.[3]

A few great capitalists and philanthropists like the Agha Khan, Annenberg, Carnegie, Duke, Ford, Getty, Gulbenkian, Mellon, Nobel, Nuffield, Procter, Rockefeller, Solvay, Wallenberg and Widener, have made huge donations to higher education, medical research, the fine arts and better international relations. They are the exception proving the general rule that capitalist countries show little regard for minor needs which all people, without exception, must satisfy, wherever they are and whether or not they are wealthy.

The social conditions discussed in Part IV may be considered, in part, to be outside the pale of economics and not the concern of business people. But while being social conditions, they must enter into the equations of economics: they are all benefits or deficiencies occurring according to the ability and willingness of the economy to provide them.

There is no need to add to the massive recent publicity about starting to admit everybody to American hospitals if they need medical care and not just those who can pay the extremely high price charged for it. Emergency wards were always open to penniless people arriving on the point of death, but they are cited as obstacles to the proper 'business traffic' and the cause of severe overwork on medical personnel. This was the subject of an honest film on American cable TV, which also revealed the persecution of hospital staffs by random attacks from predatory litigation lawyers. However, the USA may be in the vanguard regarding the sympathy shown and the facilities provided to handicapped people. It was ironic that in 1995, Robert Dole, leader of the US Senate, yielded to pressure from employers to reduce their obligations toward the handicapped under the law. Senator Dole, physically handicapped himself through war wounds, had been an author of the law.

The facilities to meet many humble human needs often seem to fall between the cracks in the capitalist system, unless they can be turned to a good profit. Much vilification has been heaped on welfare cheats, but it would appear that more public money is lost by the deceit of the aid providers, including the health care services, than by that of the beneficiaries.[4] I have seen worldwide evidence – notably with regard to foreign aid – of a working principle (to add to textbooks of political science) that publicly distributed funds flow from the top to the bottom of the administrative hierarchy, are partially diverted at each level and eked out to the intended recipients at a considerable discount. It is a practice to shoot looters at disaster scenes; discreet diversion of emergency aid continues with impunity.

The homeless

There are other problems involving public places which seem small to the majority, because they hurt a minority who are considered to be unimportant or despicable. The problem of providing accommodation and services to blacks equally with whites has been solved in many countries, though not entirely so in others. However, the problems of the homeless loom as large today as ever.

An ugly example happened recently. Harvard University has some student housing, outside of which are ground-level vents emitting stale air. This air is warm and homeless people tried to sleep across the vents in the bitterest nights in winter. Harvard security staff regularly removed them without explanation. Blockage of air circulation? Security threat? Messy sight on a handsome campus? Later, when an outcry was published in the newspapers, it was reported that the homeless were no longer being shifted.

> ## Box 4.6: Book box: The homeless
>
> *The Homeless* Christopher Jenks, Harvard University Press, 1994. Written by a Professor of Sociology at Northwestern University, this is a relentlessly logical book which strips away the dogma, though what remains looks as intractable as ever. By the late 1980s there were fewer than 500,000 homeless in America, not the 2 to 3 million often quoted. Homelessness is the product of a combination of mental frailty, addiction, bad luck and a loveless life.

If you think there can only be a few homeless people in a country like the USA, you don't need to take a down-at-heel American city such as Detroit: just look at a boom town like Atlanta, Georgia. In 1994, Atlanta alone had 7300 homeless people. Everywhere, community spirit ought to coexist with the economy's efficiency. When the economy stops charging for every single thing up-front and serves the community hospitably, its face begins to grow more human.

Handicapped workers can be excellent when work and workplace situations are made less difficult for them. We have seen how some handicapped people, when assisted prosthetically and ambiently, can perform sports with efficiency and enjoyment. Larger numbers of them could accomplish a full day's work if similarly helped. Employment can offer an escape from frustration and release surprisingly productive and fertile forces.

A similar, yet wider, accomplishment is to give all lonely adults with spare time the realisation that they can be useful in many volunteer ways and to organise the use of their energies. Some simple human and social needs can be met by people simply with their bare hands and thoughts. Don't doubt their importance simply because little money is involved in satisfying these needs.

We have now reached a conception of the level of real wages (the key to the level of family living) and of its relation to the level of real workload and job satisfaction (the key to the level of worker output and allied prosperity). It is also public good manners to care for basic human needs and not to charge for everything, even for fresh, clean air.

Wages and employment

Economists still believe that the level of wages is an important factor affecting the level of employment (as shown by the Philips' curve), though they no longer blame all unemployment on excessive wage levels. Having discussed a number of causes and cures for unemployment in Parts II and III, we discuss here the room available for the improvement of wages without incurring major risks of worsening unemployment. The scope is not too restricted, since we have learned from Keynes and Henry Ford that increased wages can stimulate the economy and represent good employment policy in strong enterprises.

A warning is necessary though: we now hear far too many employers talking as though their profits depend largely on cost-cutting – getting more out of fewer workers and giving them less for it. These employers oddly assume that reducing wages and therefore the consumers' ability and willingness to buy goods and services is of little consequence for them. They complain about quietness in their shops when lay-offs and wage cuts occur, without usually noticing the connection.

Seeking to protect their real wages, workers often urge that their wage rate (the money amount or 'nominal' rate) should be changed at least as much as any change in the cost of living and in the same direction. When the cost of living has increased – say by 10 per cent – employers are often slow and reluctant to increase wages by as much as wage-earners' purchasing power has fallen. Even this would give the workers no gain; they would simply be protected from a loss. Nevertheless, many employers will only pay a wage increase promptly if they need more workers and there is a labour shortage.

In some countries the government requires all wages to be automatically increased with increases in the cost of living: this is called 'the indexation of wages'. In such circumstances it has been found much more difficult than usual to stop the cost-of-living increases. The inflation rate then gathers momentum unless wages are tied to productivity increases rather than to cost-of-living increases.

In a recession, economic growth slows down and may even cease; the resultant unemployment can then amount to one worker or more in ten. From 1975 to 1990, national economies usually grew each year, but *real* national income did shrink in a few years, as follows:

Table 4.1

USA	1975	1980		1982
West Germany	1975			1982
France	1975			
UK	1975	1980	1981	
OECD total	1975			1982

1975 followed the 'shocking' increase in oil prices by OPEC in 1974.

In a depression there is economic shrinkage; national income falls in a succession of years and the country may get stuck in an under-employment equilibrium. In the USA in the Great Depression of the 1930s, a quarter of the workers lost their jobs. What happens to wages and the cost of living when there is so much unemployment?

Box 4.7: Ground lost by blue-collar workers

The US Bureau of Labor Statistics provides the following figures to show how manufacturing jobs have been shrinking steadily in recent years. The fall was not entirely arrested despite general economic recovery being under way by 1993; this suggests that the 1,600,000 lost jobs are unlikely all to be regained:

Year	Number of jobs in manufacturing	
1989	19,300,000	
1990	19,000,000	(−300,000)
1991	18,300,000	(−700,000)
1992	17,900,000	(−400,000)
1993	17,700,000	(−200,000)

These figures show the average inflation-adjusted earnings of *production workers* in manufacturing jobs. Unions may have helped in resisting greater real wage losses for the time being:

Year	Hourly real wages per worker	
1989	$8.22	
1990	$8.04	(−18 cents)
1991	$8.05	(+ 1 cent)
1992	$7.97	(− 8 cents)
1993	$7.99	(+ 2 cents)

The net fall in real wages for production workers was about 3% over the period. This may be compared with a fall of 10% during the same period in the real earnings of young men with a high school education − roughly corresponding to the broader category of *all blue-collar workers*. Earnings of women in that category fell by rather less.

For the first time, mid- and lower-skilled workers in the USA were in serious competition with workers elsewhere. The competition began in traditional industries like steel and automobiles, but more recently it has spread to emerging sectors. Some companies have moved production to

continued

> *Box 4.7 continued*
>
> overseas. Others have stayed, but the mere fact that they *could* move has acted as a brake on wage demands. Companies have fought competition by investing heavily in technology, especially computers. They can do the same work with fewer people. In 1980, it took 9.3 man-hours to make a ton of steel. Today it takes 5. James Howell, economic consultant suggests that the streamlining of corporate America has spread far beyond manufacturing. Department stores, telephone companies and banks are being squeezed in the same way as steelmakers. Deregulation explains the intensified competition in some cases; slower revenue growth is the culprit in others. The pain of cost-cutting is felt by workers at all levels, but it falls hardest on the lower-skilled and the less-educated.

In countries where governments once directly controlled much of the economy, they often pumped in extra money to keep an ill-structured economy going and to protect the status of employed workers. In consequence, such countries experienced what came to be called 'stagflation'. The economy was stagnant and production was low; yet people still had money to spend, so the cost of living rose. More money was chasing after the same or a reduced amount of goods. Real wages eventually fell and the unemployed experienced an even more meagre existence.

Under capitalism and free markets, things are rather different in an economic downturn. In that case – perhaps in a recession and probably in a depression – the cost of living (including mortgage and other interest rates) can fall substantially but workers may be laid-off. Workers kept in employment, however, may be reluctant to accept any cut in their wages. They think their rate of wages is 'an acquired right'. They say employers receive unlimited profits in better times to compensate them for the risks they take. Since the workers don't share in the profits in the good times, they should not have to share in the losses in the bad ones!

Box 4.8 gives some indication of the variability in occupational remuneration in the USA.

In contrast, and this time using percentage figures compared to the average (mean) wage, the variability of occupational earnings in the UK can be gauged from Box 4.9.

A more recent picture of the wages and employment interconnection in the USA, at a time of return to high employment and near-boom, is given in Box 4.10. It is clear that the major structural shift into an enlarging services sector has a huge impact on employment and earnings.

One correspondent did contend that although 'the notion that Americans are working more for less pay is firmly embedded in public rhetoric and it

Box 4.8: USA: Average weekly earnings by occupation (US dollars; July 1993)

Petroleum and coal products	812.76
Coal mining	731.87
Tobacco manufactures	670.32
Transportation equipment	650.83
Metal mining	649.30
Chemical and allied products	637.26
Oil and gas extraction	613.89
Paper and allied products	583.20
Miscellaneous services	573.25
Construction	566.83
Transportation and public utilities	546.00
All Durable goods (average)	511.26
Printing and publishing	453.77
Wholesale Trade	448.49
Finance, insurance and real estate	400.14
Hotels, motels and tourist courts	233.95
Retail Trade	214.30

Source: EBY (1994) p. 743

Box 4.9: United Kingdom: range of employee earnings (annual wages in 1990 as % of average of all wages)

Paper products; printing and publishing	133.8
Chemical engineering	118.1
Extraction of coal, mineral oil and natural gas	118.1
Mechanical engineering	108.4
Extraction of minerals other than fuels.	103.1
Manufacture of food, beverages and tobacco	103.0
Metal Manufacture	102.8
Timber and wood products	98.1
Electrical and data processing equipment	96.8
Clothing and footwear	85.6
Textiles	79.2

Source: EBY (1994) p. 740

is practically gospel that the growing American economy cannot deliver the higher pay that American workers want', statistics reveal the bulk of new jobs actually pay over the average.[6] The point to remember, before we enjoy these happy figures, is that the bulk of Americans do *not* undertake the new jobs: most of them retain their old ones. Other people (in the returned boom) are still out of work or have lost hope and have given up looking.

The new jobs created in the two and a half years to late 1994 number 5.5 million – a respectable and impressive number but it should be compared with a total labour force of well over twenty times as many workers. Frequent reports about the new jobs being less well-paid or less permanent than the old ones come from a variety of sources, most of them respectable.

We should look beneath the true statistic that 5.5 million new jobs were in occupations paying *more* than the current average of $15.50 per hour. In 1994, 72 per cent of the new 2.5 million jobs were for managers (from the chief executive to the branch sales manager), and for professionals (from surgeons and nurses to software programmers, accountants and high-school teachers). 'And despite its reputation for low wages, the service sector is adding most of the higher-wage jobs . . . Average hourly pay has risen 2.5 per cent in the early 1990s.'[6]

Economist David Wyss was quoted as saying: 'What's driving the average wage up is not so much an improvement for each individual worker but that the mix of jobs is improving.' The number of higher-paying new jobs is rising faster than the number of lower-paying ones and bigger bonuses for executives are also helping to push up pay.

We must be cautious in our interpretation of statistics on average wages:

● if you include the pay of managers and supervisors, and all pay and benefits, the rise is 5 per cent from 1980 to 1988 and 2.5 per cent from 1990 to 1994;

● if you exclude managers and supervisors and exclude benefits received by all workers, average pay fell 2 per cent from 1980 to 1988 and 1.5 per cent from 1990 to 1994.

Profit-sharing

A strong case has been made for profit-sharing with workers and for partnership in management by workers. Where it has been put into effect, many but not all of the businesses concerned have profited well from the higher productivity and better morale. A big example is United Airlines in USA.

Astute, aggressive unions are often against profit-sharing because it loosens their hold on the workers: they have 'joined management'. The unions also argue that the workers are more likely to sacrifice their wages and other benefits if that will avoid lay-offs and improve long-term

Box 4.10: Glass half full or half empty?

Median pay and employment differs sectorally as follows:

Category	Service industries		Goods industries	
	Median weekly pay 1993	Net increase in jobs 1988–1993	Median weekly pay 1993	Net decrease in jobs 1988–1993
Managerial	$635	+1.12 million	$635	–0.01 million
Professional	$617	+1.77 million	$617	–0.09 million
Sales	$314	+0.47 million		
Service	$215	+1.35 million		
Skilled, craft			$490	–0.77 million
Semi-skilled			$328	–1.01 million

Pay figures are for all industries. Goods industries include manufacturing, mining, construction and agriculture

Source: US Bureau of Labor Statistics

The new management jobs tend to be in high-growth fields, frequently at smaller firms where managers actually run businesses and develop new accounts rather than layers of bureaucracy. There is a speed-up in the new mix of jobs; in ten years from 1983 to 1993, managers and professionals filled less than half of the new jobs, whereas they filled three-quarters of the new jobs opening up 1991–1994.

Economist Robert Kuttner also warns against confusing a median with a simple average (mean). 'First, average earnings may be going up, but not for most workers . . . Second, more jobs can be created in occupations with high average wages, but most workers can still face falling earnings. Lately, inequality within occupations has been rising sharply.'[7]

prospects for profits. They thereby lay themselves open to exploitation by management. The pros and cons of this matter turn partly on the size of workers' share in profits and their involvement in the management of the companies.

However, a majority of workers under capitalism do *not* share in profits and are inadequately consulted by management. So what then happens to their wages if the cost of living drops significantly? The workers may hold out to keep their money wages steady (and therefore obtain higher real wages). Even keeping money wages steady means that they have foregone the periodic increases to which they were accustomed. They add, and with good reason, that in any case modern history indicates a resumption of inflation is sure to recur and soon.

Workers are often reluctant to work for a lower money wage even in serious circumstances such as those of the air travel industry recently. According to the International Air Transport Association, the cumulative losses of $11.5 bn the airlines have suffered on their scheduled inter- national services in the three years to the end of 1992 were greater than all the net profits earned since such services began seventy-four years ago. Employers in that kind of situation are forced to cut costs and lay-off workers because of the stiff competition with others in the industry, at home and abroad.

Long-established airlines like Pan American went bankrupt and disappeared, perhaps forever. For a long time airline workers had been accustomed to repeated pay increases and some had become comparatively highly paid. Yet in the USA, big price increases stopped from 1990 and by 1993 rises in the cost of living – when mortgage interest rates are included – had abated.

Usually, workers will only agree to a wage cut if they realise the only immediate alternative will be the sack and no wage at all. This kind of wage- and staff-cutting situation to reduce costs has been more common in the USA than in Europe. In Europe, wages are prevented from falling by laws and unions and by impediments to the dismissal of workers. European employers are therefore all the more careful not to hire more workers, nor even to replace workers who die, retire or leave voluntarily. Take the extreme case of state-owned Air France, which lost $617 million in 1992. In 1993, facing losses of $855 million, Air France tried to push through a cost-cutting plan involving 4000 job losses, but was forced by the government to hold back. There was a violent strike at Charles de Gaulle airport in Paris.

The burden of Air France's subsidy on French tax-payers remained heavy. More governments around the world are deciding they cannot afford and do not need to operate their own airlines. A few big inter- national companies will 'globalise' and carry the main traffic, with less business and luxury travel and progressively more cut-price tourism and family reunion travel. In this process, financially weak European airlines – Greek, Italian, Spanish and Portuguese – will be reduced to a more viable size.

Recent socioeconomic history

Let us look at what has happened to wages, employment and the economy in the last fifty years. Some of this ground was covered in Part II, but with a different focus: there the issue was the failure to apply Keynesian policies properly. Here attention is focused on the social incidence of economic instability and the deepening divide of inequality. The need for this historical digression is to show that our recent troubles and disquieting trends have historical, partly non-economic, roots and are not necessarily always imposed by the normal functioning of our economic system.

In the economic recovery after the Second World War, first the USA and later other large and prosperous countries boomed. Their workers became accustomed to their real wages rising spectacularly, as in the 1950s and 1960s. Those were times when the cost of living remained moderate. The established industrialists enjoyed sellers' markets. The USA, for example, produced up to ten million cars a year or more. American car workers employed on the dull, repetitive assembly lines were handsomely paid and granted excellent fringe benefits. They were not particularly skilled but had their employment protected by the unions.

The developed, power-using countries then experienced the 'oil shock' inflation of the 1970s. The cost of living went up more than wages and earnings fell overall in a recession largely caused by inflated fuel and transport costs. Car production in the USA fell and its market share fell substantially – about a third in a decade or so – as more and more well-made cars were imported from Europe and especially from new factories in Asia. Fifteen million new cars a year were bought in the USA, but a significant proportion were from non-US manufacturers.

Another recession occurred at the beginning of the 1980s, largely because money and credit supply was cut back sharply to curb roaring inflation. Interest rates, reflecting the scarcity of credit, soared to two-digit levels never known before in the USA, although commonplace elsewhere. American annual price increases were slowed down by the recession to a single-digit rate, but fewer goods were made and sold, due to shortage of credit, and people were thrown out of work.

After each recession since the Second World War, increasing numbers of those seeking work and of young people reaching working age joined the ranks of the unemployed. Some of them remained idle for long periods. Others, such as car workers, had to take jobs at lower rates of pay. In the USA, the privileged 1950–1970 period in which American workers who were only moderately skilled were much better paid than workers elsewhere came to an end.[8]

In the USA the boom of the mid-1980s was associated with a real-estate speculative bubble as mortgage interest rates dropped well below the record levels experienced earlier in the decade. Certain cities gained in the shift from 'smoke-stack', assembly-line factories, to 'hi-tech', industries which employed people with far higher skill levels. In the boom cities, there was also significant over-building of offices and facilities in the race to accommodate a growing volume of companies in the swelling services sector.

Salary earners did much better than wage-earners in the recovery from 1984. Higher income groups got tax relief whereas the small tax reductions received by wage earners were offset by increased social security contributions which left them no better off to face a period of rising prices. A 1986 revision of the federal tax code slightly diminished the privileged situation of the rich; for example, private planes and yachts were taxed a little more.

Other economically advanced countries in the 1980s saw an increase in their productivity and in their ability to compete; together with North America they swelled world trade impressively. All over the world, there were fortunate people spending more, often in speculative and extravagant ways. There were also unfortunate people spending more than they could earn and deepening their debt. It seemed to be an era of investors and big-time speculators and financial manipulators, some with little money of their own, but to whom the banks lent billions. Lenders were essentially placing their faith in the raiders' ability to merge corporations or tear them apart, giving them the opportunity to rake back from those plundered companies the money they had borrowed.

In the USA, savings and loans (S&L) institutions, the normal source of mortgages, found themselves unable to earn enough to pay the high prevailing interest rates to their depositors. Suddenly and many believe foolishly they were 'rescued' by a change in the law which allowed them to make much higher-risk investments. The risk was clearly labelled, since they bought mainly what were openly called 'junk bonds'. The government's original estimate of $100 billion needed to clear up the mess of the S&L failures proved to be far less than the total of their ultimate losses. Eventually these losses were added to the national debt and to the burden on tax-payers. The grim list, distressing to contemplate, of all of these categories of people, corporations and institutions entering into constantly heavier indebtedness is only part of the story of the 'spend now-pay later' orgy of the 1980s.

The federal government, engaged in the then accelerating arms race of the cold war, nevertheless reduced taxes without care for the uncovered public expenditure and the growing mountain of national debt. It was thus less able to help State and city governments and they too increased their massive debts. Cities in Connecticut actually went bankrupt (though that State had the highest private-sector incomes). Even New York City, with all its glitter and apparent wealth, veered into and out of bankruptcy and remains at risk. It became yet more squalid and over-burdened, with welfare cases and prematurely retired municipal pensioners.

If US government spending on social programmes had been cut in the 1980s to pay for armaments and rein in the indebtedness, as rightwing politicians were recommending, many believe that there would have been another Depression like that of the 1930s. The Great Depression had been deepened by similar politicians making similar recommendations and by the then absence of the social 'safety-net' in place in the 1980s.

From 1987 onward the speculative bubbles burst. On the New York stock exchange in October of that year the total value of all companies listed was nearly halved. From late 1989 the recession started in New England, and got under way elsewhere in 1990, largely due to investment losses and growing debts uncovered by shrinking asset values (notably of houses and office buildings). The Gulf War in 1991 was fought by the USA out of inventory without much financial strain – old arms were used up and new ones tried out – but the heroes returning home from that infested area had trouble finding jobs and some fell sick, against which the unemployed are not usually insured.

From 1990 onward, not only blue-collar but white-collar and professional and managerial employees lost their jobs and experienced long periods of unemployment. Some thought that more education would have solved the economic problem, but some of the best-qualified people found themselves unwanted. These unemployed former high-salary earners and those who were still employed but feeling insecure (some panic-stricken) all cut their personal spending. The unemployed, whose saving had stopped, used past savings and increased debts just to survive.

Looking at the private sector, we see that the recession in 1990–1993 was more than a cyclical phenomenon. It had roots in changes of the structure of the economy. We have already mentioned shifts from assembly line and smoke-stack industries to hi-tech and services' sectors. We should also recognise the corporate reorganisations currently underway. The buzz words are downsizing, decentralisation, re-engineering, a retreat from conglomerates and a return to core businesses which were the main profit centres, thereby thinning out the layers of management and shedding bureaucracy. At the same time the impacts of technology – improved communications, better data collection, analysis and dissemination – impacted on the numbers of people required and the types of skills in demand in the previously burgeoning office sector.

Many analysts thought that the improvements in productivity reduced the total number of employees required to operate the capital equipment of the economy. National, regional and local governments sought to cut their budgets and expenditure.

The cold war ended and even military expenditure fell a little, though not nearly as much as Harry Truman's sharp, deep and quick cut after the Second World War. Foreign aid, much of it consisting of 'cold war bribes', fell substantially. An effort got under way to bankrupt the United Nations. Countries getting less aid responded by cutting their imports. Countries liberated from communism could not usefully absorb much new foreign aid without making wholesale changes to their institutions and laws. All this made for a prolonged recession, not as deep as some previous ones but hurting numerous vocal people for the first time. And, as we have seen, it further enlarged the residual of unemployment which stubbornly remains despite subsequent economic recovery.

Recovery made a slow start because people and institutions were forced to service and pay-off debts before they could spend heavily and invest once again. The recession arguably first started in North America, but American recovery was slowed by the European recession, which began later and reduced American exports across the Atlantic.

In Europe, unemployment was severe and Europeans missed the relief offered in North America from extremely low interest rates. Till mid-1993, Germany kept interest rates high due to its inflationary financing of the collapsed East German economy. Other European countries, especially fellow members of the European Monetary System, had to follow suit and keep their interest rates high. Since over a trillion dollars a day pass through the world's foreign exchanges, any disparity in interest rates could cause massive destabilising currency flows. Huge sums are constantly switched from one country to another in search of the best obtainable interest rates on deposits and bonds. The other European countries had, in effect, agreed to prevent their currencies falling below the value of German money. The Europeans, in other words, had agreed not to take away markets from each other by making their currencies (and hence prices) cheaper. A currency devaluation is similar in effect to slapping heavy duties on all imports and paying big subsidies on all exports.

Under the financial and political strains from high interest rates, some European currencies collapsed. The British pound went down first. In September 1992, released from obligatory high interest rates, Britain's economic recovery started, ahead of any signs of recovery elsewhere in Europe. Unemployment remained serious everywhere, inflation slowed or stopped in many countries but real wages, that had been drooping for so long, did not in fact recover to any significant extent. Many governments have lamented the absence of any 'feel good' factor among workers and consumers during the present recovery.

Wages and productivity

The fall in real wages in the recent past has happened even though many people have been forced to work harder and their productivity has risen. For example, after correcting for inflation, in the USA the wages of non-supervisory workers have fallen 19 per cent despite a 25 per cent increase in the real gross domestic product (output and income obtained within the country).

Productivity per worker does not mean, or reflect exclusively, a worker's effort and personal achievement. It is simply a mathematical ratio between input and output, where total output is compared with only one input: labour. It is misleading when labelled 'labour' productivity, because total output really reflects the amount and quality of *all* the inputs. Perhaps the label gets used because the labour input varies more than the others.

The effort and personal achievement of the worker does, however, have some importance, especially in labour-intensive factories and workplaces. It is diminished in workplaces with a great deal of capital equipment and machinery, where workers can more easily – not necessarily more justly – be better paid than in the labour-intensive occupations, partly because their payroll is a more modest proportion of total costs. On the other hand, in places with extensive equipment and valuable machinery, any lack of effort can have significant negative effects. Workers can do immense harm to output if they wreck the equipment or just strike and leave it idle while the employer has to go on paying for it.

Minimum wages

The first aspect of the fixing of wage rates to consider is whether they should, in all fairness, have a floor applied to them. Should there be a legal minimum wage? And should that minimum be raised as much as any increases in the cost of living?

In Table 4.2 we take the legal minimum wage in the USA, and then convert it into the value of 1995 dollars. We can then express this figure as a percentage of the real value of the average private non-supervisory wage in the US over the forty-year period 1955–1995, as follows:

Table 4.2

	1955	1960	1965	1970	1975	1980	1985	1990	1995
Minimum wage	$0.75	1.00	1.25	1.60	2.10	3.10	3.35	3.80	4.25
1995 value	$3.94	4.75	5.59	5.92	5.71	5.76	4.76	4.44	4.25
%	43.9	47.8	50.8	49.5	46.4	46.5	39.1	37.9	37.1

Source: Center on Budget and Policy Priorities, quoted in BG, 29 January 1995, p. A30

First, it is important to notice the change in the real purchasing power of the minimum wage (1995 value), since it is meant to help to cover the cost of basic necessities. The real value rose until 1970 but since then has fallen from $5.92 all the way to $4.25 – its level at the beginning of 1995 – which buys less than it would buy as far back as 1960.

Second, there has been economic progress since 1965 in USA. It is therefore hardly impressive that a minimum wage worth 43.9 per cent of the average wage in 1955 is worth only 37.1 per cent of the average wage in 1995. The US Secretary of Labor, Robert Reich, said in 1994 in proposing an increase of fifty cents (to $4.75) that this would recover only part of the loss in real value of the minimum wage and was too small to make some employers lay-off the slightly more expensive labour force they employed near the bottom of the wage scale. I think it is essential to give some probably employment-neutral – and possibly employment-positive due to the productivity effect – protection to workers from cut-throat competition in the employment market of a rich country where six million children under the age of six are living below the official poverty line.[5]

The economic difference between people and machines

When an employer goes into production, let us say in a factory, he buys land on which to build the factory, and he also buys 'land' in so far as he uses air, water, minerals, plants and other natural resources derived from the land in the process of production. He also uses monetary capital to buy the equipment and machinery and to pay for the labour and 'land'. All this outlay is financed from monetary capital unless and until the output is sold. He can then, from the sales' proceeds, meet the cost of the capital. The cost of such monetary capital is the interest he pays to lenders or the interest and dividends he foregoes should he use his own monetary capital.

The employer seeks to get the best value for his money when buying the land, machinery, equipment and raw materials and paying for the personnel employed within his enterprise. 'Best value' means the quality and price required to do the job properly and not usually merely the cheapest. A wise and wealthy man has said 'I cannot afford to buy cheap things.'

An employer wants equipment that will work well and not break down and bring both production and deliveries to customers to a standstill. Similarly, he wants workers who can do the job properly and maybe a few apprentices who will take a lower wage until fully trained by his company and qualified for the job.

Equipment cannot be lazy; some workers are lazy or slow, as we may observe when they 'work' alongside us. Equipment, like a good worker, continues to do its best until it is worn out or needs repair. A sensible employer keeps spares, such as replacement parts. Similarly, he employs enough workers to take up the slack if one falls sick, until the sick worker recovers and can return to work.

It is hard to understand the meanness of employers who severely limit the number of days of sickness they will pay for. If the other inputs they use are temporarily unavailable or inoperable, they bear the full financial burden until they are available and operable again. A worker properly paid while sick and welcomed back when recuperated will be grateful, loyal and well-motivated.

When the employer buys a piece of equipment he has chosen for the job, he expects to pay the supplier's price in full without quibbling. Having got it, he will not seek to get a rebate on what he paid, though he might get repair or a replacement while the equipment is still under guarantee. The employer will take good care of all his physical plant: he will lubricate and fuel the machinery; watch the safety gauges; keep the buildings painted, cleaned, warmed, ventilated and maintained; service the vehicles; drain, fertilise and cultivate his land.

However, when it comes to giving someone a job, he normally treats that person differently from anyone who sells him equipment and supplies. He may well haggle over what he has to pay them even though he has already checked that a job applicant's qualifications and references are satisfactory. He should pay them the rate for the job. That rate should be advertised in advance and be the same for any applicant, irrespective of age or sex, just as there is a 'sticker' price on any equipment he considers buying. Just as he can return equipment for replacement or repair during the warranty period, so he might reasonably tell a new recruit there is a period of probation and retain the right not to keep the recruit at the end of that period if his performance was unsatisfactory.

Once his recruits are 'on the job', the unwise employer may display little concern about their health and morale and the extent to which the job and working conditions affect both of those qualities. He will look after his plant and equipment carefully because he has paid for it in full, whereas he is not obliged to give any worker employment for life. Any worker who is sick or injured or grows too old can just be dismissed and replaced with a healthy, younger one.

The employer may, and indeed should, be obliged to arrange medical insurance and respect official regulations and laws about working conditions and occupational safety. If inspectors are known to visit once in ten years or less, or if the penalties are trivial, he may ignore some of those regulations.

Under the Republican administration in the USA in the 1980s, there was reluctance about bothering employers with all sorts of legal requirements and adding to their cost burdens, since markets for their products were supposedly becoming very competitive. Moreover, as part of economy measures introduced by the government, there were sharp cuts in funds budgeted for official inspections. That further liberated employers' inclinations to take less good care of their personnel than of their plant.

When unemployment grows significantly and workers are desperate to get jobs, many are ready to accept poor wages. In the most recent recession, employers admitted that labour costs per unit went down because of lower wages, as well as because of lay-offs of workers and productivity improvements.

Equipment suppliers may agree to discounts in a buyers' market, but if things get worse they will have to go out of business or switch to other production lines, rather than lose money producing things that can only be sold at prices below costs. Similarly, an employer's workers in a buyers' market may have their wages cut. Indeed, at least in principle, wages may continue to be cut until workers are pushed to the point of starvation, whereas equipment suppliers will go out of business well before they are faced with starvation. This unlimited cutting of wages can, in practice, only happen when there is a large surplus of labour. Unlike the office equipment suppliers who can cut back production, the parents of the world go on merrily producing children whether or not there will be jobs (and dwellings) for them all.

In countries where all or most children have access to education and training, their parents or their teachers might identify those jobs that are increasing in number and in which pay is improving. They could then choose the appropriate qualifications for the children to acquire. But this does not help more than a few people. In parts of the world where there is such a chronic over-supply of people and where there are no schools at all for millions, the wages can fall to subsistence level or even below. This means that, unlike the equipment supplier, in such situations many desperate workers will agree to go on working even if their pay is not enough to keep body and soul together.

Setting a minimum wage doesn't stop the risk of workers going hungry. They would either be left unemployed, or employers would find ways around the fixed minimum. Desperate young workers could let their employer lie to inspectors (if any), saying that, they are members of his family who are 'pitching in to help'. Other workers might pay a bribe to get a job in the first place. Workers in isolated or backward places might be obliged to take their food, clothing and lodging from the employer, who would then overcharge them. Workers eating and living 'out' might have difficulty paying their bills and succumb to borrowing money from their employer and have to pay him a high interest rate. Not only in novels, in real life too, sexual exploitation sometimes goes hand-in-hand with economic exploitation: a man gets a job if he lets his employer use his daughter sexually, or his wife gets a job if she gives herself sexually to the employer or his foreman (probably without telling her husband).

None of these horrors or squeezes are heaped on suppliers of production equipment, buildings and land to employers, because they are providing items that are usually much scarcer than workers. In any event they are likely to be better off than workers and not nearly so desperate for a livelihood.

Today this scenario sounds extreme in the USA (though it wasn't as recently as 1933) but it does still fit the situation with little exaggeration in many less fortunate places on our overcrowded planet. 'The bottom line' – the mantra of business people – is that human beings, due to their over-supply (in relation to the availability of natural resources and capital), are vulnerable to exploitation by employers. The current trend of governments in withdrawing from the economy and becoming less able or inclined to shield and subsidise workers, visibly increases this vulnerability. Fear and insecurity are spreading like a dark cloud. Hopes and possibilities for genuine lifelong careers are withering away.

A floor can be set to wages to offer some genuine protection to workers, at least in the more prosperous countries and in more prosperous times. Whether it is set by a government or by a labour union, the economic effect is the same. In the USA, a wage not lower than the federal minimum wage is payable by all employers engaged in any business in more than one State (engaged in 'interstate commerce'). Many workers earn more than that ($4.25 an hour up to early 1995), but there are millions of others getting the minimum wage and still others earning less when working in small businesses. For example, in many bars and restaurants the serving staff may not get more than $2–$3 an hour because they are allowed to keep their tips. Tips in cash are easy to understate to the tax collector and it seems cruel and mean when tax collectors often pursue low wage-earners more vigorously than the wealthy who keep millions untaxed.

Unions do try to go further than minimum wage laws and impose on employers a structure of minima in the wage scale payable for different levels of skill. This wage-scale setting is hardly attempted by governments in capitalist countries (except for their own – public – employees, of course). However, they may connive to raise the earnings of skilled and professional workers by testing and certifying their qualifications for employment and setting the standards for employees above the level required to do the job properly so as to restrict the supply of such employees. This will obviously keep up their earnings. Examples might include those whose work is crucial to the safety, health and protection of people, such as plumbers, electricians, lawyers and doctors, most of whom enjoy earnings well above the average for other workers in parallel categories.

From a social point of view the main difference between a legal minimum and a union minimum is that a minimum wage required by law applies to all workers, whereas unions only seek to help their own members. In the USA, the 'industrial unions' set up by the Congress of Industrial Organisations each try to help all employees in 'their' industry, whereas the 'craft unions' set up by the American Federation of Labor only help their members in a single skill or occupation.

The minimum wage level

The normal and sensible thing for the government to do would be to set the minimum wage at a level coordinated with the 'poverty line'. In many developed countries and in some others, poverty is defined in law and in official statistics in terms of the minimum amount of money required to keep a family of average size supplied with the basic necessities of life. The average family today in many countries has more than one wage-earner sharing the burden of family support, so it may not be necessary to set the minimum wage high enough to support a whole family. Many non-economists would say, though, that the integrity of family and community life are more important and socially necessary than the materialistic goal of trying to overwork both parents.

In some developing countries, only a few large and wealthy foreign corporations respect the law and pay the legal minimum wages. As a result, such companies immediately acquire the cream of the labour force; the other employers paid and effectively received little. This was all right in so far as the politicians' true intention was to 'shake down' the foreigners. Taken far enough, though, it could discourage foreign investment, to the detriment of the country as a whole. Also, it is not good for business generally if a few rich businesses acquire the most productive workers.

The risk in setting a high minimum wage in a country with a healthy economy is to reduce the number of jobs offered to the least qualified and poorest workers. Furthermore, companies that need to employ large numbers of workers at low cost in order to compete – as in agriculture – may employ a lot of illegal immigrants at cheap rates. The penalties for so doing may be deemed worth the saving in labour cost. In this case, jobs are transferred from citizens to illegal immigrants. In similar vein there may be a shifting of some enterprises across the border to employ cheap labour legally there.

The essential point, ethically, is that if an employer is incapable of making a profit unless he pays wages below a subsistence level, it is arguably better to accept that the minimum wage law, properly and effectively applied, will put the sorry fellow out of business.

We might recall that when the population in most of Europe was reduced by a third as a result of the plague from 1346 to 1350,[9] the reduced supply of labour led to much better wages being paid until the population lost was replaced by natural increase. This demographic point should be kept in mind throughout this book. Solutions to many social problems may actually require a redeployment and ultimate stabilisation of world population.

Labour unions: the pros and cons

Labour unions in the USA and Canada, called trade unions in the UK, have since the last century been formed and developed to protect the economic and social interests of wage earners. At first, they were craft unions to protect skilled workers and craftsmen. Later, others sprang up to serve the unskilled. Finally, there were industrial unions to consolidate efforts and present a united front for all workers in one and the same industry. One of the first such cases was the car industry, and the car workers' hero, Walter Reuther, was history's pioneer of industrial – as distinct from craft – labour unions. In the USA the labour unions were nearly all confederated in the American Federation of Labor and the Congress of Industrial Organis-ations; in the UK they were united in the Trade Union Congress. These central organisations could confront both the central organisations of employers and the government of the country.

Alongside the wage-earners' unions, associations of salaried staffs, including civil servants and public as well as private enterprise employees, have grown up in the present century. In some cases these associations were concerned to a varying extent with members' professional interests and ethical standards, especially in the case of academies of science and music, etc. Even so, generally the much higher-paid people in our society have

Box 4.11: Recent thought on minimum wages

In the UK the Trade Union Congress, the Labour Party and the Liberal Democrats re-affirmed their intention in September 1994 of establishing a national minimum wage. Previous British experience with different minimum wages in different industrial sectors and for different occupations is ambiguous as to impacts on the levels of employment. In 1993 the government had abolished minimum rates for low-paid industries such as catering, shops and textiles. That provoked a push for a *national* minimum wage by USDAW, the shopworkers' union and by Unison, which represents many unskilled public sector workers.

A study by Low Pay Network showed that 37% of the workers in occupations formerly covered by minimum wages now received less than the old minima, with no discernible gain in employment. There were actually 27,000 fewer jobs in hotels and catering than before the abolition of minimum wages.

Roger Bickerstaffe of Unison claimed that a minimum wage could boost employment and company performance. 'It could entice someone who lived on welfare to take a job. Better-paid employees might work harder and change jobs less frequently, while employers might invest more in their training.' Economics apart, Mr Bickerstaffe says that current levels of income inequality are morally unacceptable. In New Jersey, David Card and Paul Krueger of Princeton University looked at the effect, in 1992, of New Jersey raising its minimum wage from $4.25 to $5.05 an hour, while neighbouring Pennsylvania stuck to $4.25. They found that employment in the fast-food industry grew by 13% more in New Jersey than it did in Pennsylvania.[10]

My own observation in Massachusetts is that the fast-food employers are not the weakest and lowest paying in the restaurant/café/snack bar sector. Recruitment signs in many windows of McDonalds, Burger King, etc. offer wages per hour well above the minima mentioned for New Jersey and Pennsylvania and also those prevailing in Massachusetts. Probably the lowest pay per hour is at cafés and snack bars run as family enterprises. These do not employ individuals counted as wage-earners and covered by laws for such labour.

Paul Gregg, an economist at the National Institute of Economic and Social Research in London, forecast in 1992 that the Labour Party's proposals for a minimum wage might cost 170,000 jobs. Later, he said that recent research invalidated his forecast and that a minimum of half male median earnings (£4 an hour in 1994) that did not apply to those under 21 would have no significant impact on jobs.

nearly all by now set up organisations to defend their economic and social interests *vis-à-vis* both employers, clients and patients and *vis-à-vis* governments and feel no affinity whatever to labour unions. Neither they nor the members of academies would call themselves 'workers' or their associations 'labour unions'. Hardly any countries – The Netherlands is an exception – allow military personnel to belong to or form their own labour unions.

Any reference to 'unions' in this section refers to any employee, consultant or personal contractor joined in any organisation to defend the economic and social interests of the group represented. The growth of such unions was necessary and basically sound. Everybody thus bandied together helped themselves to improve their lot and combat exploitation considerably. We have been drawing the distinctions between people and machinery and, beyond economics and business, people do matter and machinery does not: it is just a soulless heap of metal. Economists, professional and business people should remember that people do not only exist to keep their machinery running and their profits and fees flowing. People are the end of the process and economics merely the means to that end.

Workers who are not included in unions – and they are still a majority of the labour force – have gained in some ways indirectly from the battles fought by the unions on behalf of the minority of unionised workers. This is particularly true, for example, of the new and improved labour legislation they induced successive leftwing and rightwing governments to bring in, or not to amend too adversely.

Even from the employers' point of view, they have arguably gained from the organisation of employees. If an employer has no worker to speak to about the workers in general and talks instead to the first one he can pull out of the ranks, he is likely to get someone who is unable to speak accurately on behalf of all their colleagues. Consultation between employers and employees is essential for harmony of relations and for improving the productivity and prosperity of the enterprise.

At a conference in the UK on labour-management relations, I met a director of personnel of a large company. He said that early in his career he worked on the shop floor in one of its factories and gradually worked his way up to the position of foreman or supervisor. After that he was promoted into the ranks of management. He then progressed fast upward to be director of personnel. He confessed that his advancement was for some years due to the knowledge he had acquired, unique among his fellow executives, of the situation at the bottom of the pile and of the attitudes and feelings of the workers. Over time, this advantage withered away because, despite his efforts to keep in touch, he had moved to another world and had lost his intimate relationship with his old colleagues.

We can find a parallel to this in the arts. John Steinbeck wrote fine novels about poor people during the Great Depression: the down-and-out migrating to or born in California. Following his success and prosperity, he went to live in Manhattan, centre of the literary world, where he joined upper-class life. The books he wrote after leaving California invariably failed to have the same kind of appeal and tang of reality.

The same occurs in politics. In the Great Depression, even such a sensitive and brilliant statesman as President Franklin Roosevelt could not really touch base with the poor and the desperate share-croppers when he visited Arizona. He listened too much to the rapacious land-owners, who crowded out anyone else during his visit. The share-croppers felt he had just not visited them at all.

Brutally and nakedly the better-off showed little mercy or scruple as they bargained grimly with the under-class during that terrible Depression. Labour unions helped the workers in such heavy industry as steel production. Above all, labour unions were excluded by plantation owners, farmers and even by government legislation from the protection of workers in agriculture, who bore the brunt of the Depression.

Now let us look at the employers' side. The organisations set up by employers are concerned with trade and professional interests as well as with labour-management relations. Companies that grow enough to command a large share of the national or world market for their products are progressing toward monopoly. They can make an extra – monopoly – profit by the degree of control they have over prices. Monopoly strictly means a single and only seller of something: that is complete monopoly. Less complete forms, where there are several large sellers, are called mono-polistic (or an 'oligopoly' in economics' jargon). The more companies there are that join an association of other companies in the same business, the greater the possibility that they will use the association partly for the purpose of increasing their monopolistic power and profits. They can exploit buyers in that way. And they can exploit workers by saying to any worker who is dissatisfied with his wage: 'Like it or lump it. If you leave us you will not get a job with another member company in our association.' In this kind of situation the unions perform a highly necessary role to present a stronger front for the workers against the employers' bloc.

Of course, there may be occasions of connivance between the two sides. The workers' union, if strong enough, may win higher wages from the monopolistic employers (which they can afford to pay from their monopoly profits), wages higher than workers in other sectors can hope for. This is harmful to the third parties: consumers; the workers in other, less monopolistic employments; and the unemployed who will suffer more than other consumers from higher prices set by the monopolists, especially in the case of high prices for basic necessities.

All too often monopolies raise prices, reduce the prosperity of those who have to pay those prices, reduce the amount of products sold and hence reduce the number of workers employed in production. These reductions usually follow from the fact that demand falls in the face of higher prices.

Demand may not fall much (or at all) for products that are vitally necessary, such as food and water, even when their prices do go up. Having to spend more on such products, consumers will now have less money to spend on less necessary products. The workers and employers making those less necessary products will therefore have less employment and lower incomes.

The truth is that all monopolies can be potentially harmful. Unions become monopolies if they can effectively restrict, even totally control, the supply of a particular kind of labour. This situation gets worse when the unions require that none except their members can work in the industry. Some workers will retire and die but then, as happened with newspaper printing in some countries, any new workers recruited had to be selected from among the grown-up children of employees in the same industry.

Economic theorists until surprisingly recently assumed that perfect competition ruled throughout the economy. In the 1930s a theory of imperfect or monopolistic competition was developed. Nevertheless, J.K. Galbraith feels that microeconomic theory needs to go further than that and to be integrated with macroeconomic, including Keynesian theory. The latter should not be hived off in a separate compartment. He wrote that 'The dynamic of prices and wages as a determining factor in both inflation and unemployment will help to blur further the distinction between microeconomics and macroeconomics.'[11]

Excessive union control and monopoly has become abusive in some large cities where municipal unions have monopolised the labour supply sufficiently to require costly benefits – such as retirement on full pension after twenty years service, however young the retiree – which did much to push such cities into bankruptcy. This happened in New York City and could happen again. Indeed, in a number of American cities, municipal employees and their unions managed to increase their numbers employed and to feather their own nest. Some estimates suggest that more than half of the federal and State funds that city governments were entrusted with, to help poor people and provide benefits under social programmes, was 'consumed' by city employees.

At a 1994 conference of American city mayors at Harvard University, several mayors underscored the difficulties they had when coming into office and being treated as outsiders by the municipal administration. They have a lonely struggle to assert themselves over city employees, who dig in their heels and defend their own interests before municipal interests when faced by calls for reform, retrenchment and efficiency.

Governments generally strive hard to combat monopolies or control prices, especially in sectors producing vital necessities and sectors such as utilities (gas, electricity and water) where it is convenient or inescapable to have a single supplier. They are customarily obliged to exempt unions from similar regulation because, in politics, workers are in a majority and often present a solid front.

In 1995, American federal, State and municipal governments employed as many as 19 million people.[12] It is important to note that employees and their unions in the public sector in democracies have stronger bargaining power than those in the private sector. If the demands of labour in the private sector are excessive to the point where the employing enterprise becomes loss-making, the employer will either successfully resist or go bankrupt. In the public sector, the employers do not usually go bankrupt (except in the case of cities); rather, the tax-payers are obliged to cover the total costs of public employees.

At first sight it seems surprising that some members of the British Labour Party recently fought to defend that part of Labour's constitutional platform requiring the Party to push for public ownership of the means of production, or at least of 'the commanding heights of the economy'. Such members still passionately pine for nationalisation as the stairway to paradise, perhaps surprisingly after so many years of disappointment and financial disaster with public enterprises! These adherents often do not bother or care to offer justifications: rather it is an act of faith. A discreet reason lying behind the belief may be that it suits the union movement. They know from past experience that it is politically embarrassing to lay off thousands in public enterprises or to refuse wage and other demands for such reasons as the increasing cost of public subsidies.

Some workers are coming to understand that unions do not do much for non-members or for unemployed workers. They may in fact create unemployment where they make demands so heavy on employers as to bankrupt them – and even their whole industry – or frighten them away to places and countries where unions are less aggressive or non-existent. Or, in weaker situations and in recessions, they disenchant many of their members who break ranks and accept a lower wage as the only way of getting and keeping a job.

Feelings run high on these issues. Irrespective of the rights and wrongs of the matter, the fact is that the peak of union power has passed. Now in the USA, organised labour represents only 16 per cent of the labour force. In Britain, where unions never organised more than half the labour force, they were weakened and substantially reduced in the years of Mrs Thatcher's administration. Edward Heath was, arguably, ahead of his time: he tried what Thatcher successfully achieved, but he started with the touchiest target: the coal miners.

The statement in 1994 that unions are outdated and less important now that other factors, such as training, can do more for American workers' economic benefit, was surprising, coming as it did from the US Secretary of Labor, Robert Reich. We have, however, entered an era of more sophisticated and educated union leadership. They may be able to find acceptable and undamaging ways to help reduce the ominous gap between rich and poor.

We have seen that a minimum wage policy can only be of limited help.

Unions can be factors that possibly contribute to structural unemployment. They have been discussed in the context of their contribution to the labour market, both positive and negative. In the following section, they are considered again, but this time as viewed by labour law and relations specialists.

Labour law and relations

A number of the classic texts on this subject have been written by Bert Turner, Ben Roberts, Walter Galenson, Clark Kerr, Paul Dodd, John Dunlop and others. A whole new generation is now at work, though John Dunlop is still in the public eye as regards labour relations (Box 4.14). The big structural changes now ongoing call for a new look at what is happening to the organisation of labour and to the pertinent labour law

---

Box 4.12: British labour unions

On British unions Robert Taylor has written two informative but respectful books. His *The Fifth Estate*[14] remains the definitive portrait of the unions at the height of their influence. It shows how overlapping unions encouraged wasteful demarcation disputes; how shop stewards believed that the interests of capital and labour were incompatible; and how union leaders resisted the idea of rights for all workers, rather than just trade unionists'. Sixteen years later the membership of unions affiliated to the Trade Union Congress has fallen from 13 million to 7.3 million and his new book *The Future of the Trade Unions*[15] tells the story of 'a chastened labour movement striving to reform and renew itself. Mergers have reduced the number of unions affiliated to the TUC from 112 to 69, and there are far fewer demarcation disputes. The spread of "single union" agreements', has made it easier for managers to innovate. Strikes are at their lowest recorded level.'[16] This is reminiscent of the shift, decades earlier in USA, from craft (AFL) to industrial (CIO) unions.

An opinion poll in 1978 showed that 82% of Britons thought unions too powerful; in 1993 only 17% did. The leaders of the big unions now believe that their members' interests are best served by partnership with management rather than confrontation. Most of Britain's successful big companies have been willing to cooperate. In this respect both sides in the USA have something to learn. The British unions have come to see the European Union as a countervailing power to their own government in London. The EU legislation and regulation has taught British unions to accept the idea of positive legal rights for all workers, as opposed to immunities from the law only for their own members.

(Box 4.12). The London School of Economics, as usual, has been brilliantly far-seeing, as evidenced in an article on the occasion of its centenary.

In the USA the engine of society is correctly seen to be the employers or, as workers sometimes call them, 'the boss class'. The economy is capitalistic and our prosperity and most people's livelihood depends heavily on how well employers behave and do their job. That is true whether we like it or not. Theocracies are trying to come back in some poor countries because spiritual life fills the vacuum left by an absence of material benefits. In rich countries, happiness would seem to depend on wealth. Whatever your view of employers, you have to be logical in agreeing that it is in workers' best interests to have a society, a government and a taxation and legal system – fiscal policies and laws – which encourage people to be employers and to increase the number of jobs they can offer at the best possible wages.

If employers feel hemmed in, overtaxed, over-regulated, poorly served by the education and training system, losing control over the labour force they pay for, including the right to hire and fire, they are liable to contract, employ fewer people, change their address, go abroad, sell out to someone the workers may hate still more or go out of business altogether.

There were high hopes in the postwar Britain of 1946 for a 'Labour Government' and they were not all realised. The nationalisation of industries was found by many to be a red herring; labour unions' power became excessive and abusive in the enclaves they made; tax-payers (mainly workers) were left with huge bills to pay for subsidies to vast loss-making public industries that had been more generous and easy-going with their workers than they could afford. Public investment was well-meaning. Some vast projects (such as the groundnuts scheme in Africa) looked bright and rosy in the Sunday newspapers when first broached, but later flopped because of simple oversights foreseeable by scientists, local sages and other specialists. The Concorde aircraft was a marvellous bird to be proud of when it finally flew, but a massive price was paid by the masses for the dubious pleasure of moving VIPs and pop stars across the Atlantic.

British Airways is now one of the most efficient and profitable airlines in the world, but many millions were invested in it and written off over the years before it could be bought as a bargain by those in the private sector who then proceeded to run it well. Whole British industries and ports disappeared almost entirely and others were taken over by foreign managers and owners. It is only recently that investors have felt sufficiently encouraged to return to the economic environment in Britain.

So, for better or for worse, under capitalism we have to get from employers as much as they can give without smothering them with obligations and restrictions, or permitting excessive exploitation of workers at their hands. We also have to get workers to cooperate and be good teamplayers as managers struggle to win and keep customers, even where workers feel they are getting the rough end of a declining economic and social situation. And workers may well feel that this cannot entirely be blamed on foreign competition, the weather, the political party, or a dozen other external causes. Some of it is the fault of the capitalist system itself.

The unions have lost a great deal of power. Some have haemorrhaged membership and the workers, inside and outside the unions, have sometimes been beaten down and intimidated. They work hard, have often helped to raise productivity substantially, yet often seem to have been recompensed with little if any wage increase and a declining security of employment.

The labour laws are there. Strikes are not the best solution, but the unions believe that employers must sometimes be made to mend their ways. Arbitration and conciliation procedures are worth trying again and again. More people should take a close look at how and why Switzerland managed for so many decades without strikes or serious labour unrest. They have an industrial pact that works. Germany's experience with worker partnership schemes, and worker directors of company boards also merits study (Box 4.13).

Box 4.13: Worker ownership of companies

Historically, worker ownership was pioneered in Britain through the so-called worker partnership schemes. In the sixties the author met, at an annual conference of the companies running these schemes, the doyen of those pioneers: John Spedan Lewis, the founder of the John Lewis Partnership's department stores. Lewis was a charismatic character rather resembling one's image of an Old Testament prophet. Also prominent there was the Managing Director of Rowntree's Chocolates.

In the USA, the following by John Case appeared in 1994 in *The Inc. Report* (a New England magazine for small businesses):

no matter how bright the future looks, few companies will be handing out fat pay hikes, and few unions will win the kind of contracts their members once expected. In today's competitive marketplace, every company has to keep fixed costs low. So what do we do? Simple: cut employees in on ownership. They should get a share of the rewards if, and only if, their employers prosper. The fact is plenty of businesses have been quietly experimenting with employee ownership in recent years, and have found out what it can do. Some, for example, have been bought by their employees lock, stock and balance sheet, and have seen their fortunes improve dramatically. They range from biggees such as Avis (car rental) and Republic Engineered Steel (5000 employees) to everyday businesses

continued

Box 4.13 continued

such as Stone Construction Equipment, a machinery manufacturer in Honeoye, NY. Then there are the fast-growth entrepreneurial businesses, still run, often as not, by the men or women who founded them, but owned partly by the employees. Manco, a manufacturer and distributor of consumer products near Cleveland, has boosted its sales nearly twentyfold in only 15 years, to nearly $100 million. Chairman Jack Kahl is still in charge, but workers hold a 30% equity stake through an employee stock ownership plan. Finally, the most successful publicly traded companies often encourage widespread stock ownership among employees. Southwest Airlines, for instance, pays generous profit-sharing bonuses, which most employees take in the form of Southwest shares. Some veteran Wal-Mart cashiers retire with hundreds of thousands of dollars in company stock ... Thanks to favourable tax laws, several thousand American companies employing an estimated 12 million workers have set up Employee Stock Ownership Plans in the last several years. But in a country with nearly 4 million corporations and 120 million workers, employee ownership is only scratching the economic surface. What's needed is ... just a few governmental bucks for organizations that spread the word and provide information to company owners and managers interested in getting started ... Several states – Ohio is one – are already sponsoring such groups, and they have made a big difference.[17]

Profit-sharing schemes and worker-ownership of corporations are increasingly being looked at and tried out in the USA, but there remains a lot of pessimism about the chance of weaning America away from the traditional confrontational and aggressive stances on both sides in labour-management relations.

Too many laws and systems in the government sector in the USA take employers as their focal point. The business of employers is their companies' business. They are asked, even forced, to do a lot of other things that arguably should be the job of public authorities and other social institutions: for example, education, training, even daycare schemes. Although employers – especially in big companies – should be encouraged by tax and other incentives to do all they can to help the mothers they employ, it is good for society to have nurseries and kindergartens in each area open to *all* children of mothers who must work or study, including those employed by very small businesses and the self-employed (Box 4.14).

Box 4.14: Dunlop Commission on American labour

At the request of President Clinton in early 1993 a bi-partisan commission was appointed, chaired by Professor Emeritus John Dunlop of Harvard, former Labour Secretary of the US. It was composed of university economists and scholars and industry and labour representatives and it conducted many public hearings (some of them which I witnessed on TV). Its report appeared in June 1994. It found that wage distribution in America is the most unequal among the developed countries and warned that 'a healthy society cannot continue along the path the US is moving'. Productivity among US workers is in decline while (government) regulation of business has markedly increased. In one out of every four attempts to form unions in American corporations, at least one worker was illegally fired. Organised labour was losing its coercive power in the workplace and confrontations between big labour and management have declined while courts have become clogged with individual employee dispute cases.

The report stated that the real hourly compensation of American workers, once inflation was taken into account, had stagnated in the past two decades and actually fallen for male workers, a development 'unprecedented in the past 75 years in this country . . . The stagnation of real earnings and increased inequality of earnings is bifurcating the US labor market, with an upper tier of high-wage, skilled workers and an increasing "underclass" of low-paid labor.'

The present US Labor Secretary, former Harvard Professor Robert Reich, suggested to the press that the earnings gap was caused in part by a growing need for highly skilled and educated workers, a more technological society and the globalisation of the economy. 'A society divided between haves and have-nots, between well-educated and poorly educated, cannot be a prosperous or stable society'.

The Commission Report showed the number of labour disputes' cases between employees and management to have grown dramatically. This is in part because the number of federal statutes protecting individual workers has increased while the use of collective bargaining strategies by unions and workers has decreased. As a result, more workers are using the courts rather than the unions to address their grievances.

'This huge surge in litigation,' admitted Reich, 'undoubtedly uses up vast resources.' (Here again we see the heavy toll of a legal system way beyond cost control gradually ruining modern society.)

Dunlop suggested that some of the new techniques used by corporations to promote better relations between managers and workers, seen in the forms of 'collaborative work systems' and 'alternative dispute resolution procedures', may be the answer.

continued

Box 4.14 continued

Dunlop said his findings supported less antagonistic workplace relations than occur today. 'We're interested in those that are most effective and they should be encouraged. Our goal is to resolve the conflict between the high quality (techniques) and the concerns people have over the litigation that may ensue.'

'The Dunlop Commission's findings make clear that we can and must do more to promote genuine partnerships between workers and employers in American workplaces', said Thomas Donahue, AFL-CIO Secretary-Treasurer.

Social security, pension and health care schemes should not depend heavily on employers' help, either help with their financing or help with their administration. There should be no risk whatever of falling between the cracks, of losing health care coverage or pension rights or other benefits simply because a person is changing jobs, is between jobs, has long-term sickness, is undergoing retraining or is marrying and changing address, maybe going to another country. These systems should be centralised and financed by contributions from *all* people whether they are employed or not. Those with very low incomes and no earned incomes should receive earned income credits (subsidy incomes granted by the federal government on the basis of tax returns from the poorest) large enough to be able to pay their social security and health care contributions.

Box 4.15: Latest views on labour unions: who needs them?

Steve Early is a labour journalist and lawyer in the USA who works as a union representative on the Dunlop Commission (see Box 4.14). The following are excerpts from an article he wrote in June 1994:

'Many trade unionists had hoped that [the Dunlop Commission] would boost labor's long-thwarted campaign to strengthen workers' rights under the National Labor Relations Act, before mid-term elections produce a Congress that may be even more unfriendly to Clinton initiatives ... Instead the commission's 150-page report calls for further public debate on "ways to modernize the legal framework" for union organizing, contract negotiations, employee participation and dispute resolution ... [Commission members] Dunlop, Paul Weiler and Richard Freeman ... will resume their behind-the-scenes search for a "consensus" about what

continued

Box 4.15 continued

labor-law changes Congress should consider. Despite ample evidence of corporate America's zealous pursuit of further reductions in that portion of the work force that's unionized – now under 16% and dropping – commission members believe that employer hostility to unions can be lessened if labor makes itself more flexible and compliant, and management just realizes the benefits of having a union.

Freeman's 1984 book, *What Do Unions Do?* (written with Harvard economist James Medoff) argued that giving workers a union voice can actually make workplaces more efficient by allaying shop-floor discontent, reducing turnover and raising skill levels through union-negotiated job-training programs. But this useful study apparently failed to convince their Kennedy School of Government colleague, Robert Reich, who now serves as Clinton's labor secretary. He asked the Dunlop Commission to conduct further research on the link between employee organization and competitiveness because, in his view, "the jury is still out on whether the traditional union is necessary for the new workplace".

'For most employers, the verdict is already in. They're convinced that a union doesn't "add value" to a company, regardless of how "non-adversarial" it is. They prefer to run their business themselves, without the collective intervention of their workers. Dealing with a bona fide labor organization that has independence from management, its own outside resources and the legal right to bargain involves too much sharing of power and loss of control.'[18]

The notion of maximum salaries

Historically, the gap between the lowest and the highest paid has always been large. In India, a single high civil servant was paid more than the total pay of three thousand wallahs standing ready beside doors to open and shut them for less money than would buy the electricity required to open doors in a modern advanced economy. In the latter half of this century we thought we were becoming more egalitarian in the democracies. It was certainly said to be so in 'the peoples' democracies'. It is now patently obvious in the great cities around the world that the rich are getting richer and the poor are getting poorer, irrespective of the system under which they live.

Since the American and French Revolutions, the assets owned by 1 per cent of the population of the USA have varied between a quarter and a third of all national wealth and are now exceeding a third. In Britain today, more than three-quarters of the land is owned by 4 per cent of the people.

Since the time of 'Mr Five Per Cent', the original Gulbenkian, the world's richest people have thanked their lucky stars for oil. Petroleum has given some of them a personal income exceeding the national income of most Third World developing countries. In less-developed countries, heads of state like Mobutu in Zaire and Marcos in the Philippines have personally pocketed sums exceeding the combined income of five to ten million of their citizens.

Let us look now at 'ordinarily' rich workers in the latter-day prosperous countries. American wage and salary earners raised their eyebrows when hearing that Michael Milken, who invented and sold 'junk bonds' for billions of dollars in the 1980s had received a salary of $550 million in one year (Box 4.16), and not much less in the other years before he went to jail and his employer went bankrupt. Milken was not alone in the front line of the salary stakes. For example, it usually takes just a few months to make a film. When filmstar Jack Nicholson acted in 'Batman' he received a salary of $50 million, apart from other benefits. He did not have to appear for work every day during production as he was not in every scene of the film. At the box office and through a wide variety of commercial promotions based on it, 'Batman' earned a billion dollars. Nicholson got less than a tenth of that, so he only had about $150 million for a few months' work: say $50 million a month. Actor Tom Hanks' share of box office receipts from 'Forrest Gump' soon reached $10 million. The writer of the story got a quarter of a million: handsome for most writers.

Ordinary mortals in high positions, such as chief executive officers (CEOs) of large or lucrative corporations in the USA and other wealthy countries, are accustomed to a salary of at least $1 million per annum. Moreover, this seems to be a kind of guaranteed minimum. Many CEOs found their were salaries increasing – and rarely being cut – even when the corporations they headed were suffering serious losses. Many readers will recall those individuals who were notoriously rich and vastly renumerated yet not only failed in business but, worse than that, defrauded the public at home and abroad. Recent examples include the pension-raiding scandal linked to the Maxwell publishing family; the vast losses suffered by account-holders in the Bank International for Credit and Commerce, and the gross negligence of the managers of the old Barings Bank regarding the gambler on their staff in Singapore, who charmed them while he was still winning.

Box 4.16: The cost of talent in the USA

Here are some exceptional annual earnings (salaries and bonuses in one year or in year quoted):

Maurice Milken (junk bond king)	= $550 million (1987)
Lee Iacocca (saviour of Chrysler)	= $20 million
Michael Eisner (booster of Disney)	= $45 million
Steven Ross (Time–Warner take-overer)	= $78 million
Leon Hirsch (head, US Surgical Corp.)	= $118 million (1991)
Top ten trial lawyers (range)	= $6 to $450 million (1988)
CEOs of 200 biggest corps. (average)	= $3 million
Neuro-surgeons (average)	= $339,000
Cardiovascular surgeons (average)	= $420,000
President of USA	= $203,000
Ceiling imposed on public officials	= $115,000
Male economists	= $67,000
Female economists	= $53,000
60,000 Americans	= $1 million and over p.a.
600,000 Americans (total assets)	= $1 million and over (1980)
1,500,000 Americans (total assets)	= $1 million and over (1990)

It pays to be in a corporation: for example, contrast surgeons, mere professionals, with Leon Hirsch, head of US Surgical Corporation, who earned $118 million in the first year of the last recession and told the public 'I'm not paid enough.' It is also hard to beat lawyers, who neither complain about, nor mention, their earnings. The President of the USA has a joke salary but gets free room, board and transportation! (Even so, poor Bill Clinton's meagre personal resources have by 1996 been used up to the point of bankruptcy by the legal costs of defending himself against political persecution about what are peccadilloes – by Washington's standards – or nothing at all).

What matters are real earnings. The following figures show how earnings were affected by increased cost of living from 1972 to 1990:

	1972	1980	1989	1990
CEOs of 500 Fortune corps.	100	130	222	200
Surgeons		100	110	141
Public school teachers	100	80	107	108
Top career civil servants	100	70	70	

Source: Derek Bok.[19]

continued

Box 4.16 continued

Real earnings change over space as well as time. If you take a job paying $25,000 in Cleveland, you would earn more or less as follows elsewhere: San Jose +23.1%, San Francisco +18.4%, New York +16.8%, Boston +9.6%, Chicago +6.6%, Philadelphia +2.7%, Atlanta +2.2%, St. Louis –1.7%, Raleigh-Durham –2.1%, Tampa –6.2%, Norfolk, Va., –8.4%, Colorado Springs – 10.2%, Laredo, Texas –23.%.

A religious writer comments:[20]

> The enormous income disparities between the top echelons of corporate America and the bottom rungs of the economy simply cannot be justified by differences in class background, education, opportunity, or even ability. How do we square the enormous polarities with the ultimate moral worth that our ethical and religious traditions would ascribe to each individual?

The personal differences mentioned above do not justify the economic inequality, but they may help to explain it. The moral worth of an individual is, however, very different from his material worth, usually called his 'net worth' (because his wealth is what he owns, net of his debts). People who think that someone's moral worth justifies or explains their material worth betray their ignorance of morality and their misunderstanding of the way net worth is usually amassed. If Somerset Maugham's play 'Our Betters' is revived, do go and see it: it conveys a bitter portrayal of the gap between material and moral worth in practice. Maugham depicted the British upper class in the 1920s. Today a bitter author might write in today's jargon that gross income inequality does not square with moral worth in so far as poverty undermines human dignity and cripples the human capacity for generosity on the bottom rungs of the economy. Affronts to human dignity abound on those bottom rungs.

Wealth can also make a person undignified. We have seen examples of some of those destined by inheritance for the top rungs of the economy who have grown up from being odious teenagers into monstrous adults. There is a debate as to whether the unscrupled are sprinkled thicker among the 'new money' crowd than the 'old money' crowd. Possession of wealth over several generations may have had a civilising influence and helped produce some dignified people. But the new money people may themselves remember what it was like to be poor and thereby retain some sympathy for those who are still down and out.

Box 4.17: USA: Executive salaries

From 1 January, 1994, American companies could only count as business expense on their tax returns salaries not exceeding $1 million per annum. Any amount paid above that level to any employee henceforward must be paid out of profits, or added to (non-deductible) losses. In 1993 the average salary of a chief executive of a large corporation (with published accounts) was $3.8 million, or more than 150 times a typical factory worker's pay. Thomas F. Frist of Hospital Corp. came first in the USA, with a salary of $127 million, demonstrating that medicine is indeed a business. In Britain, executives prefer fringe benefits which may not be considered part of their income and are therefore not subject to personal income tax. American executives have all kinds of benefits beside salaries: Lear Jet planes, for example, are common and corporations pay up to $50 million for the more expensive jets (e.g. ones built by the British). But the Americans do not seem to worry about large salaries as well. It remains to be seen how much of American salaries above $1 million dollars are translated into other benefits which can still be counted as deductible items, at least on corporate tax returns. By 1996 a salary of $1 million looks low for the head of any large American Corporation.

On what economic basis can people be said to be overpaid?

If their company is losing money, should the top executives not take a cut in pay, along with more junior staff who are either earning less or laid-off? Though it is often shareholders' money that is risked, the CEO or entrepreneur who organises and operates any economic future performs a vital, complex function. He deserves a competitive salary for that plus a share in the profits, especially if, as in most cases, he is also a shareholder.

Any salary is justified if it is less than the wealth its earner personally adds to the company's or the nation's total. Unfortunately in some cases it is hard to prove what part of a gain achieved, or loss averted, would have been better or worse, as the case may be, if the responsible executive were withdrawn from the scene. Due note should be taken of the view of J.K. Galbraith expressed in 1967 and repeated in 1994:

> *With age and an increasing scale of operations, it has long been observed, power in the corporation passes from the stockholders to management. The Board of Directors, nominally the voice of the stockholders, becomes the passive instrument of the management that, indeed, selects it. Then, not surprisingly, since maximization of return is the avowed incentive in the market system, the management comes to pursue its own goals, to maximize its own return . . . Responsible to*

itself, protective of its own position, the servant of its own interest, the management is interested in compensation, security of tenure and perquisites. Defending management interest in personal reward against hostile takeover attack and extending management power through merger or acquisition take precedence over efficient operation of the corporation

When management attention is diverted from such efficient operation, the modern large corporation becomes subject to a bureaucratic stasis, an inner-directed bureaucratic immobility. Thought and needed change become subordinate to established policy. Initiative is diffused through the organization and is tested not for its effect but for its conformity with what has been done before.[21]

Mainstream economists have not lost as much faith as Galbraith has in the corrective influences of shareholders' interests, consumer preferences between corporations' outputs, and market forces – plus possible government intervention in some countries. But the fact is that large global corporations do have considerable powers, consumer preferences are influenced by expensive advertising campaigns and market forces are subjugated by monopolistic influences.

Many people of fine character, high skill and a long life of hard work and valuable experience deeply resent the huge fortunes made by people in the world of entertainment or finance, while they have earned a comparative pittance. A few such fortunate individuals themselves sometimes feel guilty about their earnings. Michael Caine, for example, was rueful as he reflected, after pocketing massive earnings from his first successful movie, that in a few weeks he had gained more than his father had earned in a whole lifetime of heavy but humbler work. Ironically, in the case of the entertainers it is often much easier than in the case of business executives to verify that they have personally created more wealth for others than for themselves.

Business executives and financiers do have the help of their staff. Filmstars are immensely helped by film directors, by the script writers who create dialogue contributing powerfully to the charisma of their on-screen personality and by other colleagues. Nevertheless, the huge sums earned by a few films are largely due to its star. The film 'Basic Instinct' earned a great deal of money from millions of filmgoers avid for the sexual delights unfolded by Sharon Stone. A minor star when she was hired, Sharon was paid a tiny fraction of the 'Basic Instinct' earnings. Due to her success and surge in personal popularity, she was paid a princessly sum for her next film, 'Sliver', perhaps a film with less substance than 'Basic Instinct', which nevertheless again enabled her to prove her box office success. It is not just a question of her body: there are plenty of similar ones in California. Like those other sudden commercial successes, Julia Roberts and Geena Davis, Sharon has personality, character and intelligence.

Further proof of the personal earning power of entertainers is when, for instance, a long string of films, each employing different casts, earn far more money than other films, having in common only one factor: one person is involved with them all, like Steven Spielberg. His talents as a film director earned far more money for others than the large sums he personally earned. His successes made possible the production of many other films which did not cover their costs but provided good entertainment and welcome employment for their production workers. One might say the same for the writer Michael Crighton, though some of the films of his books were directed by Spielberg.

Many entertainers and performers have to suffer long periods of unemployment and, especially the women, may be forced into retirement at an early age. Without the rates of pay when employed, which carry performers through 'quiet' periods, the public would not enjoy such a choice of talent.

In the summer of 1994 in the USA there was much anguish among baseball fans because of the threat of a nationwide baseball strike in mid-season. At issue was management's proposal that the salaries of baseball players should be subject to a cap, to avoid bankrupting the game. Few tears fell for the players when it was revealed that the average salary of each member of the National Baseball Association already well exceeded a million dollars a year. They are the main beneficiaries of the revenues earned from spectators, televiewers and advertisers. The salaries of the best players are bid up by the keenness of each team owners to come out top. The best is the enemy of the good.

Bystanders also get hurt when the giants fight. It was estimated that the baseball strike deprived of employment many thousands of drink and candy vendors and other participants and auxiliaries, with losses of about $30 million spread over their small earnings. Those earnings were needed to raise the income of many of them to a level their families could just live on. The players looked annoyed and aggressive; all these others looked frightened. When British Rail is shut down by strikes, thousands of small station vendors have to shut down too, without financial compensation.

Entertainment stars in Britain also earn well, but executives there earn less than in the USA. Once, the heads of British global companies used to earn lower salaries than a few of their juniors in foreign branches in countries where pay was better. That reflected a response to the wastage of paying high salaries in socialist Britain when most of the money would go to the tax man rather than to earners. Income taxation has now been markedly reduced in Britain and senior executives and bosses now get better paid (Box 4.18). International competition induces the highly industrialised countries to reduce the differences between them as regards the rates of taxation of wage and salary earners. An exception is Canada, where taxes of all kinds and public debt are so excessive that the economic future of the country is gravely threatened.

> **Box 4.18: High pay in the UK**
>
> The table outlines the total remuneration package of the highest paid director of selected institutional investors in 1993 (converted at £1 = $1.55):
>
> | | |
> |---|---|
> | Gartmore | $1,464,750 |
> | Prudential | $1,292,700 |
> | MAM | $897,450 |
> | Legal and General | $733,150 |
> | Commercial Union | $553,350 |
> | Standard Life | $494,450 |
> | M&G Group | $434,000 |
> | Postel | $252,650 |
>
> *The Economist,* which drew the above figures from company reports, noted that 'many of Britain's company chiefs are overpaid, including some of the ones booted out of their jobs. Other bosses deserve more'.[22] A view gaining much support is that Britain's executives should have lower salaries but higher options to buy stocks in the company they head. This would relate their pay more closely to their performance.

Coming back to the thousands of intrinsically fine human beings who help make our society so much better and who never become rich, we should note this. The people who *do* become rich mainly do so because they place high utility on wealth and also – a severely restrictive additional requirement – because they have rare personal advantages or talents that correspond to the tastes and values of the mass of people who spend their money to get what they want.

People not only get the government they deserve, especially in an ostensible democracy; they get, under what economists call 'consumer sovereignty', the distribution of wealth which largely reflects how well the leading players in the economy have given them satisfaction. There would be jealousy of such leading players whether they were highly paid or not. In fact many people do not resent the wealthy: they idealise their lifestyles, appreciate their cosmetic merits and are grateful to them for what they have done to amuse the masses and indulge their appetites. Resentment does, however, grow wherever people come to realise the extent to which they are being exploited by groups or individuals conferring few benefits to society at large.

People distinguished in less stellar ways, the unsung heroes and the saints in our society, may not care about wealth or even prefer to avoid it. Many of them will certainly have other valuable private and public rewards. They may sleep well at night. They may envy no one. They, their family and friends, may be able to enjoy life much more because of their personal qualities. They may be highly respected and loved by most of those to whom they become known. They may have qualities that do not fade with age. They may not be dependent on a single quality that could be lost, but feel secure in a multiplicity of abilities and achievements.

American doctors, who are no more capable than doctors in some other countries, have an average income from their work four times the average income in the nation as a whole. Doctors in other wealthy countries have an average income which is simply double the national average.

American dentists do somewhat better than American doctors. They may need extra compensation as theirs is a stressful life: patients are unhappy when visiting them; dentists' divorce, depression and suicide rates are higher than for those in other professions. Most mysterious is the elevation of the high fees demanded and received by orthodontists.

The President's wife, Hillary Rodham Clinton, criticised the medical profession and government aid programmes on 7 November 1993 for pushing young doctors into specialities at the expense of general practice. She said the trend must be reversed. She told a conference of medical educators that the primary care physician is the key to the success of the administration's proposal to revamp the nation's health care system and provide care for all Americans. Several medical students told her they saw no advantage to going into general practice, where the pay and prestige are less than that enjoyed by specialists. She replied: 'The characterization is unfortunately an accurate description of the situation in the medical profession today. The administration's health care reforms are meant to reverse that description by raising the status of general practitioners.'

One student said to her: 'I come from a poor family, I had to struggle to get into medical school and feel disadvantaged all over again by having to commit myself to a primary care practice to get a low-interest education loan.' Mrs Clinton replied: 'It's about time that we start thinking about the common good, the national interest, instead of just individuals in our country. I'm sorry if you feel personally disadvantaged.'

In Britain, people were once brought up to consider the insurance industry as a noble one. It enabled the whole community to share in alleviating the burden of a few people who are hit by crushing disasters. There were even quotations available from the gospels to support the principle of insurance. The huge British insurance companies had a long, distinguished history and could always be depended upon to remain secure and serve the public. Even Lloyd's insurance market was bloodied but unbowed after its enormous losses from wartime shipping, foreign hurricanes, floods and other disasters in recent years.

I was shocked to discover that insurance companies in the USA were not immune from the nationwide process of famous corporations rising and falling and constantly changing, merging and going bankrupt. Many thousands of retirees and handicapped people faced financial ruin and worse as their life-insurance companies failed, but were seldom rescued by the public sector.

Mrs Clinton complained to a meeting of the American Academy of Pediatrics on 1 November 1993 about misleading advertisements against health care reform being put on television by the insurance companies:

What you don't get told in the ad is that it is paid for by insurance companies who think their way is the better way . . . They like being able to exclude people from coverage because the more they can exclude, the more money they can make. [She was indignant at the] gall of the ads by the very industry that has brought us to the brink of bankruptcy because of the way they have financed health care . . . Enough is enough. We want our health care system back . . . As you know better than I, they second guess doctors' medical decisions every day, narrowing and limiting their choices and undermining their autonomy . . .The industry is spending millions of dollars to scare the American people . . . in order to block changes that would cut into their profits.

On 8 November 1993 Mrs Clinton told twenty-three health care reporters: 'I have no doubt that the forces of the *status quo* will dig in their heels and do everything they can, while praising the potential of reform, to try to undermine it even before being enacted.'

Arguably the worst offenders now in anti-vocational practices and opportunistic profiteering are the lawyers, especially the litigation lawyers, and the system of law and 'justice'. Lawyers do not easily shock the general public, because few people ever see a lawyer and few ever held them in particularly high regard.

Business people might be regarded as being in a similar situation of not having started out with much of a reputation to maintain. In the Second World War, many excelled themselves in public service and acts of honour and many have gained fame from their philanthropy. Hence the public is more shocked by the spreading realisation that, inside public corporations today, there are chief executives who succeed in dominating their boards of directors and arranging continual improvements in their remuneration unrelated to the performance of the business. Shareholders have failed to stop this. Some of this handsome remuneration is organised to reduce an executive's personal taxation and to continue payments to him or to his estate for many years after he has left the corporation.

To remedy this shocking abuse, one step supported by President Clinton is the notion that a maximum salary should be officially recognisable, in the sense that any remuneration above that level should not be a deductible item as a business expense, prior to corporation taxation. If salaries above the maximum continue to be paid, that excess non-deductible remuneration would eat more heavily into the after-tax corporate income available for distribution as dividends.

In the USA the figure that has been considered as a maximum salary for corporate tax purposes is $1 million per annum: again an indication that that figure is becoming established as a 'minimum wage' for the upper classes. In 1995 the Republicans in Congress discussed tax and other benefits for the middle class and sought to give relief to those with incomes below $200,000. There is a major difference between the cost of middle-class life within major American cities and outside them. It is hard to maintain a middle-class existence in such cities as Boston, New York, Washington, Los Angeles or San Francisco with a family income, before taxes, under $100,000. It is also hard for a husband and a wife each to find and keep a job paying more than $50,000 anywhere in the USA except Wall Street.

Fixed incomes and profits: parity of esteem

A wealthy man used to be one with a million dollars. Today, that would not be enough to pay for one of his houses. A person who gets a public name simply for being wealthy has to have a billion dollars. There were about one hundred and thirty-six billionaires in the USA in 1995. There was a similar number in Germany and Japan combined.[23] There are billionaires elsewhere in the world; also various species of royalty or head-of-state billionaires. A leader of the Colombian drug trade had three billion dollars until he was killed by gunfire. He could not take the money with him.

None of the American billionaires have grown that wealthy from salary-earning alone. They have so-called 'un-earned' incomes and, more important, capital gains. These both come from capital investments: shares in companies, possession of buildings and equipment that are leased out, or bought and sold; and from the ownership of natural resources: land, oil and mineral reserves, forests and plantations.

Property owners, possessors of immense wealth, have always received great respect; nobody ever thought or had the courage to question their right to it. Great military leaders often seized wealth, believing themselves to be more feared and respected when seen in their trappings of wealth on top of their armed might. People who earned wages and salaries were seen as the servants of the wealthy. The best paid were seen as sharing some of the glory of their rich masters.

As civilisation progressed, knowledge and science spread. Some of the more senior salaried people began to earn respect and prestige for their command of the facts and of the philosophy and management arts of great enterprises. Nevertheless, most people are still ready to say that a salary above a million a year looks excessive. It is too much to be fully deserved. Yet, when they hear of a private income of ten million dollars or more, it is different. It is 'all right' if it comes from possessions someone built up in a period of hard work, risk-taking and perhaps gambling-type activities given euphemous names from 'Lady Luck' upwards to 'judicious placements'. Equally it is often regarded as still tolerable if the same massive income, or more, comes from 'Daddy'. That is how it should be if you were a dutiful and loving son or daughter and preferably blessed with good looks, refined tastes and charitable inclinations: in other words 'old money' with a sense of decency and duty. Reactions might be different if you got the money as a mistress, sycophant or nurse who took advantage of a rich old man's weaker moments in his declining years.

We are still at the point where, however meritorious and devoted to work a person may be, they have much more of an uphill task to justify a large fixed earned income than an equal or larger income from honestly acquired or inherited wealth or from betting on the right horses. More oddly still, a fixed income earned in the private sector is rarely deemed to be too much until it exceeds well over a million dollars a year, whereas one earned in the public sector is readily questioned as soon as it exceeds a hundred thousand dollars a year. Public servants are paid from 'tax-payers' money' whereas corporate officials are paid from corporate incomes earned from 'consumers' money which they spent voluntarily'. As we have seen, two-thirds of the value of what corporations produce is bought by consumers.

Consumers and tax-payers are often the same people. However, they respond differently to different external events. If, say, civil servants' salaries are increased modestly, perhaps even less than the rise in the cost of living, tax-payers often seem to personally resent it. However, if the top executives of a corporation get a salary increase of 20 per cent and a bonus issue of company shares on top, few consumers write letters of complaint to a newspaper (except where the corporations are public utilities!).

Consumers should never forget that any benefits going to corporate personnel are ultimately derived from the price they pay for the company's products. These benefits to corporate personnel might include any money spent on corporate seminars in Hawaii or on a fireworks display in New York harbour, or on irritating advertising, or on a side-payment (bribe) to a congressman. Even if a company overspends, borrows heavily from banks and then goes bankrupt, the consumer will still pay for it all. The bank has to cover its losses on the company's unpaid loans out of its earnings from consumers. If the bank itself goes bankrupt and cannot give depositors their money back, the government – i.e. the tax-payers – has to refund the depositors (through a money-losing institution called the Federal Deposit Insurance Corporation). The point is that wages, salaries, profits, dividends, capital gains – *all* the sources of income – should arguably have parity of esteem and be judged on the same basis and measured against the same standard of entitlement.

Public employees can only get salaries – there are no profits to draw from. Employees and executives in the *private* sector can take out their incomes in a variety of ways. If high salaries shock the public and also incur heavy taxation, those two painful reactions from the outside world can be avoided by taking incomes and personal benefits in other and often hidden ways. The man in the street is often unaware of such practices in the private sector. However, the salaries of public employees are widely known, involving uniform scales of pay which get daily scrutiny from a jealous, though often more highly paid, labour force in the private sector.

Why should top public officials carrying responsibilities and employing numbers of people greater than those in the largest corporations be paid salaries in five figures, whereas corporate executives get six, seven or eight figure incomes out of their occupation? People are inclined to judge harshly the performance of government departments, which have to work in the open. People are much more tolerant of the performance of private corporations and regard their unrevealed internal affairs as their own business secrets.

In reality, large corporations can be as bureaucratic as government agencies. The latter might become more efficient if their top staff were better paid and respected and if they were less frequently pestered with disruptive investigations by parliaments and by the media. The top public positions in the USA carry immense responsibility and involve the employment of millions of people and the deployment of billions of dollars. The jobs are at least as complex as the management of huge global corporations and should attract similarly outstanding people. Where governments fall down badly on the job, getting little done, doing it painfully slowly and not at all well, it may be unjust to underpay and revile the public employees. Much of the blame may really lie with the political leadership and with a patronage system that allocates public jobs to cronies.

In Part IV we have seen that there are:

● money wages and salaries;

● real wages and salaries, amounting to what cash earnings will buy today;

● differences in income and welfare between workers including their working hours and holidays, their protection from injury and ill-health on the job and their working conditions.

People hold various opinions about inequality of incomes, some of which are odd, inconsistent, illogical and emotional. Among the passions aroused, jealousy looms large. These views and forces often lead to unjust policies affecting remuneration and thereby the distribution of income.

Why is inequality of incomes increasing?

In 1995 the US Census Bureau published a new measure of inequality in income distribution. This includes capital gains, but excludes transfer payments from government. In 1986, the private sector income was distributed as follows: just 1 per cent for the lowest quintile (i.e. the bottom one-fifth of the US population, merely a 1 per cent share of national income); 8 per cent for the second quintile; 15 per cent for the third or middle quintile; 24 per cent for the fourth quintile and 52 per cent for the highest quintile. The top quintile gets more income than the total amount going to the remaining 80 per cent of people. Put another way, the bottom fifth get only $1 out of each $100 whereas the top fifth get $52 out of each $100.

The average American has become poorer in the last ten years or so. From 1960 to 1973 the median family income (in constant 1985 dollars) rose by 43 per cent. But then, from the peak in 1973 down to 1985, median family income fell by 5 per cent, and has continued to fall since then. The whole time the rich got richer, though they have not done so as rapidly since 1973 as before. In 1960–1973, the richest 5 per cent of people – one person in twenty – had a 48 per cent income increase, and in 1973–1985 a further 7 per cent increase, all in constant dollars or real terms.

Total accumulated *wealth* in America is even more unequally distributed between families than is income. In 1983 the richest 10 per cent of US families had 72 per cent of US wealth. The superrich, that is the top 0.5 per cent of families – one person in two hundred of the population – owned 35 per cent of US wealth. The only type of wealth distributed to a large number of families is home ownership. In fact, if we exclude the value of home ownership, the superrich had 45 per cent of US wealth, while the top 10 per cent of families had 83 per cent of the wealth. In terms of the *types* of wealth, the superrich owned 36 per cent of real estate (excluding private homes), 47 per cent of corporate stock, 44 per cent of all types of bonds and 58 per cent of all business assets (including corporations, unincorporated business, farms and professional practices). At the same time, the richest 10 per cent of families owned 78 per cent of real estate, 89 per cent of corporate stock, 90 per cent of bonds and 94 per cent of business assets.[24]

In contrast, what is the lot of the workers in the USA? Since the wealthiest 10 per cent of families have 94 per cent of all business assets and other property, most business or property *income* goes to the top 10 per cent. The 90 per cent of the population who are less well-off are workers, whose income is almost exclusively their earnings from their employment – their wages and salaries. In the period from 1949 to 1982, nine people out of ten (i.e. 90 per cent) received 7 out of every 10 dollars (i.e. 70 per cent) of national income. The richest one person out of ten (10 per cent), in contrast, received unearned income or property income which brought them three out of every ten dollars in the national income (i.e. 30 per cent): in other words, roughly two-thirds of national income for nine-tenths of the population and the other third of national income for a tenth of the population.

This is all income before taxes. Tax rates are heavier on the rich than the poor when applied, but the rich evade paying more of the tax due than do the poor. So although incomes are rather more equal post-tax than pre-tax, tax evasion lessens the impact that a progressive tax regime (taking more from higher earners) would otherwise have on income inequality.

Over a much longer period in the USA, namely from 1780, what did push up the share of wages in national income was the increase from 20 to 80 per cent in the proportion of income-receivers who were wage and salary earners. What happened in the last two centuries was that many small farms were combined into a few large ones. The same happened with small firms, which were being amalgamated into, or displaced by, large corporations, as when small shopkeepers were replaced by large stores and chains. As a result, many independent people formerly in business entered the labour force and became employees. The observed long-term increase in labour's share in national income was in part due to this trend toward agglomeration.

Why do the rich get richer and the poor get poorer?

Here we first consider the views of Robert Samuelson, a distinguished economics reporter in Washington, quoted and summarised in Box 4.19.

Samuelson's analysis mainly helps to explain the growing inequalities among people who *work* for their living – from the humblest worker to the top CEO or filmstar – as distinct from explaining the broader canvas of deep income inequality between rich and poor in general. When it comes to explaining that glaring rift, there is on the expenditure/saving/investment side a major and simple (endogenous) factor at work.

Everyone has certain minimum irreducible needs and, beyond that, many people have other 'conventional necessities' which oblige them, like the poorest, to spend nearly all of their income. They neither save much, nor acquire much money from other family members (e.g. a wealthy spouse) or from a lottery. In contrast, among the rich, we normally have families whose incomes rise far above their expenditure. This is especially true of the 'old money': heirs and 'trust fund kids' who consolidate and carry forward wealth for centuries (with the exception of family spendthrifts, gamblers and speculators). These families accumulate savings, make sound investments which pay-off and build up ever more capital. Most of us, studying arithmetic at school, have seen how a simple savings account, left to itself, will grow at compound rates of interest; metaphorically it can

Box 4.19: 'The new inequality'

Robert Samuelson writes under the above heading:

Explaining extreme wealth and poverty isn't hard. More single-parent families and immigrants have bloated the poor population. Between 1969 and 1989 the number of single-parent families jumped from 6 million to 13 million. Meanwhile, salaries for the best-paid entertainers, executives and athletes have risen sharply. TV means that sports and entertainment reach larger audiences; salaries rise. Global markets mean bigger companies and higher executive compensation.

What's less understood is the creeping inequality affecting everyone else. The gap between skilled and less-skilled workers has grown. Among 30-year-old men, college graduates comprised about 20% more than high school graduates in the 1970s. By 1989 the gap was 47%.

Apart from widening educational gaps between workers, Samuelson investigated other possible factors increasing inequality. He reviews a number of 'popular theories' which he said *can't* account for the greater inequalities. There is the trade effect, but trade is not such a large part of the US economy. The 'minimum wage' stayed stuck at $3.35 between 1981 and 1990, but only 8.8% earned a wage at or below that level in 1981 and even less, 3.1%, earned at or below that level in 1990.

Samuelson prefers an explanation arising from changing employment policies of businesses. They were optimistic and hired amply for all conceivable needs for 30 years after 1946. Then, the possibility – and the actuality – of recessions reared their heads, and in the 1980s optimism evaporated. There was a deep recession. Competition intensified from imports and deregulation. Corporate takeovers mushroomed. Firms became obsessed with cost-cutting, as opposed to sales growth, to boost profits. Cost pressures focused heavily on new workers. It's easier to trim wages for entry-level jobs than to engage in demoralizing across-the-board salary cuts. Companies also cut costs by contracting out jobs they had once done for themselves . . .

Although this process tended to work against the young, it didn't always. Some companies eased older workers out and replaced them with lower-paid, younger workers... This sort of substitution may explain the one area where inequality has not increased: between men and women. In 1992 women's earnings were 71% of men's, up from 60% in 1980. As women gain more job experience and seniority, their incomes rise . . .

A rising tide still lifts most boats even if not – in the nautical metaphor – all equally.[26]

become an oak tree out of an acorn. Wealth leads to power; power is used to consolidate, protect and augment wealth; and there you have it.

The poor have a floor to their poverty: death from starvation or exposure. There is normally no ceiling to the potential of the rich to add to their wealth. Slim possibilities exist of it being seized by government, pillaged by others or given away by the rich themselves.

It is interesting to note the explanation of inequality by another economist, Robert Kuttner, who is politically to the left of Samuelson. He sees the matter as:

> *The sources of inequality are multiple. They include competition from lower-wage countries, technology displacing blue-collar jobs, corporations squeezing out middle managers, unions losing bargaining power, increased immigration of people who work cheap [he means cheaply], deregulation of once stable industries, and the rise of a more entrepreneurial economy with a few big winners. If your remedy is simple, it's wrong.*[25]

Both Samuelson and Kuttner's remarks illustrate an American tendency to think of most people as workers. Perhaps because of the old nightmares of McCarthyite persecution, as well as the lingering myths about American democracy, they are afraid to think or speak in terms of acquired situations or, put another way, 'class'.

PART V

THE PARADOX OF
PROSPERITY AND DISILLUSION

Malaise and optimism growing fainter

In late 1994 *Time* magazine and Cable News Network jointly released the results of a public opinion poll revealing that Americans were sceptical about their economy despite its progress and the USA's world leadership in size and competitiveness. *Time* said the prospects for the US economy were among the brightest they had been since the Second World War. It quoted a statement by Allen Sinai, a leading Wall Street economist, that the United States was 'in the midst of a long, durable and sustainable expansion' that could prove to be 'one of the longest and healthiest upturns in the modern era'.[1]

Nevertheless, 29 per cent of those polled saw this economy as stagnant and a further 9 per cent said it was in recession. Some of the latter, though generalising, may have been influenced by relatively poor conditions in their own area, because 54 per cent of those polled said they thought the recession had not yet ended in their area and only a minority (40 per cent) thought the recession was over. In general, some 55 per cent of those polled did not feel better off, while 37 per cent found their situation had improved. The 'gloom' reflected at grass-roots level hardly squared with the optimism of analysts such as Allen Sinai.

Maybe some individuals, although not personally experiencing progress, were not necessarily badly off, because an astonishing 81 per cent answered that their family finances were doing either fairly or very well. Answers are often affected by the wording of questions. You could imagine yourself answering positively to a question about 'family finances' if you were not heavily in debt or if you had some savings set aside against a rainy day.

The survey responded to a point, already made here, about a single statesman being unable to turn the economy around. In answer to the question who should get credit for the economic upturn, 28 per cent said the Clinton administration, 19 per cent cited congress Republicans and 43 per cent said neither deserved the credit.

Twenty-five years ago, Charles Reich wrote *The Greening of America*, a best-selling book that appeared just as the decades of economic difficulties and downturns began in 1970. As a lawyer-philosopher he did not foresee those difficulties and his view of America's future was then cheerful and optimistic. Now Reich has published a follow-up called *Opposing the System*. He has said about his new book: 'I hope it will explain why the country has gone so far off course in the last 25 years.' His explanation, briefly, is this.

In the nineteenth century, Americans thought along the following lines: 'Success is determined by character, morality, hard work and self-denial.

They do not accept that organizations predominate over individuals ... or that social problems are due to something other than bad character.' That attitude, he notes, 'led to robber barons, business piracy, ruinous competition, unreliable products and false advertising, grotesque inequality and the chaos of excessive individualism'. Then, 'in the twentieth century, consciousness built its value structure upon the organization with the help of liberal intellectuals, the educated professionals and technicians, middle-class suburbanites, labor union leaders'. However, in Reich's opinion, this was equally as unlikely to solve society's ills as the nineteenth century value system.

Reich keeps his sociological view that, already in 1970, there was a hint of the emergence among educated young people of a new consciousness that 'declares the individual self is the only true reality'. Those sensing it 'do not compete in "real life"'. They do not measure others, they do not see others as something to struggle against. People are brothers, the world is ample for all. There is a revolution coming.' Non-violent, 'it will originate with the individual and with culture, and it will change the political structure only as its final act'.

In his new book Reich contends that we are governed by an 'invisible system that . . . represents a combination of two kinds of government – public government and private economic government, functioning together'. Private economic government (corporations and businesses) has more control over the lives of Americans today than public government (elected and appointed officials), because the private sector controls our ability to earn a living. We are governed by a managerial élite that moves freely between the corporate and public worlds and shares the assumption that economic growth is always good and that society will always prosper if market forces are allowed to run their 'natural' course. The resulting 'managerial economy', prizing efficiency and growth above all else, has human costs that are unacceptably high, ranging from decaying schools to a damaged environment, from social strife to individual despair. The way out of our morass, he argues, is via a 'new map of reality' in which we realise that 'human beings . . . matter and an economic system is just a machine'.

In America today, Reich finds we have a:

> map of reality created by enormous corporate money. Never before was there such a carefully designed ideology that governed this country. The majority of the Republicans in Congress now sound like they've been to class and learned the part: less government, less entitlements. And behind this ideology there is also a philosophy, namely that each person can take care of himself. That philosophy was not present sixty years ago. Critics would argue that it is a barely convincing philosophy today. Look at your world; it's dominated by giant corporations. If you don't have government to protect you, nobody will protect you.

Looking back over the twenty-five years since *The Greening of America* appeared, Reich now says: 'Just about everything that was an issue then is an issue today – dehumanization, a crisis of values.'[2]

Few honest, realistic people will argue with that. Reich may be the right man at the right time. Of course, many of his ideas emerged earlier than Reich himself. Karl Marx, whose ideas are believed to have strongly influenced the education of Japan's contemporary business and public leaders, stated that government is the executive committee of the capitalist system. Other classic writers who were forerunners of Reich might arguably include: James Burnham's mid-century *Managerial Revolution*[3] which seeks to explain how and why modern management should have and is having the upper hand; Anthony Jay's *Management and Machiavelli*[4] which shows how corporate CEOs are like feudal barons: their word rules in the workplace; workers may only fully enjoy constitutional freedom and human rights when they get out in the street; and J. K. Galbraith's *The New Industrial Estate*[5] which focuses almost entirely on the power of corporations to dominate the economy, controlling demand from the supply side and conniving with governments to augment their reach and influence.

I beg to differ with the view that the mighty corporations rule the world. Their power is considerable but governments and international organisations can get the upper hand in the global market by a policy of divide and rule, the ancient political maxim adopted by Machiavelli. This can be achieved by working to preserve genuine competition in the global marketplace and by combating corporate interference and other restraints on the implementation of new inventions and technological developments. A major change in technology can and does build up a small company overnight. It also has the potential in a technocratic era to break the back of a mighty corporation.

We now discuss several current trends in the economic system which have influenced both the amount and terms of employment and contributed ambivalently to both human happiness and misery.

Changes in the economic system

There are three parts to the world economy. They almost coincide with the primary, secondary and tertiary sectors mentioned in Part III, but they differ from each other in another way. They are characterised by varying markedly as regards the degree of labour intensity and job creation per dollar of investment and per acre of land.

First, there is the early **rural economy** dominated by agriculture. This is, at least traditionally, markedly labour-intensive. Second, there follows **traditional industry**. This is much less labour-intensive and, in the course of time, becomes increasingly capital intensive, even up to the point of automation. Third, there emerges the new **services industries encapsulated**

within a knowledge-industry environment. These service industries bring a return, though in an ultra-modern context, to a labour-intensive workplace. However, this sector differs from labour-intensive agriculture in several ways. It is indoor, not outdoor activity. It lends itself much less easily to mechanisation. It uses more costly labour and is afflicted by Baumol's disease.[6]

The executive director of the *Financial Times* wrote in 1984:

In the OECD (rich) countries an extra 19 million people found jobs in the period 1975–79, some 17.3 million of them in service industries and only 3.6 million in traditional industry. As for agriculture, two million jobs disappeared during that period. The same trends continued in the years 1980–81, at a far slower pace; a fall of a million jobs in agriculture and 1.3 million in traditional industry was barely exceeded by a rise of 2.7 million in service jobs.

He then quoted ILO research showing that Third World countries are experiencing much the same phenomenon. He concluded that the former tendency for industrial employment to replace agricultural employment and the subsequent tendency for services to be the new focus for employment was not 'a luxury affordable only by rich countries'.[7]

In this context, we might examine employment figures in 'traditional industries' in the broadest sense, including some officially located in the 'primary sector' such as mining, quarrying and extraction, as well as manufacturing, construction and public utilities such as water, gas and electricity. This broad part of the economy has been the 'location' in which wages and labour conditions have traditionally improved in 'modern times', due in large part to the raised productivity flowing from capital investment and technological progress.

How is the level and quality of employment holding up in the 'post-modern' era? Table 5.1 below offers some hint as to the situation between 1985 and 1994. The countries included in the table were selected from a much larger number: they are countries employing at least one million workers in mining, quarrying, extraction, manufacturing, construction and utilities in 1994; and they are countries for which figures were available with the same coverage of industrial occupations in both 1985 and 1994 (with two exceptions, China and Italy, marked *).[7a]

China and Italy were included despite the fact that their figures for 1985 did not include employment in utilities or in mining, quarrying and extraction, though their figures for 1994 did include those sectors. They are, however, of such industrial importance, especially China, that it was considered necessary to represent them in the Table despite this statistical limitation. The substantial 'increase' in Chinese employment in the early 1990s is largely due to the adding in of more occupations in the figures for 1994.

The total world employment figures in full are 322,320,000 and 383,847,000 respectively. They suggest that there was a growth of employment totalling 61,527,000 jobs over the ten-year period; an increase of some 19 per cent. But much of that 'increase' is, due to the adding in of full figures for China only in 1994. If China and Italy are excluded from the Table for both 1985 and 1994, the totals for all the other countries listed would be 242,023,000 in 1985 and 267,657,000 in 1994. That reveals a more accurate picture for employment growth in the 'traditional industries' sector of 25,634,000 over the ten-year period, or nearly 11 per cent. There probably was an employment growth of that proportion or more in China, as we could see if we had the full earlier figures for China.

In the eighteen current or former Third World countries, the employment growth in the traditional industries sector was substantial. Should those countries succeed in raising their lowish labour productivity, however, the further growth of industrial employment might become slower or even negative – while increasing output substantially.

In the more economically developed countries, the employment pattern for the traditional industries sector has been much less promising. For example, its growth has been negligible in the UK and the USA; and the sector has actually shrunk in France and Germany. It also shrank in Poland. Perhaps there, and also in former East Germany, surplus labour on industry was jettisoned in a market-driven quest for lower costs and profit.

The totals of employment given in the Table are less than the aggregates for all countries in the world; but not substantially less. The countries with more than one million employees in the traditional industrial sector in 1994 which had to be excluded for lack of comparable 1985 figures were only the following: Argentina, Bulgaria, Hungary, Nigeria, North Korea and Romania. Their combined 1994 industrial employment level was a mere 18,298,000. Add that to the countries included in the Table and we have a 1994 grand total of just over 400 million employees in the traditional industries sector. Perhaps surprisingly, this figure is less than a twentieth of the world's labour force.

The American 'traditional industrial' employment, as a proportion of the totals in the Table, drops only slightly, from 13 per cent in 1985 to 12 per cent in early 1994. Bear in mind that the USA experienced recession in the latter period, or the figure would have been higher. That proportion of world industrial employment is impressive, in so far as the USA has only 5 per cent of the world's population. Moreover, the USA's rate of population growth is lower than in many of the other countries, whereas the productivity of its workers is higher than is the case in most of them. That productivity gap steadfastly remains.

Different countries have developed along pathways involving varying degrees of industrialisation and the expansion of services, with the USA prominent in services development. In Table 5.2, America's income share from services is shown at 41 per cent. The figures are from the early 1980s;

Table 5.1   Employment in Mining, Quarrying, Extraction, Manufacturing, Construction and Utilities in Selected Countries, 1985 and 1994 (figures in thousands)

	early 1980s	early 1990s
Australia	1,971	2,025
Austria	1,292	1,333
Bangladesh	1,486	7,742
Brazil	10,675	14,040
Canada	2,971	3,233
China	(72,700)*	109,275
Colombia	1,049	1,473
Czechoslovakia	3,437	4,410
Egypt	2,183	3,092
France	7,242	6,422
Germany	15,341	14,401
India	30,946	32,710
Indonesia	6,810	9,738
Iran	3,035	2791
Italy	(7597)*	6,915
Japan	19,650	22,270
Korea, South	4,020	6,546
Malaysia	1,074	1,399
Mexico	4,856	7,047
Morocco	597	1,453
Myanmar (Burma)	1,383	1,406
Netherlands	1,433	1,645
Pakistan	5,223	6,280
Philippines	2,518	3,816
Poland	6,239	4,822
Portugal	1,450	1,570
Russia plus	47,048	41,540
South Africa	2,196	2,887
Spain	3,742	4,716
Taiwan	2,862	3,417
Thailand	2,322	6,544
Turkey	3,072	4,489
United Kingdom	7,319	7,076
United States	32,300	32,123
Venezuela	1,198	2,031
Yugoslavia	3,083	1,170
Totals	322,320	383,847

Source: The figures were calculated from tables on employment given in the Encyclopedia Britannica Yearbooks published in 1986 and 1995, drawing on ILO and official national statistics for a year just before those years. Regarding 'Russia plus': the USSR figure is used for the 1980s, whereas the 1990s figure is obtained by addition of the figures for Russia, Belarus, Kazakhstan, Ukraine and Uzbekistan. The German figure for 1985 is the addition of the figures for East and West Germany. The Czechoslovakia figure for 1994 includes the separate Slovakia figure. *For China and Italy see pp. 194–195.

they are not recent but offer wide international coverage and permit the inclusion of the USSR before its economy crashed.

Table 5.2   Industrial Origin of Domestic Products
(percentages of gross domestic product)

Country	I	II	III	IV	V	VI	VII	VIII	IX	X	XI	XII
Agriculture	2	4	3	19	4	32	3	22	20	2	46	6
Industrial Activity:												
Total	28	28	25	30	28	18	34	21	46	31	7	36
Manufacturing	21	18	16	12	25	13	30	18	NA	21	6	16
Construction	4	6	5	4	6	5	8	5	10	5	3	5
Trade	17	15	9	13	12	13	12	15	18	12	7	9
Transport & Communications	6	7	7	7	5	5	7	7	6	6	4	12
Other (inc.services)	41	39	40	21	35	16	35	20	NA	31	20	29

I.	USA (1983)	II.	Australia (1982)	III.	Canada (1983)
IV.	Egypt (1983)	V.	France (1983)	VI.	India (1983)
VII.	Japan (1983)	VIII.	Pakistan (1983)	IX.	USSR (1983)
X.	UK (1983)	XI.	Tanzania (1983)	XII.	Venezuela (1982)

Source: Statistical Office of the United Nations, New York,
1983/84 Statistical Yearbook.

Sectors with large shares of GDP could mainly reflect inefficiency – for example, low labour productivity in agriculture or industry services – rather than specialisation. Contrast Australian agriculture with Tanzanian agriculture, for example. National income mainly adds together income received by various groups: it tells us little in itself about their productivity.

The *Economic Report of the President*, transmitted to Congress in February 1995, presents statistics about the US economy which are more reliable and up-to-date than those included in international comparison tables. Table B.44 of the President's report shows an increase 1946–1994 in the number of workers in 'goods-producing industries' from 41.7 million to 115.1 million. Compare this with employees in 'service-producing industries', who increased from 24.4 million to 91.2 million over the same period. So American workers making goods increased by 176 per cent while American workers providing services increased over the same 1946–1994 period by a more substantial 274 per cent.

The civilian labour force of USA as a whole increased by much less – 143 per cent – in that period. What happened to 'other workers'? They were mainly in agriculture and their numbers decreased substantially between 1946 and 1994, mainly due to their increased productivity. However, over much of this period these 'displaced' workers were able to find employment in the non-agricultural sector.

Let us look in Table B.44 at 'services' in the narrow sense, i.e. excluding transportation, trade and finance, insurance and real-estate, which brings us down to the bulk of professionals such as lawyers, health care personnel, teachers and accountants. The increase of employment in these more narrowly defined services was a huge 592 per cent over the period 1946–94.

The increase of employment in government employment (federal, state and local) was 243 per cent, also involving many professional workers. The increase of employment in manufacturing alone was a mere 24 per cent, i.e. less than one sixth of the growth in the whole labour force.

Not only have services, both broadly and narrowly defined, become a larger part of the labour force in the USA than in most other countries; they have also proved themselves to be characterised by high costs and prices. The service categories generally comprise the most expensive groups of employees anywhere, even when compared with countries that have a much higher cost of living and more expensive currencies than the USA. For example, Japanese medical care is much cheaper, yet its achievements as revealed in longevity, mortality and morbidity statistics are equal to or better than those of American health care. American managerial services are also expensive. American top executives are the most highly paid in the world, although numerous global corporations run by other countries are comparable in size to America's largest. The USA holds the world record as regards monetary settlements paid in damage suits. Since lawyers take half or more of those settlements – even when settled out of court – American litigation lawyers are the world's highest paid.

Although the USA has not spent as much of its national income on its armed forces and its governmental machinery as the former Eastern bloc countries or those under military regimes, it should not be thought that its public sector is economical and efficient! In general, it may be concluded that in the USA, health care, the rule of law, the practice of management and administration and the operation of the American systems of government, defence and foreign affairs, as well as other major service sectors, have costs which place a heavy burden on the country's economy and particularly on consumers and tax-payers.

In a nutshell, it might be argued that most American goods are the least expensive and best value for money in the world. On the contrary: most American services are the most expensive in the world but are not the best value for money. Professor Baumol himself calls 'his' disease 'the cost disease' – and it is spreading rapidly in other countries. Many British lawyers are now incurably and happily afflicted. Frauds and rapacious settlements are cracking the shoreline of the insurance industry worldwide.

We have examined the roots of the current malaise in terms of global figures and cost levels.   We now delve beneath this cost burden to appreciate how it is seen and felt by the ordinary citizen. Many Americans are still called 'rich uncle' by their relatives abroad. Why do they now feel so poor and exploited?

The illusion of the low American cost of living

On my return to the USA in 1983 after thirty years' absence, I became concerned about many people's ready acceptance of the American economy's entrance into a post-industrial phase, thereby downgrading the manufacture of goods and accentuating the provision of services. This was in the land that invented the assembly line and mass production and fed the American population and millions abroad with its large-scale agriculture. Was this not still true? However, in regard to this structural change towards services, in this way as in so many others the USA actually leads the way. Much of the additional value ascribed to the service sector arguably reflects the high-cost provision of modest quality services rather than a super-efficient, forward-looking sector.

Before 1939, the word 'service' meant useful, reasonably priced human attention and personal care for everyone's basic needs. It recalled such things as house calls by general practitioners; appropriate dental care (short of replacing all teeth, bad or good, by crowns at $1500 each); postal and many other desired deliveries to your door; clean, safe, prompt and frequent public transport; house and car maintenance and repairs at prices low enough to avoid forcing, as now, even the busiest people into do-it-yourself antics at the sacrifice of their limited leisure and holidays. Services then meant people rather than machines answering the phone – the kind of people who listen to what you want. Never a robot voice, nor a live voice saying only: 'will you hold?' meaning 'you will hold!' followed by music of 'their' choice garnished with 'their' advertisements.

The truth, unmasked within weeks of arrival in the USA, is that contemporary America distinguishes itself by its almost total lack of that kind of service many modern Americans now call the 'bad' old labour-intensive kind. Such service is too often deprecated by modern Americans because it depended on and was characterised by unselfishness, vocation and, admittedly, an element of subservience at the bottom of the pile. It was certainly not 'market-driven' by handsome remuneration. Many doctors during the Great Depression did not press poor families to pay on time or even at all.

Services after the sea-change

Services in the new American sense, especially those which are now becoming the mainstays of the American economy as evaluated by financial rather than substantive measurements, are arguably arrangements for the social élite to enter monopolistic professions and prise large amounts of money from the economy. Such services are notably 'manned' by doctors, lawyers, leaders and specialists in finance and insurance, bureaucrats, politicians, lobbyists, promoters, communicators and diplomats. They have at their beck and call clerks, acolytes, para-professionals, nurses, secretaries, handlers and even the underworld! Thrown into this melting pot, we have another great wedge of super-prosperity: the stars of entertainment, the media, commercialised sports and their human entourage. Added together, these groupings account for much of the growing tertiary section of the economically active population.

Below the élite level of professionals and stars and alongside the pyramids of subordinates on which they squat, a sub-élite has also arisen. Its members are often glorified versions of former traditional and smaller occupations. A sub-élite of vocationally skilled workers and technicians, they continue to prosper with the help of craft labour unions and their certification and licensing by public authorities. They have often assimilated themselves within the associations and regulations which shelter the full professionals, including entry restrictions to what are essentially monopolistic occupations. Plumbers and bricklayers are among the minor princes of the sub-élite.

However, this sub-élite is more vulnerable than the professionals to the recurrent recessions. Ninety per cent of bricklayers in the Boston area union were unemployed in the first recession of the 1990s. Plumbers do better: you must repair a leak immediately, yet bricks can only be laid when housing and other infrastructure demand is buoyant. Most, but not all, craft-related labour unions have grown far weaker (Box 5.1).

Cheap labour in America has now shrunk to the ranks of the fairly numerous illegal aliens and racial minorities, often segregated in certain districts and regions. Others who might normally tackle the millions of humble jobs left undone prefer life on better-paid relief or find that in fact crime does pay.

The good bits

This services grandiosity is counterbalanced by numerous exceptions striking to a foreign visitor's eye, which are presumably still a residual source of satisfaction for those Americans in a position to enjoy them. What catches the attention of visitors to America are its extensive enclaves of beautiful houses and gardens, glorious nature and scenery; fairly happy children in schools staffed by people who have the bright and novel idea that people can do their best if given encouragement and have their self-confidence enhanced. Most people you meet smile. Most people already know, use and never forget your first name and habitually make remarks in

Box 5.1: The pot calls the kettle black

Professor Barry Bluestone (University of Massachusetts) put union membership at only 11% of all workers nationally in the private sector, down from 36% in the 1950s. He said:

Unions are down everywhere but in sports. Mathematically, they are a shadow of what they once were. I have been astounded by the tremendous solidarity of ballplayers. The better-paid players are making the sacrifice for those coming along.

Mike Mezo (President, Local 1010, United Steel Workers of America) commented:

Unions are more than organizations that bargain. They have social and political agendas. You help your class before you help your union. What the hell have [baseball players, notoriously on strike and wrecking the 1994 season] done for the vendors? Couldn't they do something for the people trying to make ends meet by selling hot dogs (at the games)? ... They have no social or political agenda or concept of what their class might be. They're just greedy people seeing how much they can get. That's what doctors do. That's what lawyers do. That's fine. Just don't call yourself a union.

BG, 30 September 1994

the general areas of cheerfulness, best wishes and kind regards about you and the coming days and nights. Neighbourliness is the most genuine, sincere and valuable service remaining and newcomers get solid help and quick and unassuming hospitality from the day they arrive to the day they leave.

In the shops there are magnificent arrays of all kinds of foods, drinks and goods at mercifully low prices (incredible in Europe). Newcomers on their first shopping day can be forgiven for thinking that they will soon be rich at such low prices. Such attractive prices – even house prices are lower than in Europe – when compared with American salary levels and lower taxes give foreign visitors the idea that this is indeed a land of plenty! Good 'Scotch' costs less, three thousand miles from Scotland, than it costs in London, three hundred miles from Scotland. Gasolene is cheap. The prices of computers and other electronic goods fall through the floor while prices of traditional goods no longer go through the roof.

Swings and roundabouts

The low prices for goods stand in stark contrast to the outrageous prices charged in the new kind of 'service grandiosity'. Medical and dental care are prompt and painless if you pay cash in three or four figures before leaving. There are lawyers who call you 'Mr Billable Hours' almost to your face. People of all sorts promise they will do something at no charge except for 'a surprisingly low one-time fee' – actually more surprising than low. Merchants speak glibly of what is 'affordable' (in truth, a euphemism for 'expensive'); 'affordable' typically inserts itself in contexts where you are actually getting less for paying more. It has become as dishonest as the word 'creative', the fashionable slang for slick or dishonest practices.

The high prices for services and the low prices for goods in modern America help to explain a shocking statistical fact. By 1995, no less than 69 per cent – more than two-thirds – of the USA's GNP was coming from services in the broad sense, contrasted with a meagre 29 per cent – less than one-third – from manufactured goods and a pathetic 2 per cent from agriculture.

The GNP is the sum of incomes, which depend in part on the prices charged for what income-earners provide. If you think of that in real terms, this is a monstrous portrait of a bank hold-up:

● all those millions of lush American acres feeding the world, yet only drawing back to farmers a miserable 2 per cent of America's annual wealth;

● all the giant factories, furnaces and refineries – including Boeing building airliners inside the largest building in the world – drawing to themselves no more than 29 per cent;

● both together receiving less than one dollar in three from the national income; whereas

● a lion's share of America's annual income – 69 per cent of it – goes down the plug-hole through myriad little pipes into the laps of an anonymous, almost invisible, army of doctors, lawyers and financiers hidden in high towers, middle-men, media moguls and general hot air merchants, consultants and con men. They are precisely the ones who have to emphasise how affordable they are because in fact they are so unaffordable and all too often provide poor value for money (Box 5.2).

We hear a cry from a retired army officer: 'How about the fleets of bombers, fighters, rockets, aircraft carriers and warships? They are all services too and we thank God for their solidity.' Yes, indeed, solid and essential they are; and in appearance they do have the mightiness of agriculture and industry. The burden of the armaments race almost ruined a poor USSR, but the total cost to the USA of its worldwide armed forces never took more than one dollar in twenty since the 1970s and they have shrunk to much less than that today. And they are different: they are part of the public sector of the economy. That sector as a whole embraces a significant share of the USA's total investment (such as in education) and a still larger share in the USA's total consumption. Incidentally, America's military might again recalls its industrial might. In the Second World War, between 1 July 1940 and 31 July 1945, the USA produced 86,338 tanks, 297,000 aeroplanes, 17.4 million rifles, carbines and side arms, enormous quantities of artillery equipment and munitions, 64,500 landing vessels and thousands of navy and cargo ships and transports (at the end, one every twenty-four hours). They cost $186 billion at the high value the dollar then had.[8]

Box 5.2: The veil of money

When summing up the goods and services and activities in the economy we are adding a mixture of apples and pears. We can say the total is so many tons of fruit and feathers and still be far away from reality. We get closer to it by talking about so many dollars' worth of drinks and diamonds. But even looking at amounts of money is like looking through a window which is made misty by steam and distorted by flaws in old glass. This is why we say that money draws a veil over the economy, providing a translucent rather than transparent image.

Let us look at some examples of the measurement of economic 'progress' and 'growth'. In 1950 an experienced, well-trained plumber comes to your house to replace a faulty valve on the pipe feeding water into your clothes washer and charges $2 for this five-minute job, including a replacement part costing $0.82. In 1990 an average plumber comes to do the same thing and charges you $71; he took seven minutes instead of five and charges you $21 for the part (it cost him $12) plus $50 for one hour's labour, which 'has to be the minimum charge' since he is coming in an equipped, radio-phone truck and 'providing a house-to-house service on call'.

In 1950 your child falls sick. Nothing dramatic but has a temperature of 102° and you ask your doctor to make a house call to see him during his rounds the next day, for which he charges $5. The same illness occurs in 1990. The doctor's office says you can bring in the child several days later, when there is a space for an appointment, and you know the flat fee for a visit is $70. You need a general family doctor but this doctor, like most, is a specialist at something and charges the specialist rate. But you are a worried mother: you drive the child to the emergency ward of the

continued

Box 5.2 continued

hospital, wait around there two or three hours until a doctor is available and while numerous tests are done 'just in case'. Over a period of weeks hospital and specialists bills come in through the mail, finally totalling $450, but they go to your insurance so you don't see them. They include charges for two medicines and one test. If you had the child picked up in an ambulance, the charge would be $300 just to get to the hospital.

In 1950 your car breaks down and needs a new part. It is fixed in ten minutes for $3.50: $2.50 for the part and $1 for the labour. In 1990 you need the same thing; the mechanic is learning on the job and takes forty minutes, working in a much more complicated car of the same make. You pay $52 minimum for one hour's labour plus $20 for the part. That was low because the garage happened to be honest and did not invent extra unnecessary work and parts.

The economist totals the three bills and corrects them for the percentage increase in the average cost of living for all consumers' goods and services over forty years (since the base year of the index is only forty years back). Plumbers and garage mechanics use parts whose cost rose over the period 1950–90 by a smaller percentage than the cost of living (due to genuine economic progress in manufacturing) but the labour cost rose by more than the cost of living. The doctor or the hospital use equipment and tests which have risen in cost by more than the cost of living has increased and charge more than that increase for their labour. So we see that between 1950 and 1990 there has been 'economic growth' in skilled and professional services because they cost more, thereby taking a larger share of a larger national income. In reality the plumber and the mechanic were less experienced; the doctor had a lot of specialised knowledge about diabetics, but the simple non-urgent case did not call for that.

The two messages of this book

The sharpness of these criticisms of the USA were deliberate in order to raise American consciousness about two grave threats, one to the whole world and one to the developed world.

Here are my two urgent messages about them.

1. The never-ending exploitation of human beings by each other and particularly of workers by a powerful, wealthy minority, has in this century become more widespread as a result of an over-supply of poor people and the growing wealth and power of the minority. Increasingly

large numbers of workers are becoming surplus, compared with the capacity of the economy to employ and support them. Those that do find employment often acquire less secure and less remunerative jobs, unless they are exceptionally skilled and educated.

2. The massive shift in the structure of the US economy toward over-priced and less efficient services, only partly replacing the income and employment formerly obtainable in agriculture and in industry, is by no means an unmitigated benefit; it is also harmful. The harm started showing in the 1970s, when the rate of growth in the American economy tapered off to the slow pace maintained ever since. Economists cited the stark increase in the cost of oil and reduction in supply, but if the oil price increases of the 1970s were capable of killing off the powerful boom of 1950–1973, why did the major oil price drop in 1986 not have the power to stave off the puncturing of the speculative boom, forewarned by the massive stock exchange crash of 1987? The more powerful factor, growing since the 1970s, is the predominance of the service sector in the economy. It increased mainly in terms of employment and cost, rather than productivity, so slowing real economic growth nationwide. Demand within the American economy for services will be constrained because of their high cost and the inadequate purchasing power of the mass of workers and their families.

Here problem 2 links up with problem 1. The falling purchasing power of worker families may be aggravated by increased exploitation, by the growing economic burden of high unemployment and by a progressive shift of wealth-holding from the poor majority to the rich minority. American workers and the American economy must seek to mitigate such tendencies by the strengthening of education, training and research; and by promoting and applying technological advances throughout the economy.

Critics will probably object immediately to Message 2. How absurd to speak about any cloud hanging over the economic future of the United States! Its economy is booming, it is richer and more productive than ever, it is regarded by business people in many countries as the most competitive in the world. True, it runs a heavy deficit in foreign trade, but only until the unfair trading practices of Japan and other countries can be stopped! To this, we reply that the USA will remain rich and strong, but the primacy of its economy will slip relatively to other emergent economies that are looming large and it will soon lose still more business to those countries.

The foreign earnings of America's services sector are often referred to by economists as 'invisibles'. They include such elements as capital transfers and financial, insurance and transport services, all of which may be regarded as general, worthwhile and profitable American economic activities. They also include the large earnings attributable to entertainment – mainly royalty payments and sales with respect to US movie, TV and music products. English is now a universal language: British and American production and exports of books and other media using that language are considerable.

A little more precision may help here. 'Services' has become an overworked, diluted term, rendered vague and ambiguous. It has almost entirely lost its roots in the kind of personal, home-centred assistance familiar to our ancestors. For example, a car is a 'good' or a 'product'; a taxi is a 'taxi service'. 'Goods' are certainly things you can drop on your foot, though some of the output of services is also frequently called 'a product'.

Let me briefly cite the situation in Massachusetts. Industry has been disappearing fast from Massachusetts since the early part of the century. For example, in the five years from 1988 to 1993, the number of manufacturers employing more than 1000 workers dropped from 128 to 43. Yet Massachusetts now boasts of being a pole of growth (*pole de croissance* in French economic theory) and especially of growth of services. In this respect it is more of a professional than a business State: it is first in the nation in terms of the number of doctors per capita and second in terms of the number of lawyers. The *Boston Globe* concludes:[9]

> *Massachusetts has matched the nation in job creation, a feat few would have thought possible. The job growth has come exclusively from the service sector, powered by the expansion of businesses ranging from software to consulting to engineering.*

'Software' is a major and genuine product important to the present and future economy of the world. To an increasing extent, computers are sold with software already installed. Yet software is no more a service in the traditional meaning of the word than is a hard disc or a monitor. Suppose you have been hired as a temporary consultant. All too often we consultants enter the premises of our client and, within a few days, find ourselves blowing dust off a report of another consultant lying on a shelf in a back room – perhaps the room reserved for visiting consultants – and we see in that report much of the same advice that we still consider pertinent. It was not followed last time and the problems remain. The output of this particular consultancy 'service' would hardly, in such circumstances, seem to have raised society's welfare!

Yet consultants whose advice did bring about permanent changes for the better can be regarded as providing worthwhile services, meriting names such as 'innovators', 'pioneers', 'inventors', 'discoverers' and, best of all, 'geniuses'. The Nobel and the Macarthur Foundations mark them with prizes. Many of them are asked to stay with the company; that, too, sets them apart from consultants who are simply temporary and supplemental help or pawns in the game of company politics. Indeed, American experts and consultants at university level are exportable. So are engineers, chemists and other natural scientists who go abroad to help industries as well as governments. American social scientists are perhaps rather less exportable because of the differences of culture and economic infrastructure in other countries. American economists and managers are in a different situation. Many have travelled since the end of the cold war to help develop capitalism; the jury is still out regarding their lasting results.

Returning to America's internal economic affairs, the bottom line is that the transition from goods to services is marked by a more intensive input of human capital. This is not at all the same as 'labour intensity'. Labour intensity increases wherever it does something more cheaply than a machine or, as in Baumol's disease (see pages 111–112 and Box 5.3), it does something that a machine cannot do. Human capital, particularly intellectual capital and associated research and development (R&D) is something astute and qualitative. It can transform a good or product or business or a person (as in the education service) into something new, permanently changed and better.

Seven big bills

Our focus must return to the worker's direct and personal experience. It is pay-day. He has learned to pay his bills or hand over money to his wife before joining the guys at 'Cheers' bar. He knows his income is already earmarked and there are always seven mandatory bills to be paid before he can go out and have any fun. What are the mandatories: the must-be-paid-on-the-dot bills?

These are the Seven Big Bills:

1. Taxation, social security contributions, fees and fines

These are concocted and collected by the public sector. No one enjoys paying them, but the sensible majority knows that a bankrupt government reduced to corruption and inflation in order to survive would be miserable for the citizen. The eventual disappearance of government means a Beirut, a Somalia, or worse, in a place like the USA where the number of guns in the hands of a majority of the population is more than enough to arm every American over the age of puberty. But many people worldwide already find taxes excessive. There are many complaints in the USA about supporting nearly twenty million public employees and paying interest to wealthy bond-holders on a national debt of five trillion dollars, which is four-fifths of the annual income of the whole nation. In other countries, too, similar situations prevail.

2. The cost of the systems of justice, law and order

In the USA, much of that cost is not covered by tax receipts and is borne by the public. Lawyers cost progressively more; refinements in due process and rampant litigation also increase the total legal cost burden. An unmeasured part of the burden is jury duty. Millions of hours daily are taken away by jury duty. These are mainly business hours because courts also recess and rest during weekends. A nominal fee is paid to a jury member, yet if they head a small business or if they are a key employee, there can be serious consequences for the firm. Yet no compensation is paid.

Few people enjoy using lawyers, yet many feel they must turn to them for protection, compensation or vengeance. Many Americans who need their support unfortunately cannot afford to use them at all. Fear of damage suits has caused widespread harm to Americans: a whole range of valuable, harmless activities have now been stopped by such fears. Parks, ponds for swimming and skating and playgrounds are now closed. Stockholder suits against disappointing profit performance have become notorious. Businesses and the jobs they offer are sometimes wiped out by malicious suits. Gynaecologists are extremely hard to find in Florida due in large part to crippling premiums on insurance against malpractice suits. Anaesthesiologists are in a similar situation.

3. Rent or mortgage payments for a home in which to live

Many Americans live in a pleasant house, helped by the ready availability of cheap wood, vast power, excellent tools, plumbing that is a national pride and cheapish land. House-building is inherently labour-intensive. There is much scope for technological progress to economise on housing costs were it not for fragmentary and monopoly protecting regulations. Further cheapening of the costs of housing is also prevented by the extreme inequality in the distribution of income and wealth in the USA, which keeps millions of the poorest outside the house-purchase market.

The following figures about personal consumer's expenditure are expressed in terms of the value of the American dollar in 1987, so that readers wishing to look up increases in such expenditure since 1959[10] can know about the real increases, excluding the effect of price changes – mainly increases. The figures are in billions of dollars.

In 1994 in the USA, expenditure on housing, household operation and furniture and household equipment totalled $983.2 billion, some 27 per cent of personal consumption expenditure. Total private expenditure on the construction of new residential buildings was $208 billion and another $5 billions was spent by the public sector on housing and redevelopment construction. Living in your own home is certainly a pleasure – for a happy, functional family. If you rent, landlords with their rules and fussing and their failure to provide or repair what they should can be unlovable. Eviction for defaulting on the mortgage or rent payments, when involuntarily unemployed, is a widely shared pain in America.

4. The costs of transport and communications and associated pollution

The average American family spends 18 per cent of its income on private car transportation. The real cost of an American car has risen since 1985 by more than the cost of living. The new cars became more techno-logically advanced but, with some parts less durable and an increase in the number of electronic and other parts crippling when down and costly when repaired, many buyers economised by less frequent purchases and more buying used cars. In terms of the value of the dollar in 1987, between 1984 and 1994 Americans' expenditure on all consumption goods rose by 87 per cent (from $2526.4 billion to $4728.9 billion). Their expenditure on motor vehicles and parts increased 74 per cent (from $149.3 billion to $259.3 billion). In 1995 they spent $88.8 billion on gasolene and oil and another $135.4 billion on other transportation. There are 147.5 million cars in the USA for a population of 260 million; the poorest and some central city dwellers have none, while most other households have one or more. The wealthiest households own an average of seven vehicles, divided between the several residences most of them have. A few of them have more than one private plane or helicopter.

Even with crowded roads, people worldwide love private cars too much and, blindly as all lovers, pay an increasing charge for the excess cost of private transportation rather than the potentially low cost per passenger for universal door-to-door, floor-to-floor, public transportation. Telephoning, generally a blatantly overpriced state monopoly abroad, is pleasantly cheap in the USA.

5. The cost of health and medical care

These costs have risen and will continue to rise much more than the cost of living in general. Such expenditures consume a sum, largely paid by employers and government, approaching a fifth of the national income. The part (less than half) paid by consumers from their own pockets amounted in 1994 to 13 per cent of all their expenditure. Traditionally, much of this was paid for lucky employees in large companies but most employers, despite obstinate strikes and strong reactions, are now shifting more of that cost on to employees. The fraction of Americans not covered by health insurance is gradually rising by the year. The bipartisan panel of health-policy experts has foreseen that the 39.7 million people without health insurance in 1995 will rise to 66.8 million in 2002 because of federal budget cuts and eroding employer-based health coverage. That is an increase from 14.3 per cent of the population to 24.1 per cent.[11]

Congress may 'solve' the health care problem, but only in the sense that the reduction thus caused in demand and payment for health care would force the providers to lower their charges. (A few providers might change profession and fewer newcomers might train for medical service.) The poor make their first visit to hospital when it is time to die. The best hospitals in the world abound in the USA, but they are for the best people; moneyed foreigners get visas with ease and pour in by the plane-load. Yet infant mortality rates in the USA are at a Third World level.

There have been Americans (some in Congress) who have said that there is no health care problem in the USA, meaning that what is provided is excellent and immediately available if you can pay for it and that you have no right to it if you cannot pay for it. Paying $800 to $1200 a month in medical insurance for an urban family of four is way beyond the means of many families. A cure for Baumol's disease in the medical sector would indeed be healthy (Box 5.3).

6. The cost of education and training

Primary and secondary education of indifferent quality is provided without charge from municipal tax revenues. However, roughly half of Americans enter some form of higher education and training, although far fewer graduate. Such higher education is costly in the public sector and prohibitively costly in the private sector which owns nearly all the world-class American universities. Annual cost increases have been cut from double to single digits of per cent, but continue to rise faster than the cost of living.

Education is fun for the brightest and the curious and for many a passport to a job in an increasingly technocratic labour market. Ignorance is a misery like homelessness. Innocent children denied a good education and a chance for a career are one of the major sources of sorrow today for American parents and relatives.

7. The cost of credit and retirement

Money is borrowed to meet cash-flow problems and to spread out payment for most or all of items 1–6, especially for 3 (mortgages), 4 (instalment purchases of cars), and 6 (loans for higher education). Retirement is financially feasible only if all the retiree's loans are repaid, savings and investments have been accumulated and social security and other retirement pension rights have been acquired. Other savings are essential because American pensions are normally not increased to cover cost-of-living increases. It also helps retirees if their dependants become independent. In poor countries, though, you retire if your children will take on the obligation of feeding you.

For most families, items 6 (only partly paid by government) and 7 have to be paid for out of their unspent income and savings. All American

Box 5.3: Baumol's disease and health care

Baumol's disease was described above (Part III, pages 111–112). Professor Baumol much impressed Senator Moynihan with his point that health care is one of those inherently labour-intensive 'handicraft' industries whose costs rise persistently faster than the national economy's rate of inflation (Senator Moynihan has been a key figure in Congress's efforts toward health care reform and is a respected writer on social problems.) In a speech in 1994 Dr Baumol argued that none of the major industrial nations, whatever their health care system, has been successful in preventing the rise in costs beyond the rate of inflation. The United States is not the best or the worst performer, in his view. His starting point was that 'indispensable requirements' are two-fold: one, universal coverage and, two, no one can be dropped when their treatment becomes exceptionally expensive. He stressed that attempts to control health costs must not impinge on the quality of health care, nor must progress in surgery and pharmaceuticals be slowed. Small insurers must not be allowed to get away with coverage only for those who don't need it. There is a danger of creating a 'permanent army of unemployed' in proposals that oblige the government to pay health insurance for those out of work.

Features of the Clinton plan he found positive included the following: competition among providers will keep prices from going too high and 'health alliances' will provide the information consumers will need to make judgements on comparative costs and service quality of different providers. The market mechanism will help to prevent deterioration in the quality of services, because overchargers and underchargers for cheap and shoddy services will be avoided. But, Baumol conceded, there are several features in Clinton's plan that are more problematic. He cited experiences in Japan and Canada as evidence of the perils of price controls, annual fees, and penalizing large firms. For example, under the Japanese system of unit payment it is common for doctors to see 100 patients a day. Where doctors are paid an annual fee, as in Canada, the number of consultations or operations is far lower than in the USA for a given number of patients.

Dr Baumol concluded that 'the huge complexity of Clinton's and other programs is not merely bureaucratic territory grabbing, but an honest effort to grapple with real and difficult problems'.[12]

employees have 9 per cent of their earnings left over after their total personal consumption. This margin amounts to $340.2 billion a year. Wealthy families also use unearned income for these items. That helps, for example, given the need for an expenditure of around $35,000 per year per child at university.

After paying all seven bills, how many Americans have money (discretionary income) left over for real pleasures like holidays, a shopping spree, dinner out, getting happily married or proudly buried (proper weddings and funerals cost in the range of $12,000 to $30,000)? No wonder holidays are short. It is no surprise that retail customers are as indebted and fickle as they are, or that fast, cheap, fatty food is displacing slow, well-cooked, healthy food.

Perhaps a symptom of the malaise is that gambling is one American 'pleasure' which is growing immensely in popularity. The poorest can spare one dollar and one minute at least to buy a single lottery ticket and go to sleep American Style dreaming of becoming a multimillionaire overnight. Some of those that do win are known to say to the press, sooner or later, that they will keep on with their old job. 'What else is there to do?' they explain.

PART VI

REFORM AND POLICY

We return here to the point made at the end of Part I: that until recently, concentrations of power and wealth in both the private and public sectors often occurred along chains of seizure and conquest and the subsequent amalgamation of the spoils. There can be little pretence or illusion that such concentrations came about through a process of hard work and well-earned success. An effort began in the nineteenth century, in reaction against the 'robber barons', to achieve honest government based on universal democracy. As an example, the civil service was entered by relevant examinations rather than through networks and family contacts.

Good government grown fat and senile

The First World War, initially called the 'Great War', was, up to that point, the largest public undertaking in human history. Governments were obliged to assume a prominent role in the running of the economy and acquired a larger share of the national income because of the demands of the war effort. Tax receipts lagged behind government spending so that the national debt appeared on the scene and grew like a eucalyptus. It was soon noticed that additional public expenditure reduced unemployment.

The subsequent inability of the capitalist system to overcome the Great Depression of the 1930s made obvious the need for a government role to reinforce recovery, though little was actually done. Unfortunately, in Britain, the government returned the country to the gold standard in 1925, with the gold price pushing the foreign exchange value of the pound painfully above the level at which British exports could compete in world markets. Such exports now proved too expensive until internal deflation forced by the overpriced pound brought all other British prices and eventually wages down.

By 1936, the widely acclaimed writings of J. M. Keynes began to make it progressively clear that the business cycle could not be cured without government intervention.[1] Many reflected on the fact that the increase in government involvement in the First World War had brought prosperity and full employment.

By 1939 that and other lessons learned from the First World War, provided a basis for better and fairer management by government of Britain's war effort and of civilian welfare during the Second World War. A similar path was followed by the Roosevelt administration in the USA through the Great Depression (when Roosevelt was more innovative than the British political leaders) and the Second World War.

From 1943 onward, governments sought to win the peace through the United Nations and by creating social justice for the people and the soldiers who would survive and return home. Notable in the UK were Sir William Beveridge's report to the British government on a postwar social security system and his book on achieving full employment.[2] The insertion of the words 'free society' in its title expressed an early awareness that the Soviet Union's solution to the employment problem was far from the whole answer.

In 1944 came the setting up of the World Bank and the IMF at Bretton Woods, of the UN Food and Agriculture Organisation at Hot Springs and, in 1945, the renewal of the International Labour Organisation at Philadelphia. ILO's Philadelphia Declaration stated that poverty anywhere was a threat to prosperity everywhere. It envisaged economic and social goals of full employment and prosperity which were subsequently embodied in the economic and social chapters of the United Nations Charter adopted at the San Francisco Conference in 1946. These international leaps forward demonstrated how much government thinking about political economy and social justice had advanced.[3]

After the long postwar boom of the 1950s and 1960s, the economic burdens of the arms race and cold war cut cruelly into the pockets of tax-payers and workers everywhere. Though 'political economy', in its modern meaning, covers much, it does not cover all of what economists are doing, especially since the scope of what they do undertake has continued both to broaden and to fragment into a number of specialised fields.

The main recommendations of this book are contained in this Part. They all pertain to political economy. First, we consider a number of reforms required in the body politic in order to make the following recommendations feasible and applicable.

A wide public recognition that government now needs basic reform has forced mainstream parties into much 'me-too-ism' and produced hysterical swings between political extremes, arising from the people's desperation for radical reform and relief from the burdens (the seven big bills) they carry. Policy recommendations made here can only be effectively implemented if government itself is reformed, along the lines suggested in this section.

Lessons from recent history

Governments and political parties, especially the party or the coalition in power, have much influence for good – and for harm – in the economy. Failure by successive governments is in fact a large and intractable problem, often compounded by an inability or unwillingness to understand properly complex economic and social issues and an over-emphasis on interests narrower than the public interest. We might add to this list elements of inefficiency, irresponsibility and extravagance.

Economic failure underlies the collapse of many Eastern bloc regimes that claimed to be on the path toward a communist society. They collapsed from several causes but an economic inability to satisfy the growing demands of their people was mortal enough. China has only forged ahead economically since the death of Mao, who became a misbegotten god and cruel leader for his people, but even in this case, corruption in China has reached the very top. Nevertheless, in the next century China may well rival the USA as a Great Power (Box 6.1).

Box 6.1: China's economic history

In 1750 the Third World (principally China and India) accounted for 73% of world manufacturing output; as late as 1830 its share was still over 60%. By 1913 it had plummeted to just 15% as China and India were left far behind Europe's technological revolution. The share of world manufacturing output produced by 20 or so countries that are today known as the rich industrial economies jumped from about 30% in 1830 to almost 80% by 1913.[4]

China has been the world's largest economy for most of recorded history. It had the highest income per head until around 1500 and was still the biggest economy until 1850, when it was overtaken by Britain. As late as 1830, China accounted for 30% of world manufacturing output. After two centuries of long eclipse China is now re-emerging as an economic leader. If China's GDP per head grows by 6–7% over the next fifteen years, the increase in its share of world output, from 4% in 1980 to 15% in 2010, would be similar (in percentage points) to that of America in 1870–1900.[5]

In between the USA and China, an instructive example of all the other countries worthy of some attention is Sweden. A gentle country widely admired for the prosperity which is widely shared within its borders and through its foreign aid, Sweden has long propounded outstandingly humanitarian aims. However, it has been criticised, internally and externally, as embracing excessive government intervention, much of it too spendthrift and erroneous in direction. Two-thirds of the Swedish population are either employed or subsidised by the government. The large majority benefit from privileged treatment by the government which has made it hard for the Swedish people to correct their situation through elections. In fact the Swedish case illustrates a widespread danger in the world. Wherever the proportion of the population living at least partly on government subsidies or relief, together with the proportion of officials whose livelihood depends on spending government money, grows large enough to dominate in a democracy, the working population in the productive private sector can become permanently 'victimised'. The workers may then lose a large slice of their earnings through government taxation and transfer payments to support the mass of 'unproductive' (in a market sense) people. Their only hope is to stimulate a large proportion of the population to vote and thereby defeat the embittered passenger class at the polls. Economist Robert

Samuelson, debating on Independence Day 1995 the chances of big changes in America, seems to suspect that the US also suffers from the Swedish virus:

> *In short, Big Government has become too woven in the society's fabric to be unthreaded. It does too many people too much good and has created too many defenders. The central argument concerns the practical limits that people wish to place on it. This is a vital debate that could affect many groups and regions. But the larger question about Big Government has been – despite rhetoric to the contrary – essentially settled.*[6]

Argentina once caught and spread a worse virus than the Swedish one. Peronism characteristically shifted economic privileges away from a minority, the landowners, and toward a much larger minority, namely the urban working class and the army. It is extremely difficult then to turn the government towards policies providing a fair treatment of the whole population and to restore the positive features of the landowners' managerial role. The latter had arguably been the layers of Argentina's golden eggs, cultivating and husbanding its vast fertile soils under a temperate climate and kindly sky. That had brought Argentina's national income to a level as high as that of Canada at the end of the 1920s. Argentina then declined, while Canada advanced. Today, however, Canada seems to be moving in the Swedish direction whereas Argentina is partially reformed.[7]

The experiences of France, China and Japan in shaping the most propitious role for government are worth careful study, with one caveat. Though France's natural wealth has postponed its day of reckoning with its spendthrift public policies and manifest labour problems, the recently uncovered examples of corruption have proved devastating. France has sophisticated human capital to supplement its landed wealth and is certainly capable of better! The secret of China's success, little known to ordinary people in the West, lay in following a step-by-step approach towards reconstruction and a market economy. However, it must soon face the challenge of reforms embracing the top echelons of a corrupt official apparatus while seeking to become less emotionally attached to its traditional gerontocracy and to be less tolerant of a plutocracy which threatens to emerge in high places. Japan's path toward improvement, till now government-and-establishment dominated, should probably include further moves towards becoming more internationalist, embracing the virtues of other cultures worth emulating in addition to aspects of its own.

Reforms needed in public life

The USA's natural and developed wealth has, until recently, helped to carry the burden of its wasteful public sector. However, there are both healthy and unhealthy signs of powerful political trends toward clean-up, streamlining and a better 'bang for the public buck'. Vice-President Al Gore has reported on the enquiry he led into 'reinventing the government'.[8] It is indicative of the political skewing of the public's attention that this mammoth work obtained so little attention and credit. The appendices give long lists of policy recommendations and sources used. Enactment of the recommendations would produce savings of $108 billion over five years and reduce the federal workforce by 12 per cent, to below two million officials for the first time since 1966. Despite daily cries in Congress for cuts and reforms, action has been slow and inconsistent. As for unhealthy signs, we have already noted what Charles Reich has said about some Republicans in Congress (see page 192). Behind them there are shadowy forces like the non-philanthropic billionaires and what many regard as a wolf in sheep's clothing: the Christian Coalition. Perot and Powell may come and go.

Box 6.2: A male Thatcher sighted in Philadelphia

Edward Rendell was elected Mayor of Philadelphia in 1991, largely by saying that its 30,000 city workers were pampered and overpaid. When he took office in January 1992 the city was just weeks away from bankruptcy. He imposed on city workers a two-year pay freeze, cut four of their fourteen public holidays, reduced the city's contribution to their health benefits and replaced hundreds of city workers with private contractors. His new four-year contract with the unions involved saving an average of $93 million a year on a total city annual budget of $2.4 billion, of which 60% went to meet labour costs. His speeches portrayed city workers as, by-and-large, lazy feeders from the public trough, protected by inane work rules. He derided such practices as sewage workers shovelling sludge out of one truck on to the ground and into a second truck; custodians being paid to wash floors but not wash the walls; park-workers being prevented from operating power tools. The President of one union of city workers was sent to prison for corruption. Although Philadelphia ranked near the middle of large cities in terms of the number of public employees per resident and in worker salaries, it still came up with a plan to save $200 million without hurting workers.

Philadelphia now has a balanced budget and Wall Street has upgraded its credit rating. There are more police, but trash pickups are less frequent and the city has curtailed aid to libraries and museums.[9]

The implementation of adequate and appropriate reforms is awaited with shrinking patience. The natural resentment of the people could be more constructively directed if many voters were not so ignorant of public affairs. While keeping them in the silent majority, this ignorance does not stop their whimsical or backlash voting.

Economics with a human face cannot be fully achieved under *laissez-faire*, unbridled and unaided capitalism, even should cultural progress touch the rawest capitalists and move them to be as public-spirited and caring as they are efficient. (More characteristically, their immediate reaction to the unselfish is contemptuous: 'knee-jerk liberals and born-again types'.)

A number of inherent flaws in public sectors must be removed if the role of government intervention is to be enhanced.

Governments to obey the law of the land

Governments have put themselves above the law in a variety of ways. Emergency rule, martial law and military intervention are frequently adopted, under which laws are set aside because of a supposed need for prompt, *ad hoc* intervention in an urgent crisis. Recent history shows that armies are frequently used to attack their own people rather than to defend their country from an outside enemy. All too often they become notorious for subjugating the representatives of the people and intimidating the weak and poor. Armies can safely be dispensed with in small, unthreatened countries with brotherly neighbours, as Costa Rica has done; all soldiers – especially generals and would-be 'Pinochets' – should be constantly reminded that it is the poor people who feed them and that they are owed due respect for that.

Under the normal rule of law in democracies the people are generally ignorant of the extent to which government institutions give themselves privileges and exemptions and disobey laws with impunity and without publicity. A broad welcome has been given to the action of the US Congress in January 1995 to resolve that any laws it enacts apply equally to Members of Congress as to others. The unfettered actions of public industries in the 'peoples' democracies have now been revealed as polluting their countries and endangering the health of their citizens through the emission of poisonous wastes, hazardous nuclear power generation and, in the case of the military, nuclear testing.

Even in the USA and other 'law-abiding' countries, where private industry was once tightly controlled in these respects, the public and military sectors have caused abundant damage and have left lurking hazards. Careless handling of nuclear materials and wastes and cold-blooded experiments on human 'guinea-pigs' with radio-active substances are increasingly being uncovered. More minor infractions of law and practice by the American authorities, probably true *a fortiori* elsewhere, include the ignoring of fire and other safety regulations in public buildings and state vehicles, which cause damage and injury without concern for innocent victims or payment of compensation.

The need for any government to police both itself and raw capitalism has been illustrated:

- by department stores collapsing and hotels burnt to the ground in Seoul, South Korea;
- by modern bridges in Rome that have developed ominous cracks whereas bridges built to carry chariots over the River Tiber also carry heavy motor vehicles today without trouble;
- by the collapse of new buildings during the Armenian earthquake because of official corruption diverting steel supplies away from them when they were built;
- by dams and other structures in China developing faults because the 'engineers' responsible for their design and erection had a ten-year gap in their education during the cultural revolution;
- by suppliers of meat for hamburgers in the USA not ensuring that the carcasses of animals slaughtered for the purpose are properly cleaned. (This is a less publicised but greater risk to public health than 'mad cow' disease.)

Although citizens are normally innocent under the law until proved guilty, tax-payers are liable to being found guilty until they can prove their innocence. Tax collectors do not recognise property rights and arrogate to themselves powers of debt collection far beyond those allowed to the private sector. In 1995 they decided they would pick out thousands of innocent, busy citizens at random to question any aspect of their lifestyle and oblige them to explain how they pay for it.

Cost efficiency in the public sector

Two major recommendations are made here with full emphasis, and have wide application to national and international life.

1. Try to achieve economy without impairing efficiency

All authorities are rightly pressed to make economies: cut overall expenditure and obtain cost efficiencies at all levels. However, it should be recognised that it is not at all money-saving just to cut projects in half or lop off a quarter of them. If you cut a horse in half, the two halves will be dead. If you just cut off the horse's head or only two legs, it will still be dead. Maybe it would be better to replace the horse with a bicycle, car or truck, or walk or use public transport. The same principle applies to government departments and agencies. Zero budgeting means asking again, before formulating each new budget, whether any unit in the government is worth maintaining at all. If not, close it down. Never merely cut it in half or by some prescribed percentage which is likely to render it operationally ineffective while still costing the government substantial sums of money.

Some departments, we hope, may be found to be so valuable that they are allocated still more staff and/or equipment. Do not cut inspection and audit services so much that some will calculate that they can take the risk of ignoring regulations regarding any fines payable as akin to insurance premiums or self-insurance provisions.

Vice-President Quayle did some valuable work in a commission to improve the competitiveness of American businesses. Nevertheless, one fault was carried over from Reagan's reign: namely, reducing the likelihood of business being bothered by inspections. This provided a positive inducement for both government departments and private corporations to ignore safety and other regulations.

2. Do not try to keep dead jobs alive

In political life, a powerful way of defending the existence of anything, whatever its cost, is to state how many workers it employs and how many would lose their jobs if it is cut or eliminated. True, it may be worth subsidising the continuance of something temporarily if it is useful but has run into a problem; a problem that can be solved within a reasonable time, thereby enabling a return to full usefulness. However, it is scandalously costly and ultimately ineffective to keep any useless and money-losing activity going without any time limit merely for the sake of continuing the employment it generates. This practice remained so widespread in Russia that it was fast ruining the country. Almost any other way of subsidising employment would be cheaper. Of course, in labour-intensive, start-up and 'infant' businesses and industries, it can be worthwhile to partially subsidise the payroll during a gestation period, as for example in support of training an inexperienced labour force.

Box 6.3: Big, and big losers

Bankruptcy is a tragedy for the owners, employees and pensioners of a company. It is often less of a loss for the economy: the remaining assets of the failed company can usually be sold, which provides cash to pay off redundant employees and creditors. The remaining financial assets can be used by the new owners to replace much of the production and

continued

Box 6.3 continued

employment of the previous company. Some of the old employees may well be re-employed in the same industry.

Subsidised industries, while providing jobs to employees, impose costs on the economy which has to bear the burden of the subsidies and arguably on consumers who might otherwise get cheaper goods and services from more efficient and profitable industries.

The losses among a majority of the world's largest steel producers are listed below: the first three had outputs over 15 million tonnes in 1993; the rest produced 10–15 million tonnes in that year. The losses sustained (in millions of dollars) are indicated by minus signs:

Nippon Steel	−287	US Steel	−164
Pohang	+368	Sumitomo Metal Industries	−319
Usinor Sacilor	−1024	Kawasaki	−363
British Steel	−195	Magnitogorsk	+400
NKK	−262	Steel Authority of India	+180

Many of the steel producers receive subsidies in one form or another, though these are often covert.

In world agriculture, the subsidies are more overt and quite enormous:

Country	Subsidy as % of value of production in 1993	Subsidy in $billion in 1992
Norway	78	2.7
Japan	70	35.0
Sweden	50	1.9
European Union	47	79.6
Canada	29	4.8
USA	25	28.4
Australia	7	1.0
New Zealand	3	0.1
Total		153.5

The net losses by the steel companies mentioned above were $1.7 billion, compared with total subsidies in agriculture of $153.5 billion.

The subsidies to agriculture in OECD countries involve a combination of direct payments, cheap loans and guaranteed prices (called producer-subsidy equivalents, or PSEs). PSEs amounted to $163 billion in 1993, or 42% of farmers' total income and averaged $98 billion annually from 1979 to 1986, providing 34% of farmers' income.

Money-takers spend carefully, as earners do

'Easy come, easy go.' It is too easy for governments to seize money. Some have swamped themselves with it to the point where they developed an illusion that their country was more wealthy than it had ever been. All governments seize and spend too much money; in doing so they are grievously harming the economy and may well be grinding the face of the poor. Not only do they overspend; they spend carelessly, destroying and wasting society's assets.

This is another reason, on top of the rapacious behaviour of armies, why most people around the world and through history have mistrusted their government. They may not say so, but the fact remains. As evidenced by numerous opinion polls, the silent majorities often mistrust governments. Even some of the millions now living at the expense of the government and the general public, object to their 'enforced' dependency.

Little need be said about the proliferation of bureaucracy in the present century; the ever-swelling ranks of civil servants, from the hundreds to the thousands and even to the millions. So much has been written in serious and jocular vein on this theme. Even the Parkinsonian humour comes painfully close to the truth. In his own career, Parkinson was an astute observer of the growth of the British Admiralty. I saw such tendencies in microcosm in the increasingly bureaucratic United Nations system. In Washington almost $40 billion is spent annually on duplicative, partially inefficient, spy-ridden and sometimes mischief-making intelligence agencies. Americans are appalled by the ocean of money in which Washington keeps well afloat throughout the severest depressions; whereas those within the beltway are becoming as ignorant about the shabby life of ordinary people beyond it as Marie Antoinette.[10]

In contrast, we are reaching a situation where most people worldwide are getting desperate about finding and keeping jobs, whether bureaucratic or not. Public offices and contracts provide many jobs. They offer interesting and reasonably paid employment to well-educated people. Indeed, we now have – both in developing and developed countries – university graduates who can no longer count on serious employment, despite the years they and their families scraped and saved for the hard and costly study to get a university degree. The patronage in terms of jobs offered by the public sector has proved extremely attractive.

Do not print money to seize wealth

Here, figuratively speaking, 'printing money' includes that form of money (the majority of it) consisting of figures in books. The government can encourage and enable both the central and the profit-making banking system to juggle with figures – to extend more credit – thus 'printing' an increase in all supplies of money. This has happened ever since money was no longer confined to coins made of gold and other metals in limited supply and since 'fiduciary' monetary systems replaced them with bank notes and mere records of bank balances. Such money works only while we can keep our faith in it.

The recent and welcome combating of inflation in the West may not be long-lived. The piling up of public budget deficits and the swelling of national debts, combined with the resistance to increased taxation, tempts politicians to erase the deficits and debts invisibly by printing money to pay them off. In real terms, it should be remembered that this seizes wealth from those who have bought the government debt. The bonds they bought become worth less and less if inflation is the result of an over-zealous printing of money. Inflation and debt accumulation actually seizes wealth from everybody engaged in large or small saving activities, whose hard-won earnings will buy progressively less and less.

We might think that inflation as a method of 'tax collection' would cause an outrage. In fact, this is rarely the case. Printing money is easier than other forms of tax collection and far less noticeable to the person in the street, at least initially. Anyone with heavy debts will welcome the fact that they become easier to pay off as the real value of debt declines. That welcome is accentuated, in so far as their income initially rises at least as fast as prices. Inflation often starts as a secret and gradual disease.

Equal terms of public and private employment

Many governments offer their employees both security of employment and security of financial support in the future through a 'generous' pension system, in the belief that these attributes promote loyalty in public and military servants. These 'benefits' help to retain in public service the skills often gained at public expense and encourage the public servants to accept lower rates of pay than are available in the private sector.

There is no harm *per se* in those objectives. Let us face squarely the fact that capitalism has major faults: they arguably involve the economic insecurity it imposes on society, the alienation of people from each other and 'incentives' towards the erosion of the spirit of cooperation and community. These are faults less endemic in the public sector; that sector is seen by many as an asylum for the refugees from the raging waters of capitalism. Rather than the public sector being a source of refuge, there should be a smooth and stimulating flow of employees back and forth between the public and private sectors.

Whatever our terms of employment, they should be applied equally in the public and private sectors. Nor does the growth of public sectors occur in a vacuum. In Washington, there is a parallel growth of the private sector (lobbyists, lawyers, lovely women, light-fingered con men, loquacious persuaders, leaders of the media) to match the swelling size of the government machine it seeks to influence (Box 6.4).

Box 6.4: Arrogant capital

The District of Columbia bar had fewer than 1000 members in 1950; now it has 61,000. The number of journalists in Washington soared from 1500 to 12,000 over the same period. The staff of Congress has roughly doubled since 1970. On one estimate, 91,000 lobbyists of one sort or another grace the Washington area with their presence. Kevin Phillips finds the arteries of the American system are hardening with age, and a bloated, arrogant capital city is seen by him as a symptom that the country is suffering from the degenerative corruption typical of empires in decline.

Arrogant Capital, Kevin Phillips, Little, Brown, 1994

At the top end of the employment market, we often see the brightest, the most innovative and adventurous individuals going into jobs in the private sector which pay considerably more than the top jobs in the public sector. The public jobs may actually carry far heavier responsibility, with many more peoples' lives and large proportions of society's economic assets being in the hands of public servants. Yet they are often poorly remunerated. In the USA a comparatively low maximum public salary applies to the chairman of the Federal Reserve Board, which is probably less than the entertainment allowance of many of the bank presidents he deals with daily.

The result is that the positions of cabinet minister and ambassador can only be taken by 'outstanding' men and women with their exceptional attributes including, as a necessary condition, a large private income! A new wrinkle: the prime remedy for personal financial loss in public service is the publication of memoirs on leaving office. The practice of becoming highly paid consultants is arguably more harmful than this; Ross Perot, though a loose cannon, correctly castigated many high public officials who become consultants to foreign governments, including unfriendly governments and public enemies, the day after retirement from public office.

It is disturbing to see press reports daily in the USA of politicians spending money on their federal and state election campaigns so far above the total salary they would receive during their full term.

Downsizing government and bolstering community action

This is a painful subject because it may appear to people of conscience as a licence to savagely cut vital programmes needed to support people and children least able to help themselves through no fault of their own. A distinction should, however, be kept clear:

- **deleting programmes and ministries** is a device for budget deficit reduction where the end may well justify the means. If you cut immunisations now, you hit your grandchildren now. If you protect all programmes and ministries and fail to cut the national debt, you hit your grandchildren later.
- **downsizing government** is reducing the number of government employees down to those genuinely required to attain effectively the goals of any programme with sufficient merit to be preserved.

The first of these may save money, sometimes wisely but not always; the second of these almost invariably saves money in an overall beneficial way.

In the USA and probably also in Britain citizens feel that many important things are best done by actions chosen and managed at a community level, which may often be as low as a village level. Their cry is: give us the money and we will do the job. Volunteers, community leaders, school teachers and the like living close to many problems feel that they understand the problems and solutions best and should be given a free rein to tackle them. It may help if a little advice is given to them about experience gained and experiments undertaken elsewhere. What local communities object to is to be put under a massive, distant bureaucracy which imposes aims, designs projects and devises regulations and controls based only on a hazy, generalised notion, often conspicuously ignorant of local variations, needs and circumstances and frequently flawed or warped by political interference intended to serve special interests foreign to the community. If such bureaucracies are unnecessary – indeed, an actual hindrance – they should be removed and government employment could thereby be reduced.

In the matter of government employment there is a further consideration, namely Baumol's disease. Civil servants, even though relatively poorly paid, are often expensive because they work – indeed, they may be obliged to work – labour-intensively, missing opportunities to utilise technological progress (apart from a degree of computerisation) which would raise overall productivity.

Immunising governments from bribery

In the USA, public officials, including the President, are not allowed to receive valuable gifts. However, gifts might be received at times and in ways which are officially acceptable. For example, Ronald Reagan, after leaving office, was given a splendid house in California by friends who could well afford to, denizens of the wealthy who did best under Reagan's tax reforms and other gestures to the rich. Equally, after leaving office, he went to Tokyo and gave a single lecture which netted him two million dollars. That is a fairly good hourly rate of pay, even for a film star. This is all 'honourable': it is among the time-honoured practices handed down to us by history. Kings of olden times conquered land and distributed a substantial part of it to their cronies and partners in battle.

If democracy is to overtake plutocracy now, political action committees should be abolished. The need for massive donations to political parties and their candidates for office should be shifted and met by more generous support from public funds for public election campaigns. A nationwide television channel, numbered one, might be made available on a 24-hour basis for official statements and official election campaigns; it should never be open to any commercial or even charitable or religious use or available to anybody speaking in a private capacity. Billionaires like Ross Perot can still buy another channel to say what they like but could only use Channel One gratis if and when they are a serious candidate for elective office.

In particular, it is intolerable for the US government to suffer any longer the indignity, on occasions when important policy speeches and statements must be made, of having to borrow time from commercial networks. It is shocking to have the President of the United States at one moment speaking to the world, to be followed the next by an anonymous but soulful voice urging the public to buy a cure for constipation or diarrhoea. There is no guarantee that, should the Pope be speaking to the UN General Assembly, he will not suddenly be superimposed by a female model exhibiting cut-price but uplifting brassieres!

Downsizing dissimulation and hypocrisy

Public leaders should earn and keep the respect of the public. Their private life should be inviolate. The media and lobbyists have become too intrusive and aggressive and must be cut down to size. 'The people' arguably do not 'need to know' anything about the sex life of any person or any other element in their private life which is not illegal. The right to privacy, including the principle that the body and mind of each human being belongs exclusively to them is as sacrosanct as the human right to be told the truth and to be spoken of only truthfully. Politicians would do well to realise that whenever they descend to scurrilous attacks on the personal lives of other people in public life they are underlining their inability to criticise constructively the major policies and actions of the people they target. Good public actions speak volumes louder than personal peccadilloes; we are not best served by a government of inept and inactive goody-goodies.[11]

Total expenditure and borrowing

Government expenditure should be pruned. It should not exceed revenue by so much that growth in the public debt becomes chronic and endemic with the result that initiatives to work and to innovate are stifled by the burdens and impediments of government. However, government expenditure may exceed government revenues with a view to stabilising the value of money and aggregate effective demand in both private and public sectors. The capacity for governments being able to do this will require a reorganisation of government activities, especially with a view to reducing mandatory expenditures.

This is recommended along the following lines:

- reduction in the national debt, thereby lowering the annual interest charges payable on it;
- elimination of the permanent tenure of public employees so that short-term changes in their level are possible when required;
- achieving economies in the benefits and privileges accorded to public servants and legislators when required;
- reductions in foreign aid, diplomatic expenditures (including support of international organisations and armies) and in domestic social relief as a last resort when further economies are imperative;
- strict economy and efficiency at all times and a suitable scepticism to help avoid panic measures and paranoia in connection with demands for increased defence and military expenditures. This is a huge area of financial leakage and is almost the only one where the US Congress sometimes throws more money at the military than even they want. As long ago as the farewell speech of President Eisenhower we were warned: beware the military–industrial establishment;
- judicious restriction of any legislation which will lead to massive increases in public expenditure, as in the health care, law and order, penal and social defence sectors;
- attempts to bring the social security system, including its administration and conduct, within a strictly insurance basis. The very poor can be safeguarded by the American 'earned-income-credit' device: a kind of negative income tax;
- subsidies in support of minimum standards for essential public services should not be guaranteed for periods longer than five years. This will give greater flexibility in policy-making, especially when downward adjustments in expenditures become imperative.

Much of government expenditure should have the character of increasing (or at the least not reducing) the tax base: namely, the capacity of the economy to yield revenue to the government. This means that government should be directed towards promoting prosperity and higher productivity in the country as a whole and in other countries that are, or could be, trading partners. This is the politically easiest and economically healthiest way of raising government revenues. Economies, governments and countries can become much richer by learning how to conquer the business cycle.

A part of the solution to offset cycles involves stabilising the value of money, i.e. avoiding either inflation or deflation, thereby sharply discouraging speculation and narrowing the scope for it. Such a policy was once urged by the monetarist school of economists as all the economic policy you needed for any purpose. However, it was said of interest rates that you can pull on a string when raising them but lowering them is like pushing people with a length of string. Changing money supply and its price (interest rates) may not be possible or indeed have the intended effects on consumer behaviour.

Reform of the taxation system

Direct taxation – taxes on incomes and property accruing to central, regional and municipal governments – has led to excessive public expenditure from the time it was introduced in the last century. It is regarded by many as costly to implement, oppressive to the citizenry and discouraging to human effort and initiative. It is widely evaded, thereby creating an acute sense of injustice (Box 4.10). It should be abolished, say its critics. Politicians usually claim that to be impossible. They press for many costly things, but often not because the people want them but rather because special interests and the military–industrial establishment press for them. There is a big debate about whether taxes should increasingly shift from direct taxes towards indirect taxes on purchases. It is often argued that the latter at least reflect the choices of what people decide to spend their money on.

Many believe it is sound to continue to increase the direct taxation of real estate as a source of municipal revenue. Real estate is tangible, visible and easily identified and such taxation is collectable without heavy and costly administration. Real-estate taxation should be based on the value of property. The value may be fixed in part by what was paid for it historically and in part by what is currently paid for similar property. Thus what is payable would increase with inflation but should not be further increased when a rise in the value of property results from improvements being made to render it safer and healthier. This latter safeguard would be a major innovation. At present all improvements are discouraged by increases in the percentage rate applied via property taxation.

Objects of expenditure

The municipality should receive money from inhabitants and from higher levels of government to cover the costs of the public education of children resident there and not attending private schools. Municipal subsidy for poor children to switch to private schools at will is undesirable because it diminishes the economies of scale of the indispensable public education system. A more selective subsidy to poor children who are extremely bright might more easily be defended, so that they could enjoy an accelerated and broadened education, thereby helping to exploit their high capacity to serve society.

Federal assistance to poorer municipalities is needed to reduce inequality in standards of education throughout the nation. State assistance for this purpose cannot promote national equality. In public education, the ultimate aim in the USA should be to have a uniform national examination for graduation from secondary school, at least equivalent in standard to comparable examinations in European and other advanced countries. After immense efforts, by the next century as many as three-quarters of American children might pass this examination. Self-deceptive practices like advancing all children annually by one grade and then graduating them all, when as many as one in four cannot properly read or write or calculate without a calculator, should be dropped as unworthy of a great nation.

Smaller countries that are economically developed are often better governed than the dinosaurs such as the USA, Russia, Brazil, India and China. The UK is relatively small and arguably would be better governed if there were more decentralisation of government. Some have suggested downloading government in the UK on to five administrative areas: London; the rest of England; Scotland; Wales and Ulster, with limited powers for strictly local affairs lying with municipalities.

Much of the money raised under the following recommendation concerning charities could, with great advantage, be channelled to support communal voluntary activities managed by local people.

Relief of the vulnerable poor and the involuntarily homeless should be exclusively a central government responsibility, as regards both its financing and its administration. It is understandable but unfair that the needy migrate and crowd themselves on certain cities seen as being more 'generous' than others. Street parking is often restricted to residents and relief should also be restricted to residents. There is no room for more in either respect. It is costly and undesirable for the needy to be accommodated in cities. They should be maintained in the areas of the country where it is least costly to help them.

Illegal aliens should, however, be an exclusively federal responsibility: to keep them out as far as possible; to salvage them temporarily; and, where appropriate, to deport them. Immigration laws should be changed so that it is no more difficult to deport an illegal alien who has crossed an American border than it is to refuse entry to an undesirable alien at the border. Applicants in good faith for entry are now treated more harshly than illegal aliens who have entered. It is not fair to expect a few States to carry a heavy burden of salvaging illegal aliens; it can produce a backlash which may ultimately prove dangerous to the aliens themselves.

Asylum for political refugees is a privilege when granted. For practical reasons it cannot be a right because it could then exceed a country's absorptive capacity and become an occasion for abuse, as has happened in Germany due to the fine ideals embodied in its constitution. It should be subject to the following general principle. Since legal aliens are taxed equally with citizens, though they have no representation and cannot vote, it is only fair and wise that under tax laws and beneficiary legislation legal aliens (including refugees) and citizens should be treated equally in every respect. It is hypocritical of governments to heap on refugees additional benefits and privileges not granted to citizens and then to accuse citizens of bigotry when there is a natural backlash and resentful jealousy. Discrimination should be neither negative nor positive, but simply non-existent.

Radical change in taxation

As a provocative base for fruitful debate, the following radical changes in taxation are proposed for governments in all countries which choose to entrust their economy to a private enterprise free market system. Several of these proposed changes have recently been mooted in one form or another in the USA and elsewhere (for example by Bill Bradley, Steven Forbes and John Kerry in the USA; by Lord Kaldor, David Miliband and Stephen Tindale in the UK).

A. Upper revenue limit: one dollar in four

The proper roles of government, efficiently performed, should be limited to what can be done efficiently with not more than a quarter of the national income. More is needed only if you choose to push the capitalist system aside.

The Tax Foundation has estimated that the typical American family allocates 40.4 per cent of its annual expenses to taxes: income taxes, sales taxes, excise taxes, meals taxes, airport taxes, capital gains taxes, payroll taxes, estate taxes, property taxes, cigarette and drink taxes, petrol taxes. 'It's a burden that comes close to legalized theft,' writes Jeff Jacoby. 'The best way – and the right way – to accomplish . . . good and useful endeavours . . . is through cooperation and commerce and community and church. Not the punitive coercion of taxes, which nearly always gets the job done less well and more expensively.'[12]

Government expenditure beyond the limit of a quarter of national income is either due to extravagance and inefficiency; or, if it is due to aims considered worthy, then a retort might be that these cannot be afforded immediately and will have to await growth in the national income nurtured by a healthy and tolerable taxation system. Proposed government policies and programmes should be placed in an order of priority, with only the least important and less urgent being left out through economy measures.

B. Simplification of the tax code and other official regulations

Regulations to implement legislation in the USA should be drastically simplified. Vivid indications of the excessive weight and cost of combined executive and legislative action can be found in the size and complexity of public manuals recording regulations and detailed orders. Their weight is such that President Clinton organised a display of some official volumes and manuals to be delivered by bulldozers and piled in a ring of several heaps head high on the White House lawn. Their immensity demonstrate:

- injustice. No one can read all the words therein, although they directly affect nearly everyone. Yet the doctrine is that no one can plead ignorance of them for expulcation, despite frequent errors contained within them. For example, many millions of dollars of social security money go astray. Recipients, if overpaid, are expected to spot erroneous payments immediately and are punished for cashing such cheques. From time to time the press reports on the significant proportion of IRS officials who cannot answer questions accurately in internal tests about the IRS' own regulations. It is also revealed that not all IRS staffers are even high-school graduates. Educated or not, they tend to be polite; nevertheless, the IRS computers send through the mail monstrously threatening, cold-blooded, unsigned print-outs;
- undercover dictatorship and sleight-of-hand. No legislator or departmental chief can read such a volume of regulations before approving them all;
- gross wastage and make-work. Millions of officials have enough time to write all this stuff.

The federal tax code alone runs to more than 9000 pages and is administered by 130,000 officials in the Internal Revenue Service. Every day the IRS heavily penalises tax-payers who cannot prove they have followed every particular requirement in those thousands of pages, which hardly any citizen has ever seen. It has been publicly admitted that, with presidents and politicians promising not to raise any tax (unless they can change its name to a 'fee'), the government is thirsty for the additional revenue it collects from the IRS being successful in tripping up tax-payers and collecting enormous penalties. The whole IRS operation costs the US economy about $100 billion a year.

C. No income taxation

There should be no income-related taxation of either individuals or corporations, for many reasons. Here are five:

1. Income taxes are evaded by individuals and corporations, notably the

rich among each. Evasion unfairly raises the amount that must be collected from the honest.

2. To encourage employment, including socially valuable part-time employment. People will work harder to earn more if they can keep all their earnings. Employers can afford to employ more staff if earnings are not inflated to yield sufficient take-home pay after direct taxation.

3. To encourage efforts to earn more money and to save and invest a good part of earnings, thereby accelerating the rate of economic growth. That growth can occur if investment decisions are wise and if recessions, wars and other wastages of the economy can be avoided.

4. To avoid the administrative cost and demoralising harassment of citizenry involved with direct taxation.

5. Because it is quite feasible for governments to scoop up not more than a quarter of national income simply by using other and better methods of revenue-gathering.

Without recourse to direct taxation but using indirect taxes from purchases of products amounting to one dollar in four from the people, the 'new world' will look like this:

First and foremost, the government no longer requires any direct dealings with citizens about taxation during their lifetime. It need only be involved after their death with the heirs to their estates. In a single stroke, this immensely increases public toleration of government. This would be most welcome in the USA, where it has become part of the culture to detest officials.

Employers would be emancipated from much official pestering and discouragement. They could focus on hiring more workers, including those preferring part-time employment (Box 6.5). There would be no payroll deductions for any purpose. Affordable universal health care would be necessary but it would be financed by families being insured directly with government-subsidised health insurance schemes and not involving any employer as a third party.

Box 6.5: Book box: 'Reinventing the Left'*

This book, edited by David Miliband, chief adviser to Tony Blair, leader of the new Labour Party in Britain* includes a chapter by Stephen Tindale of the Institute for Public Policy Research which argues convincingly for a shift in taxes from 'good' things, such as employment and savings, to bad things, such as pollution, waste and resource depletion.

*Polity Press, London 1994

Employers would have to bear the full cost of job or unemployment insurance schemes since they and their profit-driven (not market-driven) system would be seen as causing much of the unemployment. Such schemes would be obliged to vary the premiums charged to each employer according to his or her success in keeping lay-offs and dismissals down to a minimum.

In some countries there are already levies on payrolls to finance training systems. However, payment for the benefits employers enjoy from the country's education and training system could be financed from other government revenues, including notably those gathered under the next measure recommended.

D. Estates over $10m: 50 per cent to charity and community

There need be neither taxation of inherited wealth nor of capital gains. No compensation would need to be paid by government to any individual or corporation suffering capital losses. However, it would be obligatory for half of the net value of all estates above $10 million to be donated to any publicly approved charities. The choice of charities could be made freely by the deceased in their will, or by executors appointed in the case of death intestate, except that the government would insist that a proportion, not exceeding a quarter, be distributed to voluntary communal activities for the common benefit.

Since there would be no income tax there would be no deductions from income before tax. This would reduce contributions to charities, but the contributions from estates would more than make up that loss – and should prove to be a substantial, but slow and relatively painless, reduction in the inequality of wealth. Contributions from estates would also reduce objectionable inequalities in incomes since they would greatly diminish unearned incomes derived from inherited capital, as distinct from savings that were *earned* by the recipient. No earnings would be taxed if saved and invested, nor would the income from investment be taxed; earnings would only be taxed when they are spent on non-vital goods and services.

It would be important to keep family businesses going and not force them to shrink or close down in order to sell assets to meet the contribution of half of the inheritances to charities. The establishment of the net value of estates for distribution would therefore be calculated to avoid injury to ongoing businesses and their employees: ownership of shares of capital invested in ongoing family owned private companies which belonged to deceased family members would be divided among all full-time employees of the company with at least two years' seniority, including surviving relatives, in proportion to their total annual income earned from the company.

This 'estate transfer tax' may be subject to objection before the Supreme Court as being unconstitutional as an 'unusual or cruel punishment'. But would it be? Let us assume that a man dies leaving a fortune of $1 billion. Of that, under the estate transfer tax, $500,000,000 goes to charity. Then, say, $350,000,000 goes to his son, a good golfer who will continue in the family founded corporation as a moderately efficient vice-president. The remaining $150,000,000 then goes to the deceased's much-divorced, drug-addicted, childless daughter, of no fixed employment or address other than luxury hotels. Would it be cruel to let her have only $150,000,000 – producing a tax-free income – instead of, say, $300,000,000 with income heavily taxed?

Fortunes would not be decimated. New ones would grow rapidly with no income or capital gains tax. Only the *idle* rich would be financially euthanased over the next two or three generations.

E. Value-added tax (20 per cent) on non-vital goods and services

Vital goods and services are those which people would soon die without, or at least be reduced in health and employability. In the production and distribution system, only non-vital goods and services would be subject to a 20 per cent value-added tax. The following vital necessities of low-income groups would be exempt from the tax:

- food and non-alcoholic beverages;
- medicines and services recognised by the government as contributing to better health;
- materials used in the production of cheap clothing;
- house rents and mortgage payments up to a maximum annual amount should be set according to what can be afforded by a family head or individual in the lowest quartile of incomes. Transfer of the ownership of houses should be free of tax and not be encumbered with unnecessary formalities incurring expenses for legal or other services burdensome to families with modest incomes;
- services provided by self-employed persons, both because some, such as doctors, provide services which are vitally necessary and should be as cheap as possible and because such taxation would be akin to income tax, which has been abolished;
- new products which effectively replace products which are highly polluting in their production and/or use;
- utilities – water, electricity, gas, heating fuels, telephone service – provided to residential housing;
- one car per family, priced below the cut-in level for luxury vehicles.

The value-added tax of 20 per cent would be levied on all other goods and services, except that it would be set at 30 per cent on costly luxuries and socially undesirable or harmful products.

It is important to have enough government revenue to pay off the national debt. Graduated but finally steep increases of petrol and diesel tax (above 20 per cent) can take care of that and encourage more people to shift from private to improved public transportation. Ubiquitous public transport is a vital necessity. Once it is provided as a top priority, private transport (vehicles and their fuel) becomes non-vital and taxable.

Value-added taxation is vastly preferred to the so-called expenditure tax proposed notably by Lord Nicolas Kaldor and Professor James Meade, for several reasons. The expenditure tax imposes the same costly administrative burdens on both tax-payers and tax-collectors and incurs similar problems of definition and evasion, since the tax is still levied on income; income spent instead of on income earned or received.

Value-added tax is simpler and cheaper to administer and much more difficult to evade. It is less regressive than an expenditure tax, because it permits the exemption of sales of vital and basic necessities bought by everybody, including the poor. Value-added taxation cannot be used for victimisation purposes by corrupt or tyrannical politicians in high public office. Yet value-added tax retains the economic advantages of an expenditure tax. It encourages saving and new investment. It would encourage investment even more so, if payment of the tax was also exempted in the case of selected producers' goods bought by investors developing productive capacity and services facilities. A particular advantage of value-added taxes is that everyone will pay them, including many people who, under other taxation systems, managed to evade much tax collection.

The amount of the value-added tax is suggested as 20 per cent on the supposition that the other fiscal measures D, E, F and J proposed here will yield the other 5 per cent of government revenues required to make up a maximum of 25 per cent per annum. It is important, so as to avoid economic distortions or invidious impacts on various employment opportunities, to keep the rate at the same level (20 per cent) for most of the items subject to the tax. There should not be too many different rates for items considered more or less necessary or luxurious or, by some, divine or undesirable.

Fiscal policy is one of the most complex and sensitive areas of economic analysis. It may be necessary to consider certain modifications of this broad value-added tax system. For example, instead of a flat 20 per cent tax,[13] it might be recommended to classify goods and services into two groups. One, being taxed at a lower rate (say 18 per cent), would include most services and those goods whose production requires an intensity of labour input well above a defined average in all employments. The other group, being taxed at a higher rate (say 22 per cent) would consist of all other goods and services produced by highly capitalised processes having high level productivity. This differentiation would help to compensate for Baumol's disease and would counterbalance the already gross overcharging for professional services.

In a rich society, labour-intensive supplies tend to be expensive, whereas the advance of technology makes capital-intensive and 'high-tech' goods cheap. And the gap widens over time: the prices of the labour-intensive items tend to go up, whereas the prices of the hi-tech items tend to stay down and even to fall: in some cases there are falls of several hundred per cent. They could easily bear quite a heavy tax without the tax significantly reducing demand for them.

F. All land nationalised; low-rent long leases

All land in the country would be classified as the property of the State and would be subject to a small lease payment: 10 dollars per acre per annum for agricultural and rural land; 20 dollars for urban land; 50 dollars for any land serving profit-earning activities other than agriculture. A higher tariff would be established for land used for the extraction of a list of valuable minerals and other deposits.

All existing landowners and future purchasers would be granted leases for a thousand years. These they would receive without any further payment by them (beyond the full payment they made when acquiring ownership), or to them in compensation. The lease may be immediately terminated at will by either the government or the lease-holder. The government only has the right – not the obligation – to terminate the lease if the land is either unused in any way for more than ten years, or if it is used in ways which infringe any laws of the land, including laws for protection of the environment. Land areas leased out would be clearly defined by the government so as to obviate any further expense or trouble with title searches and guarantees. Governments would not be permitted to lease out some land, such as national parks. Any usage rights sold by the government to private parties, such as grazing rights to cattle owners and water rights in irrigation systems, would be sold at the same prices as are charged by private lease-holders of land.

In future, all land sales would be sales of lease-holds, at market prices; lease-holders who were once free-holders would have no reason to expect major falls in property values because of the imposition of this new system. There need be no limit to the amount of land bought and sold, or to the value of buildings and other improvements on the land. Government might have a veto-power over sales in highly exceptional circumstances such as sale to a purchaser who is an enemy alien or country or to a criminal such as a smuggler or drug-dealer.

Customs duties are considered primarily as a device to protect trade. A country which levies customs duties as a revenue-raiser is under an illusion if it thinks it is taxing foreigners.

G. No exemptions from the new taxation system

There would be no impediment, licensing or additional taxation (nor any privilege or incentive) for individual and corporate charities of any kind so long as their activities were not found to be illegal. For simplicity of administration and accounting, all individuals and institutions, including those in the public sector, would pay the same taxes, including land taxes, as the remainder of the population and the economy. There would be no exemptions for religions, always difficult to define, some of which at present are privileged but bogus shells covering up non-religious and even criminal activities.

H. Centralisation and standardisation of social relief

The central or federal government, exclusively among the authorities in the public sector, would be responsible for the relief of destitute families, which should be mainly or entirely in kind: stamps for food and cheap clothing and government shelters on low-cost land. Destitute but able-bodied people can be required to work in national service schemes.

J. Property taxation unchanged; education systematised

There should be taxes on the value of real estate payable to town and city administrations for municipal services they provide and at a similar rate on rents paid above the minimum rent level fixed under E above. There should be no other taxes, such as on incomes or sales, imposed by municipal authorities. City taxes should arguably be much lower because the central government already subsidises education, training and other municipal activities in order to even out the inequities for children between rich and poor municipalities.

K. Power shift and endowment to community action

State or provincial governments should not have any taxation power and would be supported only by an income from the central government or from voluntary donations. This central assistance would only be paid to support activities which would be more cost-effective and better delivered by being decentralised from the central to the regional level. These activities could include democratic functions which supplement and do not duplicate such activities at central and municipal levels. Municipal administration can be honest, democratic and cheap. In principle, municipalities are necessities in the landscape of democracy and they come close to sharing the grass-roots advantages and strengths of voluntary communal and village organisations.

Modern corporations now think they can improve themselves by eliminating levels of middle management. Provincial governments might be eliminated for similar reasons; although closer than the central government to local realities, they are never as close to the grass-roots as are the municipalities.

In the USA, some politicians have clamoured to reduce the tax deficit and national debt. However, their proposals for cuts in federal government are often motivated by a desire to shift power and tax revenues from the federal to State governments. This is not a democratic movement; it is rather anti-democratic and plutocratic and promotes a kind of apartheid. States' rights were claimed not so long ago in order to maintain racial discrimination. States' rights means that each State can have maximum scope to protect and promote whatever it believes in. That includes maximum privileges for the rich in States where they predominate (New Hampshire); a happy nest for the incorporation of business (Delaware); baleful bigotry in States where one race or religion does or can predominate (the old South); carefree and sunny retirement (Florida, Arizona); and protection of the main industry, ranging from agriculture (the mid- and far-west) to gambling, divorce and prostitution (Nevada), to tobacco (North Carolina) oil and the right to pollute (Alaska) and holidaying in Hawaii. We may yet see a nostalgic collapse back into a wild west situation watched over maternally by the National Rifle Association! Indians on their tribal lands are already exempted from any restrictions on gambling and can maintain their own system of justice. Vermont specialises in peace, quiet and beauty and has dreamed of independent sovereignty like its Canadian neighbour, Quebec. California, New York and Texas already seem to be the three tails that wag the Washington dog.

Flood protection from a torrent of criticism

In the USA, right-wing Republicans may like the first taste but will ultimately spit out in horror proposal D, citing a 'half-baked' decimation of estates. They may even suggest that the land tax idea, proposal F, proves that I am either mad or a red under the bed. 'Red! as bad blood' will echo the farmers and real-estate interests, perhaps arguing: 'Land tax is as old hat as Henry George, but nationalisation of land is downright treacherous – and only exists in more primitive Third World countries.' Left-wing Democrats, an endangered species, may also condemn the switch from direct to indirect taxation as blatantly regressive and poor-bashing. Retail traders will bemoan the sales tax. Labour unions will say it is the royal road to wage-price inflation, industrial strife and recession: in a word – stagflation.

Much of what is recommended here was written before a surprising number of politicians and authors have recently begun to move with such an agenda. There is one point, however, which goes solidly against the grain of American public opinion: States' rights. Indeed, it would be easier to conquer the USA by force than, by peaceful persuasion, to achieve any diminution of States' rights. No more civil wars and no more Franklin Roosevelts or John Kennedys, please.

Furthermore, about ultimate delegation, when people murmur about less interference by Washington and by lawyers, what they most want is for community action to be given its head. However, that idea is dead in the water politically: it is perhaps too close an approach to real democracy!

Against other tidal waves in this flood of objections, I have erected a few sandbags.

Adequacy of revenues

A slick and easy way to criticise any fiscal proposal is to say: 'Ignore it folks; he hasn't done his sums. It'll bankrupt the country! He would ruin your kids by tripling the national debt.' The answer to that may be prefaced by a few words about the proper making of national budgets.

The United States is about the only rich country in the world which makes no distinction in its national budget between current and capital expenditure. This is incredibly old-fashioned accounting: everything, including the kitchen sink, goes into the national budget. Public present-ations of the US budget often include social security contributions in 'back of the envelope' additions showing how well public expenditure is being covered, thus turning insurance contributions or premiums into taxes and capital investment into cash flow.

It is simple honesty and logic for every global document on public revenue and expenditure to be clear to the reader. The following may help in this respect:

- to distinguish clearly, on the one side, general revenues from receipts of funds paid to serve exclusively specified public purposes and not to be spent on any other; and
- to break down public expenditure on the other side between general expenditure by sector and specific expenditure by purpose.

Above all, there should be a separation of current and capital items.

- Current items are expenditure recurring each year for items that correspond roughly to 'public consumption'.
- Development-budget (capital) items correspond pretty much to public investment. The latter are projects and programmes, often involving

immense purchases which will take several years to complete, years to pay for and still more years to be maintained when completed. These include the public highway system and other large-scale public works, irrigation and drainage systems and so forth. Maintenance work can be accounted for under 'development' and that and new investment would be shown as the difference between net and gross public investment.

A taxation system along the lines proposed here will expand the supply of savings and capital for investment, will keep the cost of capital from rising too much and permit the completion of items in the nation's programme of capital development as well as bolstering investments in the private sector. A proper accounting procedure is therefore to have the interest payable on the national debt presented in the 'income and expenditure statement' of the government's current budget and the value of capital projects completed shown in the government's 'assets and liabilities' balance sheet. In such a balance sheet, the projects are assets and the liabilities include the face value of the bonds and other instruments issued by the government when it borrows money.

It will be argued that a lot of public works and infrastructure improvement do not, immediately and directly, yield to the government the amount of tax revenue needed to pay interest on the bonds the government sells to raise capital for its development programme. That has been true in the past, but would not be true in future under the programme envisaged here.

Let us go back to the taxable capacity of the corporations and other businesses. While they would no longer pay income tax they will have to continue to pay real-estate taxes under point J of my taxation proposals. They will also have to pay the land rent under proposal F. Corporations will make substantial payments to the central government under the value-added tax proposal E, even if they are losing money but continuing to make sales, whereas today a lot of corporations, including large ones, escape practically all taxation. (Those in Massachusetts were recently terrified when the Department of Revenue threatened to publish their names; that was hushed up for them.)

Now, beyond the taxation here proposed for businesses, it is not fair for them to pay tax on *all* their income, because not all of it is earned with the help of the government. But they should reimburse the government for valuable services they directly receive from it. For example, here are some instances of what is euphemistically called 'corporate welfare' in the USA. Western cattle ranchers – most of whom are wealthy – pasture their cattle on government land for nominal government fees, far lower than pasture land elsewhere costs them. They should be charged in full. Similarly, irrigation systems provide large quantities of water at heavy government cost to farmers, those in California being a glaring case in point, who are charged so little for this water they make a good living even when raising crops and animals that could not normally be afforded on land irrigated with water charged at its full cost. They should be made to pay in full.

Millions of trucks are rumbling across the highways of Europe and North America, causing heavy wear and tear to them and killing and wounding hundreds of people weekly, thereby creating an economic loss to society. The taxes on fuel, etc. they pay comprise no significant contribution to the capital and maintenance costs of these highways. Modern electronic tracker systems (developed in France but ignored by the USA on the amazing grounds that France can afford them but the USA can't!) can economically track and identify all trucks using these roads. The vehicles' owners should be charged a monthly fee based on the maximum loaded weight of the vehicle and the distance it has travelled. The same system could be used to levy more modest charges on private cars. This system has two enormous advantages over the present clumsy, time-wasting toll-gate system: (i) it would never oblige any vehicle to stop or even notice it was measured; (ii) it would permit fairer charging at rates proportionate to the wear and tear caused by the vehicle to the public highway system anywhere in the country.

Due to the cost and inconvenience of current public transport, which should be reduced by rationalisation, poor people use their cars a great deal to get themselves to work and their children to school. For this reason the subsidy to public passenger transport should be increased. It is also necessary to be sure that we redress the balance currently in favour of the heavy trucks which are now the most subsidised, paying so little for highway use and the costs they impose in maintenance, accidents and congestion.

A lot of other US government services provided free or at low cost should be charged for at their full cost and paid for by the beneficiaries, not the tax-payers. The UK is now starting to charge litigants for the cost of judges trying their cases. This and the British practice of charging all costs to the losing party in civil court cases would be well worth adoption in the USA, where there is urgent need to stem frivolous, opportunistic, casino-type litigation.

Another major item has received much publicity, yet it is worth repeating: namely, the heavy costs of maintaining large American military stations in Japan and Europe. At least half of the benefit of such expenditure accrues to the countries in the theatres mentioned. Those host countries, thus protected, are not poor. They can afford and often do provide their populations with much better social programmes than the American people receive. This is unjust and should be rectified without further delay. US bases overseas of great benefit to other rich countries should be supported financially, at least in part, by those other countries.

To generalise: in many parts of the world (including the USA) governments should cease giving foreigners' help which is more generous per individual than the help they give to their own citizens and tax-payers with similar needs.

Regressivity

There will be objections that the abolition of income tax and capital gains tax and the tax exemption of estates under twenty million dollars is regressive, in contrast to existing (progressive) taxation systems which are said to favour the poor. That is not so true in the USA, where the rich wax prosperous more as a result of capital gains than by earning incomes and have already demonstrated their horror at the idea of a minimum income tax payable by every citizen without exemption (except for the poorest, who qualify for negative income tax).[14] In contrast, many people with low and modest incomes are more concerned about having any income at all than they are about the burden imposed by tax systems. They would rather have full employment, or close to it, instead of less or more taxation.

Under my proposals there is a tax on non-essentials bought by low-income groups. But they are not forced to buy non-essentials; in large families particularly, many of the 'necessities' they buy would not be taxed at all. It is arguably less regressive to have the ranks of the rich thinned out, leaving a large but more meritocratic group of high-earning people who vigorously promote prosperity. This is surely better than a high-tax, high-spending economy which permits only low levels of employment (or indeed a zero-tax, zero-spending economy, were that feasible).

The proposals would also reduce objectionable inequalities in incomes, since they greatly diminish unearned incomes derived from inherited capital – as distinct from savings that were earned by the recipient.

Impact on employment

Fuller employment, widely desired, would be likely to result from the proposed system by discouraging excessive or frivolous consumption. This would be taxed more severely, helping to discourage the consumer indebtedness so burdensome at high interest rates. Indeed, the system would encourage investment by freeing funds which are now heavily taxed but which would be tax-free in future. Government purchases should not be tax-free; public bodies as well as individuals should be motivated to consume less and invest more.

Investment creates employment now and more employment in the future, because it builds up and strengthens the economy. Consumption is merely money lost: all that remains are fading memories (and maybe overweight bodies and hangovers). More untaxed capital saved up in individual hands increases personal economic security. Unbridled consumption merely leaves consumers with receipts to put in their income tax files or in the rubbish bin (Box 6.6).

No one may be anxious to give employers and corporations a better life than they have now; but it would be a positive step to ensure that they will not be taxed and tied in knots with red tape whenever they seek to hire more people. It is also worthwhile to make life easier for small businesses. They constitute the majority of employers and they employ more workers per unit of capital than the big, highly capitalised corporations, many of which are hell-bent on automation and on a shift of production to cheap-labour countries.

Box 6.6: Investment-led recovery

Readers of the recommendation in this book for an expenditure tax must shudder, especially shopkeepers, at the thought of the overall depressing effect on our consumerist societies of the discouragement of consumer spending and the encouragement of saving (and hence of investment). We are back to the worry about the famous 'two-thirds' of demand plunging when the consumers zip up their purses and stay home. A look at what happened most recently in the USA, contrasted with what occurred in the 1980s, may cheer them a little. It is true that in the 1994 recovery indices of consumer confidence shot up, people binged again at Xmas and splurged a bit on houses and cars. But an economist of a major Wall Street Bank has argued that the American economy is shifting from consumption, its traditional engine, towards investment. Spending on producers' durable equipment in 1994 reached 13.67% of consumption, well above the 10.71% average for 1972–91. He expects that, by the year 2000, $1 will be spent on equipment for every $5 on consumption. If so, that fraction – one fifth or 20% – happens to coincide with the recommendation in this book for an expenditure tax of 20%. In his view the current recovery, unlike past consumption-led booms, may not end in inflationary misery. It is true that spending on consumer goods may be more inflationary because it includes the so-called 'wage goods': when their prices rise there will usually be demands for wage increases to pay for them. In contrast, when there is heavy spending on capital equipment, that raises productivity, which combats inflation and also tends to be labour-saving. The latter in turn mitigates increases in the demand for labour, though wages may not be too dampened insofar as it is easier to raise wages in more capital-intensive sectors.

America, in 1994, was in the second stage of a 'productivity-led' recovery, so-called because productivity growth had accounted for almost all of the 2.9% annual GDP growth of the preceding three years. Indeed, investment rose by 15% in real terms in 1993: accounting for 12% of GDP, up from 10.7% in 1992. By 1995 it is expected to reach 13.4% (a record since 1945). Three-quarters of the new investment has gone so far on

continued

Box 6.6 continued

durable equipment, rather than on new buildings. (That is healthy: the speculative boom in the 1980s led to the over-building of offices, few more are needed in the 1990s and a boom and bust in real estate perhaps can be averted this time.) Investment in information technology has led the way: spending leapt by 27% in real terms in 1993. In 1994 equipment spending broadened to include more traditional items as companies upgraded their machinery. Great American industries have thrown off their complacency and are improving their efficiency and capacity to compete globally. Demand for American exports should rise with this investment leading to better quality at lower prices. If it also gathers strength from economic recovery abroad, American companies will be able to hire more workers.

By 1995, however, many more economists and Congressmen began to propose an expenditure tax in place of income tax, since that would promote investment, which is needed to raise the productivity of the American economy, the only factor permitting improved levels of living for the majority. By 1996, this problem of slow productivity growth received much attention in Congress.

In a dangerously overpopulated, under-employed world, our most urgent need is to increase the supply of capital so that more jobs, homes and social facilities can be created. The poor countries are saying 'We have the billions of people but you rich countries, with so many less people, are consuming about three quarters of the world's income.' So then, let us have expenditure tax systems (like the one proposed here) in rich countries which, via increasing savings and investment, will ultimately make those countries richer and better able to help the poor.

Thinkers on the left will probably complain that these tax proposals are too gentle on the rich. Those who want to speed up the reduction in inequality may wish to introduce a tax on wealth which hits the living rich, as distinct from the dead rich and their heirs. An annual levy on wealth is administratively far simpler than levying income tax, if it is confined to large items for which there must be official registration of their ownership titles. This includes land, buildings, cars, yachts, aeroplanes, portfolios of stocks and bonds (except anonymous bearer shares and bonds) and private corporations. Such a wealth tax, which has long existed in the world's wealthiest country, Switzerland, might be fixed at 1 per cent per annum on the value of all property owned by each individual which exceeds a total value of one million dollars (a small sum, growing smaller as time goes by).

A major and interesting question would be: would such revenue from the wealth tax go to the local authority where the owner officially resides, or in its entirety to the central government? Central government would be the administratively simpler course. See, for example, the difficulty in knowing where billionaire Adnan Kashoggi officially resided, when his divorced wife claimed half of his net worth and had to settle, in the end, for less than a paltry $100 million. Obviously, the wealth tax would partly duplicate some of what has already been proposed above. It would nicely raise total revenues for those in Washington with big spending plans!

Balance of power, public and private

Why nationalise land? That ruined Soviet agriculture when the kulaks (small farmers) in the USSR were liquidated and the poorly motivated, cumbrous state farms were set up. Productivity increases occurred in communist China almost immediately after some agricultural collectives were replaced by farmers who were granted fifteen year leases on land allotted to them. It is agreed that farmers have no incentive to invest their money in any improvements or structures on the land they farm if they do not own it. But they will feel like owners if they hold very long leases, extending far beyond their own lifetime and the duration of their equipment and installations. The rents on leases should be set at a token level; indeed at zero ('grandfathered') for existing owners when the tax is inaugurated. Such rents will then bring the government useful revenue without imposing any noticeable charge on any businesses or families.

Realism, and the truth for its own sake

Although these proposals will meet with immense opposition, notice where the opposition is coming from and work out the real reasons for it. You will see, for example, that thousands of lawyers and accountants would no longer be needed. There is other and better work for them to do. When a major source of their business – handling a monstrously complex and proliferated tax system – disappears, their vast fees will fall as they compete for work. They may then need to seek clients among people with modest incomes who always needed them but could not previously afford them.

These proposals on taxation are intended to provoke a debate. Such a debate would be a good start. It may prove naïve to try to reform society at this late stage. There are formidable practical problems in the transition stage, even if the reform were embarked on. In the USA, for example, a country highly geared to consumerism with so many of its investments aimed at swelling supplies to every nook and niche of the consumers' market, great structural strains would arise in its economy from a radical tax reform which switched from encouraging consumption to encouraging investment.

The solution was highlighted in J. K. Galbraith's contrasts between private affluence and public squalor.[15] Could not 'the richest country in the world' begin to do something about cleaning up its public squalor? Instead of the current filth, American cities could shine with cleanliness. This is but one of several dimensions of a better quality of life in the USA to be gained through a higher level of investment. For example, the reserves of intellectual manpower now underemployed could be rewardingly absorbed into an expanded and strengthened American education system.

We might ruminate on the nature of our 'need' for many of the costly services we currently consume. We would need less health care if we took more of the well-known steps to live a healthy life. Some might argue that we would need less still if people are given the choice of dying in peace and comfort when they are ready to go. Almost half of medical care is now lavished on dying people, yet it fails to keep them alive. Perhaps their major need is to receive as much comfort as possible during the dying process rather than painful attempts to avoid the inevitable.

We would need less lawyers if aggressivity, alienation and social tensions were reduced and less still if we had fewer laws. Fewer laws and less government, with a reduction of their attendant expenses, are possible when we are more self-reliant and responsible; when we can re-establish a moral code adhered to in the land; and when blameworthy people will again be endowed with the capacity for shame and with heightened sensitivity and imagination required for their salvation.

If there were less unnecessary work to do and further technological advance there could be reduced pressure at work; more time for leisure and for activities less numbing than automated machine-like work. There might even be less need to ginger up a dull or anguished life with injurious and mortal addictions. Spectators might even leave their seats and TVs to join in the sports and entertainments!

Is all that an impossible dream?

Well, at mid-century, to save our lives and our freedom, we beat Hitler and Hirohito. We played ping-pong with the Chinese and the Russians knocked down walls so that we could befriend them too. Perhaps some economic and social reforms along the lines envisaged will not be outside the compass of a society determined to show its citizens a more human face than we have ever managed before?[16]

Notes

Introduction and Part I: Our Inheritance

1(a). 'The Winner-Take-All Society: More and More Americans compete for Fewer and Bigger Prizes, Encouraging Economic Waste, Income, Inequality, and an Impoverished Cultural Life', Robert H. Frank and Philip J. Cook, Free Press, 1995.

1(b). The usual lapse of time from completion of a manuscript to when the edited book reaches readers is a mere moment in history. However, there is now an accelerated succession of occurrences making up the stuff of history. This is due, possibly, to speeded progress in technology, transport and communications and to the current political impatience of the public. Even books concerned with supposedly unchanging matters such as 'economic laws' need now to anticipate the rapid changes and major developments. My policy recommendations looked audacious and radical when they were written, yet similar views are being expressed and gaining acceptance in the media and the political arena. The mainstream of economics is not easily or quickly switched in its course within the establishment of academic economists. As we go to print, however, their discipline, and especially the macro-economics built around the statistics of national accounting, is being jolted by a new awakening. The most recent and accessible instances of this are:

'If the GDP is Up, why is America Down?' by Clifford Cobb, Ted Halstead and Jonathan Rowe (Atlantic Monthly, October 1995);

'Benefits are being pecked to death' (Business Week, December 4 1995).

Further advanced among maverick university economists is:

'Labyrinths of Prosperity', by Reuven Brenner (Michigan University Press).

Most recently, and centrally in the mainstream, has come 'Top Heavy: A Study of the Increasing Inequality of Wealth in America', by Edward N. Wolff, Professor of Economics at New York University (Twentieth Century Fund Press, New York, 1995). Its significance led to Prof. Wolff's interview on USA's public television channel (the MacNeil-Lehrer News Hour) in late 1995. Richard C. Leone, President of the Twentieth Century Fund, concluded his introduction to it with these words: 'With a remarkably large segment of the population losing ground in wealth and income, the inevitably greater insecurity this group faces must be a root cause of the anger that is shaking the democratic system.' Equally outspoken on a renewal of the employers' tacit social contract to avoid a breakdown is 'The Future of Capitalism', Lester Thurow, New York: 1996.

2. *Critique of Economic Reason*, André Gorz, London, New York: Verso, 1989. Another brilliant book, which also delineates much of the services sector realities depicted here is by a former neo-conservative who proposes policy solutions less left-wing and Utopian than those of Gorz: see *The Next*

American Nation: the New Nationalism and the Fourth American Revolution,
Michael Lind, The Free Press, 1995.

3. For more details about other areas, see *The Economics of Subsistence*, Colin Clark and Margaret Haswell, 2nd edn, New York: St Martin's Press, 1966; London: Macmillan.

4. *Why Poor People Stay Poor: Urban Bias in World Development*, Michael Lipton, Cambridge: Harvard University Press, 3rd printing, 1980.

5. Regarding evolution in the size of communities and a future perspective, see *Global Paradox*, John Naisbitt, New York: Morrow, 1994.

6. For example, about Washington see *Arrogant Capital*, Kevin Phillips, New York: Little, Brown, 1994.

7. *The Rise and Fall of the Great Powers*, Paul Kennedy, New York: Random House, 1987. Kennedy focuses on the critical relationship of economic to military power as it affects the rise and fall of empires.

8. An academic surmise is of a world population growth (with ups and downs along the way) at .0007 per cent to .0015 per cent per year for one or two million years to reach eight million people at the end of the Pleistocene era; an acceleration to about .036 per cent per year after the establishment of agriculture, to reach 300 million by 1 AD; then growth at .056 per cent per year to reach 800 million by 1750. See *Structure and Change in Economic History*, Douglass C. North, Norton, 1981, p. 14.

9. *The Times Atlas of World History*, p. 143, Maplewood, NJ 07040–1396: Hammond, 1984.

10. See *State of the World 1995*, Lester R.Brown *et al.*, Washington, DC: World Watch Institute, 1995, Chapter I. This annual report sold worldwide at a low price is a valuable source of updated global information on population, resources and the economy.

Part II: Unemployment

1. *Economics in Perspective: A Critical History,* J. K. Galbraith, Boston: Houghton Mifflin, pp. 155–6.

2. Galbraith, op. cit., pp. 234–5. See also pages 30–31.

3. *The Pocket Economist*, R. Pennant Rea and B. Emmott, TENL and Martin Robertson, Oxford, 1983, p. 103.

4. Members of the IMF since before 1974.

5. *Traite d'Economie Politique*, Jean Baptiste Say, cited in Alexander Gray, *The Development of Economic Doctrine*, London: Longmans Green, 1948, p. 267.

6. *The General Theory of Employment Interest and Money*, J. M. Keynes, London: Macmillan, 1936. A McGill economist told me he did not know what is 'aggregate effective demand'. I say it is, at a point in time, the total amount of money all people can and want to spend on things they want now and money which is effectively and immediately spent in that way. At successive points in time, the amount goes up or down and the selection of things to buy changes.

7. See 'Psychological Economics', George Katona (reprint. ed. pap. 127.70, Books on Demand, Division of University Microfilm International, 300 N.

Zeeb Rd, Ann Arbor, Michigan MI 48106–1346). Much of the wide field of study about the role of expectations and of uncertainty in economic life, associated particularly with the pioneering work of R. E. Lucas (the 1995 Nobel prize winner) of Chicago University, lies behind what is said in this book about consumers' and investors' attitudes. One memorable and early book has the apt title *Risk, Uncertainty and Profit*, by Frank Knight, 1921, most recent edition: University of Chicago Press, 1985.

8.   See the working of the Stock Exchange described in *The Great Crash, 1929*, J. K. Galbraith, Boston: Houghton Mifflin, 1955, 1988.

9.   *The Trade Cycle*, Roy Harrod, Oxford University Press, 1936; also see Paul Samuelson, *Review of Economics and Statistics*, 1939; also 'Collected Scientific Papers of Paul Samuelson', Cambridge, M.I.T. Press, 1966.

10. *Macmillan Dictionary of Modern Economics*, edited by D. W. Pearce, London: Macmillan, 1981, 1989, p. 182.

11(a). TENL, 6 August 1994.

11(b). This view was expressed by Professor Paul Samuelson of M.I.T., in a lecture he gave on the business cycle during the 1990–92 recession, at Harvard University, to members of the American Friends of the London School of Economics.

12. Conclusions drawn from 'The culture of contentment', in *A Journey through Economic Time: A First Hand View*, J. K. Galbraith, Boston: Houghton Mifflin, 1994, pp. 236–7.

13. Since this was written it has become clear from conflicting statements by authorities how difficult it is to measure productivity properly and to agree on whether it is going up or down.

14. BG, 8 September 1994.

15. Keynes, 1936, op. cit. More recent expositions of Keynesian economics by Alvin Hansen, Paul Samuelson and Galbraith are easier to grasp. 'Economics in Perspective', John Kenneth Galbraith, Houghton Mifflin, 1987; 'Macro-economics', Paul Samuelson and William Nordhaus, McGraw Hill, 1992; 'Business Cycle Theory: Its Development and Present Status', Alvin H. Hansen, Connecticut: Hyperion, 1980.

16. *A Treatise on Money*, J. M. Keynes, 2 vols., New York: Harcourt, Brace, 1930.

17. Keynes, *General Theory*, op. cit.

18. Keynes, *Treatise*, op. cit.

19. *A Journey through Economic Time: a First Hand View*, J. K. Galbraith, Boston: Houghton Mifflin, 1994, pp. 88, 216. He may have borrowed this 'string' analogy from Keynes.

20. As a fundament to Part II here, see *The Business Cycle*, Howard J. Sherman, Princeton University Press, NJ, 1991, for a full-fledged economic analysis of the business cycle. *The Economist* speaks of *Business Cycles Forever*; see TENL, 28 October–3 November 1995, pp. 16 and 89.

Part III: Structures in the Population, Economy and Society

1.   Source: US Bureau of the Census, *Statistical Abstract of the United States: 1993*; annual averages of monthly figures.

2. TENL, 4 March 1994; about NAIRU, see also note 5.

3. *Full Employment in a Free Society*, Sir William Beveridge, London: Allen & Unwin, 1944, p. 26. He may have coined the term 'frictional unemployment'.

4. *Unemployment: Macroeconomic Performance and the Labour Market*, R. Layard, S. Nickell and R. Jackman, Oxford University Press, 1993.

5. *Structural Slumps: the modern Equilibrium Theory of Unemployment, Interest and Assets*, Edmund Phelps, London, 1994.

6. *Anxious about Jobs*, TENL, 12 March 1994, compares European and American concerns.

7. *The Business Cycle*, Howard J. Sherman, Princeton University Press, 1991, pp. 62–3.

8. I attended Viner's lectures. Viner may have published his view on this subject later.

9. 'Some thoughts for consideration or rejection', by Robert W. Cox (Professor of Political Science. York University, Toronto), quoted from a periodical (not for sale) written by and circulated among retired ILO officials.

10. TENL, 3 September 1994.

11. TENL, 10 September 1994.

12. *Competing for the Future*, Gary Hamel and C. K. Prahalad, Harvard Business School Press, 1994.

13. Op. cit., note 10.

14. Op. cit., note 11.

15. *The Information Society, Issues and Illusions*, D. Lyon, Cambridge: Polity Press, 1988.

16. *Measuring the Information Society*, F. Williams (ed.), Beverly Hills, Ca: Sage Publications, 1988.

17. *Paths toward the Informational Society: Employment structure in G-7 Countries, 1920–1970*, Manuel Castells and Yuoko Aoyama, Geneva: ILO: International Labour Review, Vol. 133, 1994, No. 1. The paper, with a similar title but extending the period covered to 2005 by projections, was presented to the Berkeley Roundtable on the International Economy in November 1992, Berkeley, California.

18. See Part I, note 7.

19. See *The Great Hunger: Ireland 1845–9*, Cecil Woodham-Smith, London: Hamish Hamilton, 1962. The British have been accused of ethnic cleansing in Ireland, though they did not introduce the potato disease and no one then knew how to cure it. The British and other landlords in Ireland did not want or try to starve their tenants. The tenants starved because they were too poor to afford any food but potatoes, so the more valuable, undiseased foods they continued to grow during the famine continued to be exported from Ireland. It was the capitalist system and nineteenth-century economic thought which starved and drove out the Irish peasants; the British government, seeking to save them, imported American corn into Ireland for famine relief. This was the only obtainable food that would not compete with and undermine the existing food trade. Britain did not seek to exterminate or expatriate the Irish (except criminals); it allowed them to enter Britain freely for residence and employment long before Ireland joined the European Union. In future, famines and suffering as bad as the Irish experience will recur in many parts of the world.

20. BG, 9 May 1994.
21. *Scientific American*, Paul Krugman and Robert Z. Lawrence, April 1994.
22. *Journal of the American Medical Association*, 5 July 1995.
23. *The New Industrial Estate*, J. K. Galbraith, Boston: Houghton Mifflin, 1967; London: Hamish Hamilton, 1967.
24. BG, 9 May 1994.
25. The annual *Human Development Report* by UNDP (published by Oxford University Press) was launched by Dr Mahbub ul Haq and is prepared with the collaboration of Sir Hans Singer and Paul Streeten.
26. See the chapter on 'Manpower planning and job creation', in *Education and Training in the 1990s: Developing Countries' Needs and Strategies*, Education Development Center, New York: UNDP, 1989, Sales No. E.89.III.B.7. Also pertinent is *Structural Change and Development Policy*, Hollis Chenery, World Bank Research Publication, Oxford University Press, 1979.
27. Although this section was abstract, consider how reform of taxation is a major issue in forthcoming elections. This book recommends that income tax, which discourages employment, be abolished and replaced by a tax on consumption, a view now shared by some of America's most respected Senators and pundits.

Part IV: 'The Poor Ye Have Always'

1. Interview with the actor Anthony Hopkins, BG, 31 October 1993.
2. *The Affluent Society*, J. K. Galbraith, Boston: Houghton Mifflin, 1958.
3. *Equality*, R. H. Tawney, London: Penguin Books, 1938.
4. Publicly stated, for example, by the Attorney-General of Massachusetts in October 1995.
5. See also 'The minimum wage debate' TENL, 10 September 1994.
6. *The New York Times*, 17 October 1994.
7. BG 24 October 1994.
8. Hard-nosed economists could argue that real wages have not gone down in the USA because American workers' remuneration in 1950–70 included a temporary quasi-rent until the rest of the world economy recovered from wars that did not injure the American economy.
9. *The Times Atlas of World History*, Maplewood, NJ 07040-1396: Hammond, 1984, p. 143.
10. TENL, 3 September 1994. Subsequently it was found that this study lacked validity for taking samples too small.
11. *Economics in Perspective*, J. K. Galbraith, Boston: Houghton Mifflin, 1987, p. 296.
12. Stated on TV Cable News Network, 24 January 1995, quoting DRI/McGraw Hill.
13. *LSE: Centenary Review*, Stephen Wood, pp. 50–1.
14. *The Fifth Estate*, Robert Taylor, London: André Deutsch, 1978.
15. *The Future of the Trade Unions*, Robert Taylor, London: André Deutsch, 1994.
16. TENL, 10 September 1994.

17. 'The Inc. Report', John Case, quoted in BG, 13 April 1994.
18. 'Look out for the Union Label', Steven Early, BG, 5 June 1994.
19. *The Cost of Talent*, Derek Bok, New York: Free Press, 1993. Derek Bok is a former president of Harvard University.
20. 'Economics as if values mattered', Jim Wallis, *Sojourners* (monthly), November and December 1993, January 1994, Washington, DC.
21. *A Journey through Economic Time*, J. K. Galbraith, Boston: Houghton Mifflin, 1994, p. 203. First expressed in *The New Industrial Estate*, Boston: Houghton Mifflin. 3rd. ed. rev., 1979 NAL-Dutton, 1979.
22. TENL, 27 August 1994.
23. Survey by *Forbes Magazine*, quoted on TV CNN, October 1995.
24. See *Toward Two Societies: The Changing Distribution of Income and Wealth in the US since 1960*, Andrew Winnick, New York: Praeger; and *The Growing Divide*, Jerry Kloby, *Monthly Review*, 39 (September), 1–9. (Both quoted in Howard Sherman, op. cit., pp. 61–2). Up to date and valuable is 'Top Heavy: A Study of the Increasing Inequality of Wealth in America', Edward Wolff, Twentieth Century Fund, New York, 1996.
25. BG, 24 October 1994.
26. Robert Samuelson, BG, 6 September 1994.

Part V: The Paradox of Prosperity and Disillusion

1. *Time* magazine, 24 October 1994.
2. 'Opposing the System', Charles Reich, New York: Random House, 1995. The remarks by Reich were quoted in the Boston Globe's Sunday Magazine during the week of the book launch.
3. *The Managerial Revolution*, James Burnham, Westport, Connecticut: Greenwood Press, 1960, 1972.
4. *Management and Machiavelli*, Antony Jay, Hodder and Stoughton, 1967.
5. *The New Industrial State*, J. K. Galbraith, London: Hamish Hamilton, 1967.
6. See Part III, pages 111–112 and Box 5.3.
7. 'Structural Unemployment', Joe Rogaly, EBY (1984), p. 29.
7a. China and Italy were included for their industrial importance, although their statistics for the 1980s did not include employment in utilities, mining, quarrying or extraction. 1990s figures did include those sectors. The substantial 'increase' in Chinese employment is largely due to the inclusion of more occupations in the statistics for the later period.
8. *American Economic History*, Harold Underwood Faulkner, 8th edn, Harper & Row, New York, 1960, p. 701; quoted in J. K. Galbraith, Journey, op. cit., p. 123.
9. BG, 8 October 1994.
10. See *Economic Report of the President*, February 1995, Appendix B, Table B–16, p. 293.
11. Analysis done by Kenneth Thorpe of Tulane University and researchers at Brandeis University, BG, 9 November 1995, pp. 1, 13.
12. William Baumol, Professor of Economics at both Princeton and New York Universities, speaking to the American Friends of the London School of Economics sixth annual dinner, New York City, Spring 1994. See *Productivity in Personal Services*, W. Baumol, American Philosophical Society, May 1993.

Part VI: Reform and Policy

1. Keynes *General Theory* and *Treatise* are cited in Part II notes 6 and 16. Keynes' impact is described in *A Journey through Economic Time: a First Hand View*, J. K. Galbraith, Houghton Mifflin, 1994, pp. 95, 97–9, 103–4, 108. In the USA, Keynes gained much influence through the language, clearer than Keynes', of Professor Alvin Hansen (Harvard University). See note II, 15.
2. *Full Employment in a Free Society*, Sir William Beveridge, London: Allen & Unwin, 1944.
3. For their history and performance see *The Specialized Agencies and the United Nations*, Douglas Williams, St. Martin's Press, New York, and David Davies Memorial Institute of International Studies, London, 1987.
4. 'International Industrialization Levels from 1750 to 1980', Paul Bairoch, *Journal of European Economic History*, II, 1982.
5. 'China's emergence: prospects, opportunities and challenges', World Bank paper by Andrea Boltho, Magdalen College, Oxford.
6. 'Fear of US Tyranny', BG, 4 July 1995.
7. Quebec will continually wound Canada's economy and polity mortally, unless and until it realises that its French culture is not threatened by Canada but by American television.
8. *The Gore Report on Reinventing Government: Creating a government that works better and costs less: Report of the National Performance Review*, Vice-President Al Gore, New York: Times Books, Random House, September 1993. Al Gore is also the author of *Earth in the Balance: Ecology and the Human Spirit*, Al Gore, NAL-Dutton 1993, and, with President Clinton, of *Putting People First: How we can all change America*, New York: Times Books, Random House, 1992.

     Reform efforts on both sides of the political spectrum suffer from inattention and ignorance. The so-called Grace Report on government reform by a commission appointed by the Republican administration, headed by Peter Grace, made recommendations on cutting government waste that could supposedly save $400 billion, but copies of it are oddly difficult to trace.
9. *Newsday*, William Bunch, columnist.
10. See Part I note 6 and pp. 226–227.
11. Turning from peccadilloes to the big picture, corruption and immorality in Washington are not a novelty. Trollope, on a postal assignment in Washington in the mid-nineteenth century, wrote about corruption in Washington, DC in terms strikingly applicable today (*An Autobiography*, Anthony Trollope, London: Oxford University Press, 1953, pp. 269–70). On the recent decline in moral stature in American government, see 'Clinton faces Kennedy myth,' by Mike Barnicle, BG, 26 October 1993 and the source quoted in Box 6.4.
12. BG, 14 April 1994. An article by Jeff Jacoby exactly a year later (also in BG), when tax returns fell due again in 1995, contained a damning indictment of the oppression of the American people by the Internal Revenue Service. His charges are serious and merit an official inquiry.
13. This should not be confused with the flat tax proposal prominent in the 1996 American presidential campaign rhetoric. Here we speak of a flat tax on expenditure; in the campaign the talk was about a flat tax on incomes. Those flat tax proposals in Congress in 1995 were in the area of 17 to 20 per cent

of all incomes and those made in previous years did not call for higher rates. The highest income receivers were supposed to be taxed 39 per cent in 1940, and 54 per cent for the most of the time from 1941 to 1970; 47 per cent from 1971 to 1979, 45 per cent from 1980 to 1986, 35 per cent from 1986 to 1994, rising to 36 per cent more recently. How many people paid these taxes if a flat tax at a lower rate alarmed them mightily? This was one of those special moments in history when the naked truth is momentarily unveiled by startling events. Another such time was in 1994 when the New York Stock Exchange started plunging within minutes after President Clinton stated correctly that interest rates on credit cards were too high and should be subject to a regulatory ceiling. They had been untouched by low interest rate policy to promote economic recovery. The American banking system, running empty at the beginning of the 1990s, restored its low reserves through usury of the most desperate borrowers.

14. Public concern has been expressed in 1995 about billionaires abandoning their American citizenship to escape taxation. More might do so to escape the proposed redistribution of large estates to charity. When the escapist billionaires die and if they leave money to heirs who are still American tax-payers, as well as money remaining in identifiable US investments, those moneys should be subject to a tax sufficient to recapture at least some part of the deceased's estates exceeding $10 million that would have been destined for American charities but for the evasion. There are a few tax havens abroad and, under the new taxation system proposed here, the USA would become one and would attract wealthy people elsewhere to settle in America. They should be entitled to US residence for their wealth alone, subject to having no criminal record nor visible and grave character deficiencies. Under existing American law, no one can regain US residence if they have abandoned it to escape taxation.

15. J. K. Galbraith, *Affluent Society*, op. cit.

16. Throughout this book much has been said about capitalism, including its faults, notwithstanding its outstanding superiority as an *economic* system. The question, Can capitalism be chameleon? has been answered by Dr. Robert Cox (Professor of Political Science and International Relations at York University, Toronto): 'One may try to identify various forms of capitalism which are to a degree conceived, assumed, or put into effect, in different parts of space and periods of time. There are the following different rival 'substantive capitalisms' each with its own consequences for society:

● a single model of reformed capitalism that (as assumed by the International Labor Organization (ILO) in Europe after 1919) was achieving an institutionalizing of social conflict: incorporating salient elements of civil society (trade unions and employers) among its constituent elements – an essentially European development of that time;

● a hyperliberal capitalism (Thatcher–Reaganism) that envisages a separation of economics from both politics and society, placing economics in dominance over both. It espouses deregulation, privatization and the dismantling of the welfare state. This form of capitalism is strong in North America and Britain, and in Europe challenges . . .

- a social-market or social-democratic capitalism that retains roots in western and northern Europe and is closest to the original ILO assumptions. The issues within EU over 'social Europe' and the 'democratic deficit' are about whether this form of capitalism can survive in a defensive struggle with hyperliberal capitalism (see Michel Albert, 'Capitalisme contre capitalisme');

- an East Asian capitalism which was initiated in Japan and has evolved in a variety of forms, none of which succumbed to the hyperliberal doctrine of the separation of economics from society and politics; and in all of which cultural and social practices have remained integrated with economic and political organization;

- an unstable void into which predatory, rapacious capitalisms have surged. This is the case in the ex-Soviet empire and much of what used to be called the Third World. It is being encouraged by hyperliberalism through policies euphemistically described as 'shock therapy' and 'structural adjustment.'

('The ILO of Today and Tomorrow', R.W. Cox, Geneva: op. cit. 'ILO Friends Newsletter', no. 17, May 1994. Unpublished paper quoted by kind permission of Dr. Cox).'

Index

Academe, academicians, 50
Acceleration, downs and ups, 37
Accelerator, 39
Accountants, 50
Afghanistan, 77
Africa, xv, 3, 4, 7, 77, 88, 90, 123, 167
Age (*see also* unemployment), 78
Agha Khan, 141
Agriculture, xviii, 6, 7, 13, 70, 77, 111, 194, 197, 202, 223, 236, 247
Ainshan, China, 111
Airbus, 101
Air France, 150
Airlines, 84–85, 103, 150
Air Transport Association of America, 85
Alaska, 240
Alcatel Alsthom, 93
Aleutian Islands, 6
Albania, 8
Alabama, 98
Alexander the Great, 9
Aliens, 231
American Academy of Pediatrics, 181
American Dream, xvi, 14, 17
American Economic Association, 73
AFL-CIO American Federation of Labor (and *see* CIO), 159, 166, 171
American Management Association, 86
Angola, 77
Annenberg, Walter, 141
Antoinette, Marie, 224
Aoyama, Yuoko, nIII.17
Apartheid, 240
Apple-Mackintosh, 42, 43, 44
Aristotle, 7
Argentina, 89, 121, 122, 195, 196, 218
Arizona, 82, 240
Armenia, 221
Armstrong, W.E., 4
Asia, 45

economic progress 11, Box 1.1, 122, 123
migrants, 76, 91
Atlanta, 143, 175
Atlantic City, 33
AT&T, 87
Australia, 5, 59, 71, 100, 114, 128, 129, 196, 197
Austria, 59, 71, 114, 115, 196
Autarky, 8
Avis cars, 168

Baby boomers, 55
Baja California, 81–82
Balance of trade, 97
Balance of payments, 40, 97
Baltimore, 100
Bangladesh, 122, 196
Bank International for Credit and Commerce, 173
Banking, bankers, 84, 152
Bankruptcy, 222–23
Barings Bank, 173
Baumol, William, -'s disease, xviii, xx, 110–12, 198, 207, 211, 227
Beatrice Co, 87
Beirut, xv
Belgium, 48, 59, 61, 71, 114
Bengal, 6
Bermuda, xv
Beveridge, Sir William, 70
Belarus, 196
Bell, Linda, 137
Beveridge, Sir William, 215–16
Bickerstaffe, Roger, 161
Billionaires, 31, 101, 182
Bills, mandatory, 207ff
Birkbeck College, 128
Birmingham, Alabama, 98
Black Death 'Plague' (1346–1350), 12, 83, 160
Blinder, Alan, 73

Biosphere, 83
Bloomberg Business News, 92
Bluestone, Barry, 201
BMW, 96
Boeing Company, 101
Bok, Derek, nIV.19
Bolivia, 121
Boltho, Andrea, nVI.5
Boom and bust, xvii
Boston, 175, 182
Boston, 128
  area, 41, 100, 101
Boston Globe, xx
Brazil, 6, 77, 91, 122, 196
Brenner, Reuven, nI.1(b)
Bretton Woods conference, 56
Britain, *see* United Kingdom
British Airways, 167
British Rail, 178
Brown, Lester, nI.10
Budgets, surplus, deficit, 53
Buffet, Warren, 31
Bulgaria, 195
Bureau of Labor Statistics (USA), 149
Burger King, 161
Burnham, James, 193
Bush, George, President, 56, 83

Caine, Michael, 177
Cairo, 6, 68
Calcutta, 99
California, 49, 50, 59, 76, 240, 242
Canary Wharf, 102
Canada, xiv, xv, 4, 41, 59, 79, 88, 89,
  97, 114, 122, 160, 178, 196, 218
Capone, Al, 9
Capital, capitalisation, xviii, 112–14,
  154–55, 238, 246
  human (*see also* education), 207, 248
Capitalism, xiii, xiv, 13, 23, 39, 52,
  59, 60, 67, 83, 110, 141–42, 146,
  167, 220, 221
Card, David, 161
Caribbean, 6, 29, 77
Carnegie, Andrew, 141
Cars, *see* transportation
Case, John, 168
Castells, Manuel, nIII.17
Casual employment, 25

Caterpillar Co, 101
Catholic, Roman, Church, 75
Census Bureau, USA, 52, 185
Censuses, 68
Central America, 6
Chauffeurs, 68
Challenger, Gray and Thomas, 86
Channel tunnel, 102
Charities, 231, 235
Chenery, Hollis, nIII.26
Chicago, 7, 90, 100, 175
Chile, 91, 122
China, Chinese, 4, 6, 8, 10, 13, 82,
  91, 93, 97, 98, 122, 194, 216–17,
  218, 221, 247
Child labour, 78
Christian Coalition, 219
Chrysler, 96, 174
CIA, 58
Cities, 5, 7, 80, 88, 151, 164, 182, 231
Civil servants, 68, 76, 165, 174, 183,
  219, 224, 225–26
Civil war, xvi
Clark, Colin, nI.3
Clerks, 68
Cleveland, 175
Climate, 4
Clinton, Bill, President, 23, 58, 72, 93,
  170, 174, 181, 211
Clinton, Hillary, 180, 181
Cobb, Clifford, nI.1(b)
Community action, 227
Conference Board, 49
Consumption, consumers (*see also*
  retail trade), 244
Cold war, arms race, 55, 57, 58, 105,
  153
Cole Porter, 87
Colombia, xiii, 121, 196
Colonies, colonialism, xv, 12
Colorado Springs, 175
Commerce Dept., USA, 49, 97
Common Agricultural Policy, 197
Commonwealth, xv
Communications, xv, 8, 84, 105
Communism, xiv, xvi, 13, 67
Community, – service, xix, 239–40
Comparative advantages, 7
Competition and costs, 104

Concorde aircraft, 167
Computerisation, xviii, 112
Conditions of work, xviii, 140–42
Congress of Industrial Unions, 159, 166
Conquerors, 8
Construction, 70, 197
Consulting, xix, 84, 120
Consumer confidence, 33, 34–35, 48
Contracyclical policy, 229–30
Corby UK, 111
Corporate welfare, 242
Corporations, companies (see also employers), 242, 245
Corruption, xiii, 10, 45
Costa Rica, 220
Cost efficiency, 221
Cost of living index, 138–40, 199
Cotton, 4
Commercial Union, 179
Cox, Robert W., 83, nVI.16
Credit cards, 35–36, 58
Crighton, Michael, 178
Crime, xiii, xvi, 99
Culture, xv, 69, 80, 96, 117
Cunard Co, 101
Customs duties, 238
Cyclical industries, 32–34, 37
Czechoslovakia, 196

Datta, Tappan, 20
Davis, Geena, 177
De Beers, 95
Debt, 54, 55, 56
Defence, 55, 59, 82, 87, 105, 202–3, 229
Delaware, 240
Denmark, 48, 59, 71, 114–15
Dentists, 180
Deregulation, 84
Design, xix
Detroit, 100
Devaluation, 63, 154
Digital Equipment, 41, 42, 43
Disraeli, Benjamin, 102
Disney, Walt, 174
Divorce, 240
Djibouti, 99
Doctors, 50, 111, 180

Dodd, Paul, 166
Dole, Robert, 142
Domestic staff, servants, 68
Donahue, Thomas, 171
Down-sizing, 84, 85, 86, 105, 153, 226
Drivers, 68
Drugs, xiii
Duke family, 141
Dunlop, John, 166, 170–71
Dunlop Commission on American Labour, 170–71

Early, Steve, 171
Earned income credit, 229
Easter island, 5
Ecology (also biosphere, environment), xix, 84
Economics, xiii, xvii, 14, 17
Economic independance, 106–7
Economic migrants, 75–78, 90–91
Economic planning, 126
Economic Report of the President, 197
Economic statistics, xiii
Economic structure Part III passim
Economic theory, 164
    neo-classical, 73
    of trade, 7, 8
Economists, 17, 174
Economist newspaper, xvii, xx, 108
Economy, underground, xiii
    visible, xiii
Ecuador, 121
Education, training, xix, 78–80, 105, 124–27, 145–46, 210, 230–31, 239
Egypt, 6, 10, 196, 197
Eisenhower, General Dwight, 229
Eisner, Michael, 174
Emotion, religious, xv
Empires, in general, 10, 11
    British, xiv–xv
    Chinese, 10, 11
    German, 10
    Roman, 10
    Pharaonic, 10
    Turkish, 10
Employers, 20, 46, 50, 51, 71, 74, 105, 119, 157, 162, 166, 167, 169, 232, 244–45

Employment market organisation,
    Jobmap, 127–29
Employment policy, 123–29
Employee Stock Ownership Plans, 169
Employment structure, 89
Endogenous factors, 80–81, 88ff
Energy (also see oil), 4
Environment (also ecology), 83
Entertainment sector, 110, 177–78,
    248
Eliot, T.S., 112
Eritrea, 77
Errors, 41–45, 89
Esprit de corps, 105
Estates, xviii, 235
Ethiopia, 3, 77, 122
EU European Union, xv, 50, 90, 98,
    116, 166
Europe, 37, 40, 45, 46, 49, 54, 59,
    60–61, 70, 72, 73, 77, 79, 90, 103,
    129
Europe, eastern, 91, 93
Europe, western, 97
European Commission, 98
European Monetary Union, 63
Executives, managers, 51, 59, 84, 113,
    172–82
Exogenous factors, 80ff
Exploitation of labour, 75
Exxon, 93

Famine, 13
Faulkner, Harold, nV.8
Federal Deposit Insurance Corp., 183
Federal Reserve System, 23, 48, 58,
    226
Felixstowe, 99
Feudalism, 8
Finance, 70, 198
Financial Times, 194
Finland, 71, 115
Fiscal policy, 237
Flight attendants, 68
Florida, 46, 50, 76, 81
Food, – prices, 4, 13, 54
Food aid, 19, 77–78, 121
Ford Motors, Henry Ford, 45, 46, 93,
    96, 141, 144
Forbes, Steven, 232

Forecasting, 62
Foreign aid, 142, 153, 229, 243
Foreign exchange, 46, 56, 93, 215
Fortune '500', 174
France, xv, 3, 28, 48, 56, 59, 61, 63,
    70, 71, 75, 77, 79, 90, 99, 107,
    114, 115, 122, 144, 195, 196, 197,
    215, 243
Freeman, Richard, 137, 171
Free trade, protectionism, 107–10
Full employment, 31–32

G–7 countries, 89
Gabon, 122
Galbraith, Kenneth, 50, 60, 87, 113,
    141, 175, 177, 193, 248
Galenson, Walter, 166
Gambling, 33, 240
Gartmore, 179
Gates, Bill, 31, 44, 101
GATT, 103
General Dynamics Corp, 82
General Electric, 93
General Motors, 44, 93, 96
George, Henry, 240
Georgia, 143
Germany, 28, 40, 48, 54, 56, 59, 61,
    63, 99, 102, 103, 107, 114, 115,
    122, 144, 154, 168, 195, 196
Gerontocracy, 218
Getty family, 141
Ghost towns, 7
Glen Gould, 110
GNMA, see real estate
GNP, 202
Global warming, xiv
Gold, 28, 29, 81, 215
Goldfarb, Warren, 126
Goldsmith, James, 107
Goodman, Ellen, 125
Gordon, General, xv
Gore, Al, Vice President, 219
Gorz, Andre, xix
Government reform, xviii, 215
Grace, Peter, nVI.8
Gray, Alexander, nII.5
Great Depression 1930s, 23, 27, 31,
    54, 145, 152, 163, 215
Great Lakes, 90

Gregg, Paul, 161
Greece, 28, 48, 61, 115
Groundnuts scheme, 167
Guinea, 77
Gulbenkian family, 141, 173
Guns, xvi

Halstead, Ted, nI.1(b)
Handicapped persons, 142
Hanks, Tom, 173
Hansen, Alvin, nII.15
Harrod, Roy, nII.9
Harrod-Domar model, 39
Harvard University, 44, 126, 142–43,
    164
Haswell, Margaret, nI.3
Hawaii, xv, 183, 240
Health Care (see also medicine), 46,
    171, 180, 209–10, 248
Heath, Edward, 165
Hirsch, Leon, 174
Hirohito, Emperor, 248
Hispanics, 52, 77,
History, Economic (see also Keynes)
    Part I passim,, 150–54, 215–18
Hitachi, 93
Hitler, Adolf, 9, 54
Holidays, 136–38
Holland, 48, 59, 61, 81, 93, 114, 115,
    162, 196
Homeless, 142–43, 231
Hong Kong, xv, 8, 11, 82, 91, 95,
    96
Hoover, Herbert President, 23, 57
Hopkins, Anthony, nIV.1
Hospital Corp., 176
Housing, 34, 36
Houston, 100
Howell, James, 146
Hughes Missile Systems, 82
Human development index, 122
Human rights, 98
Human resources and career planning,
    123–29
Hungary, 91, 195

Iacocca, Lee, 174
IBM, 41, 42, 43
Ideology, 80

Illinois, 50
Income, incomes Part IV passim
    discretionary, 212
    disposable, 232
India, 11, 77, 91, 121, 122, 172, 196,
    197
Indians (American), 4
Indochina, 6
Indonesia, 11, 91, 95, 122, 196
Industrial Engineering
Industry, xviii, 112, 194
Inequality, xvi, xvii, xix, 46, 110, Part
    IV passim, 185–88, 248
Inflation, hyperinflation, see
    unemployment
Information age, 103, 105, 112
Innovations, 80–81
Insurance, industry, 180–81
Interest rates, 56, 58, 60, 93, 230
International Air Transport
    Association, 150
International Bank, see World Bank
International Labour Organisation,
    24, 88, 111, 194
International Monetary Fund (IMF),
    11, 29, 56, 123
Investment, public, xviii, 45, 53, 55, 167
    private, xix, 91, 92, 93, 245
Investors confidence and expectations,
    37
Iran, 77, 196
Ireland, 48, 61, 71, 90, 115, 128
Islam, xv, 68
Israel, 55, 91
Italy, xiii, 7, 28, 48, 54, 55, 59, 61,
    62, 63, 71, 75, 77, 79, 114, 115,
    194, 196
ITT, 87
Ivory Coast, 77, 121

Jackman, R., nIII.4
Jaguar, 96
Japan, 12, 13, 20, 28, 37, 40, 41, 45,
    46, 50, 55, 56, 59, 79, 93, 95–98,
    99, 103, 104, 107, 114, 122, 196,
    197, 198, 218, 243
Jay, Anthony, 193
Jefferson, Thomas, 7
Jenks, Christopher, 143

Job creation, 47
Johansson, Don, 3
Junk bonds, 173
Jupiter, 82

Kaldor, Lord Nikki, 37–38, 232, 237
Kashoggi, Adnan, 247
Katona, George, 34
Kazakhstan, 196
Kennedy, John, 241
Kennedy, Paul, 10, 11
Kennedy School of Government, 172
Kerr, Clark, 166
Kerry, Senator John, 232
Keyes, Alan, 232
Keynes, Lord J.M., 23, 30–31, 37–38,
    46, 52–58, 60, 144, 150, 164, 215
Khmer Rouge, 11
Krueger, Paul, 161
Krugman, Paul, 108–9
Kuttner, Bob, 107, 149, 188

Labour Government, 167
Labour Law and Relations, 166–72
Labour, workers, 12, 50, 52, 59, 105,
    167, 168
  intensity (see also Baumol), xix, 51,
    114, 154, 207
Labour, work force, 67, 78, 92, 145
Lancashire, 102
Landlords, xix,
Land settlement, 76, 121
Laredo, 175
Las Vegas, 33
Law, rule of, system, 207–8, 243
Lawrence, Robert, 108
Lawyers, 50, 142, 174, 198, 202, 248
Layard, r., nIII.4
Low Pay Network, 161
Lear Jet Planes, 176
Lebanon, 28
Legal and General, 179
Leone, Richard C., nI.1(b)
Lenin, V.I., 28
Lewis, John Spedan, 168
Liberal, 57
Liberia, 29, 77
Librarians, 111
Lipton, Michael, 4

Liquidity preference, 31
Liverpool, 99
Lloyds insurance, 82, 180
Logging, 84
London, 82, 99
London School of Economics, 167
Los Angeles, 100
Luxembourg, 48, 61, 115,
Lyon, D., nIII

Macmillan, Harold, 55
Mahbub ul Haq, nIII.25
Mahdi, The, xv
Malaysia, 5, 11, 91, 95, 196
Malthus, Rev.T., xvii
M&G group, 179
MAM, 179
Manufacture, 70, 194–97, 202
Manko Inc., 169
Market(s) -driven, xvii
Marshall Plan (European Recovery
    Program), 40, 54
Martin-Marietta Co., 82
Marx, Karl, 193
Massachusetts, 50, 102, 125, 161,
    206, 242
Massachusetts University, 201
Maquiladora, 94
Maugham, Somerset, 175
Maxwell, Robert, 173
Meade, James, 237
Mellon family
McCarthyite persecution, 188
McDonnel-Douglas Co., 82, 101
Mechanisation, Ludditism, 112–14,
    156–57
Media, 59, 228
Medicine, health care, 12, 46, 58,
    111, 142, 171,
Medoff, James, 172
Mercedes Benz, 96
Mergers, 84, 87–88
Mexico, 38, 91, 94, 98, 121, 196
Mezo, Mike, 201
Michigan, 50
Microsoft co, 100
Middle class (see also executives), 36,
    46, 50
Middle East, 77, 90, 122

Milken, Michael, 173, 174
Miliband, David, 232, 234
Military-industrial establishment,
    229–30, 243
Militias, xvi
Mining, quarrying, 7, 70
Mississippi, 82
Mitchell, Senator George, 58
Manhattan, 100
Mobutu, President, 173
Money (see also unemployment), xviii,
    28, 29, 54, 56, 81, 203–4, 210,
    224–25
Mongolia, 6
Monopolies, 74, 95, 102, 104, 163–64
Mortgages, see real estate
Motorola, 96
Morocco, 196
Mozambique, 77
Multiplier, 38
Mussolini, 54
Myanmar (Burma), 77, 196

NAFTA North American Trade
    Agreement, xv, 94
Naisbitt, John, nI.5
NAIRU, 70
Napoleon, 8
National Baseball Association, 178
National debt, USA, 40, 57, 92, 93
National Labor Relations Act, 171
National Institute of Economic and
    Social Research, 161
National Rifle Association, 240
Nazism, 28
Nestle, 93
Netherlands, see Holland
Nevada, 240
New Deal, 84
New England, 7, 98
New Hampshire, 240
New Jersey, 50, 161
New York, 50, 76, 92, 100, 175, 240
New Zealand, xiv, 5, 111
Nicholson, Jack, 173
Niemira, Michael, Mitsubishi Bank, 51
Nigeria, 121, 122, 195
Nickell, S, nIII.4
Nixon, Richard, President, 58

Nobel, Alfred, 141
Nordhaus, see Samuelson
Norfolk, 175
North, Douglass, nI.8
North, north pole, 4
North America, 6, 49, 54, 243
North Carolina, 50, 240
North Korea, xiv, 11, 195
Norway, 71, 115
Nuffield, Lord (William Morris), 141
Nurses, 68

OECD, 27, 62, 71, 116, 144, 194, 223
Ohio, 50, 169
Oil, 40, 55, 81, 103
Oligopoly, 163
Olympia and York, 44
OPEC, 40, 55, 95, 97
Orthodontists, 180
Outerclass, 119
Over-investment, 45
Ozone, 81

Palestinians, 77
Pakistan, 77, 122, 196, 197
Panama, 29
Pan American Airways, 101, 150
Paranoia, 229
Parkinson, 224
Paris, 91
Pearce, D., nII.10
Pearl Harbor, 96
Pennant-Rea, nII.3
Pennsylvania, 50, 161
Pentagon, 82
Pensions, 140, 171, 173, 210
Peronism, 218
Perot, Ross, 38, 94, 219, 226
Peru, 121
Ph.Ds, 126
Phelps, Edmund, 72
Philadelphia, 100, 175, 219
Philadelphia Declaration, 216
Philippines, 11, 122, 196
Philips Curve, 144
Phillips, Kevin, 226
Phoenix, Ariz., 100
Pilots, 68
Pinochet, 220

Pittsburg, Pittsburgh plus, 102
Plaza (hotel) Agreement, 56
Plutocracy, 218, 228
Poland, 195, 196
Police, 68
Political action committees, 228
Political economy Part VI passim
Politics, 106
Politicians, 50
  Democrats, 56, 240
  Republicans, 56–58, 157, 182, 219,
    240
  Labour Party 161, 16
  Liberal Democrats 161
Poor countries, 121–23
Pope, 28
Population, xvii, xviii, 4, 5, 12–14,
    75, 76, 78, 81, 90, 93, 204–5
Population Action International, 122
Portugal, 7, 48, 61, 115, 196
Postel, 179
Potato Famine, 90
Poverty, 52, Part IV passim, 172, 231
Powell, General Willian, 219
Pralahad, C.K., nIII.12
Prehistory, 3–5
President of USA, 23
Primary, secondary, tertiary, 69, 88
Princeton University, 83, 161
Procter family, 141
Productivity, xviii, xix, 22
  of labour, 7, 8, 21, 51, 95, 153, 154,
    197
Profits, profit-makers, xviii
Profit-sharing, 148–50
Prostitution, 33, 240
Prudential, 179
Psychology, 34, 37, 48
Public utilities, 70
Purchasing power, xvii

QE2, 101
Quality of Life (see also human
  development index), 140–42
Quayle, Vice-President, 222
Quebec, xv, 4, 75, 240

Raleigh-Durham, 175
Rationing, 55

Raytheon Co., 82
RCA building, 101
Reagan, Ronald President, 46, 56, 57
Real earnings (by city), 175
Real estate, 40, 41, 48, 49, 57, 101,
    151, 230, 238
Real wages, see cost of living
Recession1990ff, 36, 50, 59, 153
Recessions, 40, 45, 47, 48, 52, 59,
    146, 151
Recovery, 47, 49, 54, 60, 153
Refugees, 232
Regressivity, 244
Reich, Charles, 191–93
Reich, Robert, 155, 165, 170
REITS, see real estate
Relief, 231, 239
Religion, 80
Rent, cost of housing, xix, 208
Republic Engineered Steel
Rest, xvi, 137–38, 210
Restructuring, 84–86
Retail trade, 46, 48, 49, 51, 104, 202,
    212, 240
Retirement, xvi
Rio de Janeiro, 83
Roberts, Ben, 166
Roberts, Julia, 177
Robbery, plunder, predators, 8, 9
Rockefeller family, 101, 141
Rogaly, Joe, nV.7
Rolls Royce, 96
Romania, 195
Rome, 221
Roosevelt, Franklin, President, 23, 54,
    163, 215, 241
Rotterdam, 100
Rowe, Jonathan, nI.1(b)
Rowntrees, 168
Royal Navy, 101
Russia, 7, 29, 196

SDRs – special drawing rights, 29
Salaries Part IV passim
  Notion of maximum, 172–82
Samuelson, Paul, 46n
Samuelson, Robert, 186–87, 217–18
San Francisco, 82, 100, 175
San Francisco Conference, 216

Saudi Arabia, 101, 122
Savings, 8
Say, J.B., 30, 54, 73
School teachers, 68
Scotland, 201, 231
Scotch whisky, 201
Sears, 101
Secretaries, 68
Security, economic, 8
Self-employed (and *see* consulting), 169
Seoul, 221
Services sector (*see also* Baumol), xviii, 89, 109, 110–12, 146–47, 193–207
Shakespeare, 7
Shanghai, 82
Shaw, George Bernard, xv
Sherman, Howard, 73, 74
Shipbuilding, 7
Siberia, 6, 82
Silicon Valley Calif., 41
Sinai, Allen, 191
Singapore, xv, 11, 91, 173
Slavery, child, xiii, 7
Slash and burn, 6
Small vendors, 178
Smokestack industries, 102, 151, 153
Smoot-Hawley tariff, 54
Snower, Dennis, 128
Social classes, xiii
Social defence, 229
Socialism, xv
Social security, 71, 152, 171, 215–16, 229
Social structure, 69
Software, 206
Solvay family, 141
South Africa, 5, 122, 196
South and Latin America, 6, 28, 37, 40, 76, 77, 88, 91, 93, 123
South Korea, Korean war, xiii, 13, 40, 55, 95, 96, 196
Southwest Airlines, 169
Space exploration, 55
Spain, 7, 48, 59, 61, 71, 114, 115, 196
Special Drawing Rights – SDRs (IMF)
Spielberg, Steven, 178
Spiritual values, xix
Sports, leisure activities, 137–38
Sri Lanka (Ceylon), 77, 136

St. Lawrence Seaway, 7
St. Louis, 175
Stabilisation, 52, 74
Stagflation, 29, 240
Stalin, Josef, 23
Standard Life, 179
Stanford, 108
States rights, 240, 241
Steel, 102, 111, 223
Steinbeck, John, 162
Stevenson, Adlai, 126
Stewarts and Lloyds, 111
Stockmarket, 34, 48, 57, 152–53
Stockpiles, USA, 55
Stone Construction Equipment, 169
Stone, Sharon, 177
Strategic stockpiles, 55
Streeten, Paul, nIII.25
Strikes, 168
Students (*see also* education), 52
Subsidies (*see also* agriculture), 71, 229
Sudan, xv, 77
Super-rich, 31, 46, 51
Surgeons, 174
Sweden, 59, 104, 114, 217–18
Switzerland, 59, 98, 114, 115, 122, 168

Taiwan, 11, 13, 91, 95, 196
Tampa, 175
Tanzania, xv, 197
Tawney, R.H., 141
Tax base, 229
Taxation, xviii, 46, 56, 57, 58, 71, 103, 151, 186, 207, 217, 230–247
Tax Foundation, 232
Taylor, Robert, nIV.14
Teachers, 174, 198
Technology, xvii, xviii, xix, 5, 12, 67, 81, 87, 106
Tensions, xvi, 52
Texas, 50, 76, 240
Textiles, 102
Thailand, 5, 95, 196
Thatcher, Baroness Margaret, 165, 219
The Inc. Report (periodical), 168
Third Wave, 102
Third World, 12, 13, 55, 68, 76, 122, 123, 194

Thorpe, Kenneth, nV.11
Thurow, Lester, 79, 105, nI.1(b)
Time-Warner Corp, 174
Tito, xvi
Tobacco, 4
Toronto, 7, 90
Toys R Us, 96
Training, see education
Trade, 7, 8, 12, 54, 70, 81, 95,
   96–97, 103, 106, 107–10
Trade Union Congress, 160, 161, 166
Transport,
   communications, general, 70, 209
   road, 86, 96, 151, 243
   rail, 82
   underground rail, 102
   air, 84–85
   water, 7
Travel agencies, 85
Trickle down prosperity, xv
Trollope, Anthony, nVI.11
Truman, President Harry, 153
Trump, Donald, 45
Tsongas, Senator Paul, 102
Tsunami, 81
Turkey, 196
Turner, Bert, 166

Ukraine, 196
Ulsan, 96
Under-class, 70
Underconsumption, 45
Underemployment equilibrium, 18, 22,
   31, 121–23, 30–31
Unemployment, xix, 12, Part II
   passim, Part III passim,
   and Aliens, 118
   Addictions, 117
   Age, 78, 116
   Chronic, xviii, 59–63, 114ff
   Contract and casual labour, 120
   Cyclical, 18, 26–31, 32–52, 60–63,
      74
   Disablement, 116
   Dropouts, 118, 119
   Frictional, 24–25
   Gender, 78
   Hyperinflation, 28
   Impact, xviii

Inflation, 48, 50, 54, 55, 56, 58, 93,
   151
International job displacement, 91,
   94, 108
Long-term, 18, 50, 52, 67ff, 70, 73,
   115
Low IQ, mental problems, 117–18
Nationality, 118
Part-time working (involuntary), 119
Politics, 22
Productivity, 21–22, 119
Race, 118
Religion, 118
Seasonal, 25–26, 33
Statistics, 20, 22
Structural, 59–63, Part III passim
Taxation, 244
Technological, 18
Trade, 12, 107–9
Trap, 117
Unemployable, 116–18
Unions, 73, 166
Unskilled, 117
Wages, 74, 79, 128–9, 144–48,
   145–47
Uganda, 77
Ulster, 231
Unions, labour, trade 71–75, 99,
   159–66, 170–72, 201, 240
Unison, 161
United Arab Emirates, 122
United Front, France, 54
UN Conference on Trade and
   Development, 93
UNDP, 122
UN Food and Agriculture
   Organisation, 216
UN High Commissioner for Refugees,
   77
United Kingdom (see also history),
   xiv, xv, 7, 12, 40, 41, 48, 55, 56,
   59, 61, 70, 71, 77, 90, 154, 99–100,
   114, 115, 122, 133, 134, 141,
   144–45, 147, 160, 167, 196, 197,
   215, 243
United Nations, 68, 95, 117, 153,
   215, 224, 228
United Steel Workers of America, 201
Uruguay, 122

Uruguay Round, 103
USA (*see also* history), xiv, xvi, xviii,
  4, 8, 12, 20, 32, 37, 41, 48, 49, 56,
  57, 59, 90, 92, 94, 95–98, 103, 114,
  122, 133, 134, 141, 196, 144–45,
  147, 158–59, 160, 197, 198–207,
  215, 243
USDAW, 161
Useem, Mike, 87
US Surgical Corp., 174
USSR, xiv, xv, 24, 57, 81, 91, 196,
  197
Uzbekistan, 196

Value -utility -exchange, 109
Vanderbilt family, 31
Venezuela, 122, 197
Vermont, 240
Vietnam, vietnamese, 5, 40, 95, 122
Vietor, Richard, 84
Viking, 7
Viner, Jacob, 83
Volker, Paul, 56

Wages (*see also* unemployment)
  General, xviii, Part IV passim
  and productivity, 51
  Minimum, 75, 155–60, 165
Wage goods, 245
Wales, 231
Wallenberg family, 141
Wallis, Jim, nIV.20
Walmarts, 100
Walton family, 100
Wang, 41
Washington, DC, 102, 224, 226, 240
Wealth Part IV passim, 175, 185, 236,
  246
Wealth Tax, 246–7
Weather, 81

Welfare, social relief, 58
Weller, Paul, 171
Wharton School, 87
Wheat, 102
Widener family, 141
Wilde, Oscar, 137
Williams, D., nIII.16
Williams, Douglas, nVI.3
Winnick, Andrew, nIV.24
Wolff, Edward N., nI.1(b)
Wood, Stephen, nIV.13
Women, sex structure, 4, 20, 67–68,
  78ff, 119, 122–23, 140
Woodham-Smith, Cecil, nIII.19
Woolworths, 100
Workaholism, 136–38
Worker management, ownership,
  148–50, 168–69
Working conditions, 140ff
World Bank, 123, 215
World Development Report, 123
World economy, 26, 123, 195
World Food Programme, 121
World Health Organisation
World Investment Report, 93
World Trade Organisation, 103
World War, First, 215
  Second, 12, 13, 40, 54, 215
Writers, 173
Wyss, David, 148

Xerox, 41

Yemen, 77
Yugoslavia, former, 28, 77

Zaire, 77, 173
Zambia, 77
Zero budgetting, 222